The Last of the Last

The Spanish Waffen SS in the Battle of Berlin, 1945

Eduardo Manuel Gil Martínez

HELION & COMPANY

Helion & Company Limited
Unit 8 Amherst Business Centre
Budbrooke Road
Warwick
CV34 5WE
England
Tel. 01926 499 619
Email: info@helion.co.uk
Website: www.helion.co.uk
X (formerly Twitter): @Helionbooks
Facebook: @HelionBooks
Visit our blog at helionbooks.wordpress.com

Published by Helion & Company 2026
Designed and typeset by Mary Woolley, Battlefield Design (www.battlefield-design.co.uk)
Cover designed by Paul Hewitt, Battlefield Design (www.battlefield-design.co.uk)

ISBN 978-1-806722-45-7

British Library Cataloguing-in-Publication Data.
A catalogue record for this book is available from the British Library.

For details of other military history titles published by Helion & Company Limited contact the above address or visit our website: http://www.helion.co.uk.

We always welcome receiving book proposals from prospective authors.

Dedication

In Memoriam: Eduardo Gil

To Solete, my love
To my parents, Salud and Eduardo
To Caco, Iñigo, Ibón and June
To Merce
To my grandparents: Mercedes, Salud, Mami, Manuel and Juan
To Ángel el Garci

Contents

Acknowledgements

Marisol García Gómez, Ricardo Ramallo Gil, Luis E. Togores, Erik Norling, Juan Arráez, Massimiliano Afiero and especially Vincent Hunt for his significant contribution.

Introduction

The book you hold in your hands aims to recount the story of a small group of Spaniards who fought in the bloody Battle of Berlin in April–May 1945, defending what remained of the German Reich against the Soviet attack. This text is entirely devoid of any political agenda and merely seeks to reconstruct the events as faithfully as possible and how they occurred, taking into account the scant amount of information that has survived to the present day. In 2011, we published an essay on the Spaniards who fought in the *Wehrmacht* and the Waffen-SS, which mentioned the presence of Spaniards in the Battle of Berlin. Fortunately, over the last 15 years, new books and publications have emerged that have expanded on the scant information available regarding the Spanish units that fought in the streets of Berlin in 1945. Similarly, new accounts of the Battle of Berlin allow us to understand their involvement with greater accuracy. But let us begin at the beginning.

The involvement of Spanish troops during the Second World War as part of the German armed forces is well known in our country, thanks to the growing number of publications that have appeared in recent years. The vast majority of these deal with the well-known Blue Division and its successor, the Blue Legion, or the Blue Squadrons (on the German side) and the Ninth (in the Allied forces). Far less well known is the fact that, following the withdrawal of the more or less 'official' Spanish involvement alongside the Germans in the war – as a result of Allied pressure on the Spanish Government – several hundred Spaniards remained in the service of the Reich. These 'diehards' have been covered to a much lesser extent in the literature due to the scarcity of information regarding their involvement following the end of the world war. In fact, the presence of Spaniards in the Battle of Berlin has generally been ignored in non-Spanish publications, but also in Spanish ones. To take just one example, a highly regarded work on the Battle of Berlin such as Antony Beevor's *Berlín: La caída, 1945*[1] *completely overlooks the presence of Spaniards in the fighting for the German*

1 Antony Beevor, *Berlín: La caída, 1945* (Barcelona: Editorial Crítica S.L., 2002).

Despite making a negative first impression on the German military high command, the Spanish soldiers managed, through their countless actions in the *División Española de Voluntarios* (DEV, Volunteer Spanish Division or Blue Division) and the *Legión Española de Voluntarios* (LEV, Volunteer Spanish Legion), to earn the respect and affection of their German superiors. (Courtesy of L. E. Togores)

capital, as does Tony Le Tissier in his works on the Charlemagne, which also saw action in the Battle of Berlin.[2]

Amongst these latter Spaniards fighting for the German Reich was a small group that took part in the final defence of Berlin. It is on them that we will base our account, using all the information currently available and drawing on the increasingly abundant literature dealing with the fighting in Berlin. We will therefore collate the information at our disposal and, as far as possible, the dates of the various engagements in which the men under Ezquerra's command took part on the streets of Berlin during the Soviet offensive on the German capital.

While it is true that Spanish participation in these battles was by no means particularly significant – unlike the intervention of French troops who, with far greater numbers, did manage through their actions to delay the fall of Berlin by a few days – they too contributed their courage and effort during the fighting. Together with troops from the *Nordland Division* or their Latvian comrades, they did indeed play a very active role for a few days in the clashes with the Soviets in the German capital.

Ambushes and assaults were the most frequent missions in which the men of the *Einheit Ezquerra* found themselves involved; despite their small numbers (which dwindled further with each day of fighting because of

2 Tony Le Tissier, *With Our Backs to Berlin* (Stroud: Sutton Publishing, 2007).

losses through death, wounds, capture or desertion), they distinguished themselves through their bravery. Clearly, their small numbers and their theoretical 'non-existence' meant that under no circumstances were the Spanish initially given any recognition in the history books, although this situation has been rectified in recent years.

In this text, we will learn more about these men who, in many cases, gave their lives to defend a land which, although not their birthplace, was the last bastion of the cause for which they had chosen to continue the armed struggle against communism; as was the case with many of the troops who defended the capital of the Reich, which included not only Germans and Spaniards, but also Frenchmen, Estonians, Latvians, Swedes, Belgians, Romanians, Italians, and others. Although these non-German contingents did not number many men, they do show us what would have been a first, embryonic pan-European Army (always under German control) against communism.

The foundations of this text are the memoirs narrated by the head of the Spanish unit in Berlin, Miguel Ezquerra Sánchez. Ezquerra published his memoirs on two occasions: *Luché Hasta El Fin* (1947 in Portuguese) and much later in Spanish.

This autobiographical work must be treated with considerable caution, as, to begin with, the events it recounts do not entirely coincide. Thus, facts corroborated by external sources are joined by others that are difficult to verify or simply highly improbable. Despite this, and with the inaccuracies that may well appear in any work of this nature, we must regard it as a point of reference that will serve as a framework upon which to delve deeper into the events that took place during those difficult days in late April and early May of 1945; what is clear is that Ezquerra was indeed in Berlin during that period.

As his memoirs cannot be cross-checked against other comprehensive accounts of the events, they have been met with scepticism by many, leading numerous historians to deny the existence of Ezquerra's unit altogether. It is certainly true that, as regards the fighting in Berlin, Ezquerra tells us of a multitude of incidents in which he and his men risked their lives, from which it seems impossible that they could have escaped unscathed, as some of them did. But Miguel Ezquerra was undoubtedly present during the Battle of Berlin, as he recounts events that someone who was not there would find very difficult to know. What we must bear in mind is that the accounts he gives of certain events – which, it is true, may be less than accurate and contain some embellishments – should not for that reason be regarded as a string of lies. The impression Ezquerra gives in some of the events he recounts is that he appropriates events he heard or saw, casting himself as the protagonist in some.

We have, of course, omitted those parts of the account that lack any semblance of plausibility and could not be corroborated with other sources. Nor, however, can it be regarded as a work of fiction, far from it. Ezquerra was a Spanish soldier hardened by years of service in the Spanish Civil War and with service (albeit brief, as he was wounded after just over a month of service) in the Blue Division, which voluntarily joined the German side despite the fact that its imminent defeat was already on the horizon. Thus we should have no doubt, at the very least, about his fighting spirit and ability, as was the case with many of the men who made up his unit. Furthermore, the nature of the Spanish unit and the timing of its creation during the final days of the German Reich, when chaos and collapse reigned not only amongst the civilian population but also within many military units, may have led to a lack of documentation regarding the unit and, consequently, to its non-existence 'on paper records' for many.

We will draw on the excellent and now classic works that tell us 'a bit of this and a bit of that' about these men as our secondary sources. These include such important figures within this little-known 'subculture' of the Second World War as Jean Pierre Sourd, with his works *True Believers*[3] *and Croisés d'un idéal*[4]*;* and the leading Spanish author Carlos Caballero Jurado, '*Los últimos de la División Azul*'[5] and *Españoles en la Wehrmacht*[6]; Wayne Bowen with 'The Ghost Battalion: Spaniards in the Waffen-SS, 1944–1945'[7]; Antonio Muñoz with various books dealing with very niche topics of the global conflict;[8] or Fernando Vadillo with his *Gran Crónica de la División Azul*[9]. To these now better-known texts we should add more recent works such as Aaron Stephan Hamilton with *Bloody Streets*[10], or what in our opinion is the most outstanding contribution in recent times: the excellent and masterful work by Ángel González Pinilla, *La Legión Clandestina*.[11]

By carefully piecing together the accounts from various sources, we have managed to reconstruct the Spanish unit's movements during the fighting in Berlin as accurately as possible.

Furthermore, thanks to Vincent Hunt (today the leading authority on Latvian troops during the Second World War), we have managed to obtain previously unknown information about the Spanish soldiers in Berlin, based on the testimonies of their Latvian comrades who fought side by side

---

3 Jean Pierre Sourd, *True Believers: Spanish Volunteers in the Heer and Waffen-SS, 1944–1945* (Rome: Europa, 2014).

4 Jean Pierre Sourd, *Croisés d'un idéal: Volontaires espagnols de la Waffen SS, Heer et Kriegsmarine (1944–1945)* (Paris: Dualpha, 2021).

5 Carlos Caballero Jurado, 'Los últimos de la División Azul: el Batallón Fantasma' in *Revista Defensa*, no. 114, 1987.

6 Carlos Caballero Jurado, *Españoles en las SS y la Wehrmacht, 1944–1945: la Unidad Ezquerra en la batalla de Berlín* (Madrid: Almena, 2011).

7 Wayne Bowen, 'The Ghost Battalion: Spaniards in the Waffen-SS, 1944–1945' in *The Historian*, 63 (2000), pp.373–385.

8 Most especially, Antonio J. Muñoz, *Forgotten Legions: Obscure Combat Formations of the Waffen SS* (Boulder Co/London: Paladin Press/Axis Europa, 1991).

9 Fernando Vadillo, *Gran Crónica de la División Azul en los Irreductibles* (Granada: García Hispán, 2008).

10 Aaron Stephan Hamilton, *Bloody Streets: The Soviet Assault on Berlin* (Warwick: Helion & Co., 2020).

11 Ángel González Pinilla, *La Legión Clandestina* (Madrid: Gutiksland, S.L. 2021).

with them on numerous occasions. In some cases, this has enabled us to confirm events that were previously considered false.

Our aim with this text is therefore to delve deeper into these events, as well as into the highly distinctive nature of the fighting in Berlin and the hardships endured by these Spanish soldiers as they defended an ideal and their military pride, despite the extremely adverse conditions they faced. And thus to rescue from oblivion the contribution of the Spanish men who fought alongside Germany in the Second World War.

Before delving into the events on which the book will focus, we shall begin by briefly recalling the presence of Spaniards on the German side during the final two years of the Second World War, so as to understand where these Spaniards came from – men who would largely give their lives amidst the ruins of the Reich's capital.

Part I

1

Spaniards in the Wehrmacht and the Waffen-SS

With the early years of the Second World War demonstrating German military superiority in Europe, Adolf Hitler and Francisco Franco agreed to send a Spanish contingent to fight under the German flag exclusively against the Soviet Union. In this way, part of the debt Spain owed to Germany for the latter's assistance in the Spanish Civil War could be indirectly repaid.

In July 1941, an initial contingent of around 18,000 men under the command of General Agustín Muñoz Grandes (who was relieved by General Emilio Esteban Infantes in December 1942) set off for Germany, entering into the German Army under the designation *Infanterie Division 250* – popularly known as the Blue Division. They fought bravely in numerous engagements against the Soviets in places such as Novgorod, Volkhov, Lake Ilmen and Krasny Bor.

Two corporals from the Blue Division pose for the camera. Note the unofficial Blue Division badge worn by the corporal on the left of the image. This type of badge was also used by some of the men of the *Einheit Ezquerra*. (Museo del Ejército/Biblioteca Virtual de Defensa)

Formation of the LEV in Stablack-Süd, with the Spanish national flag flying. (Courtesy of L. E. Togores)

Colonel García Navarro greeting one of the decorated men at a parade. (Courtesy of L. E. Togores)

Due to pressure from the Allies, the Spanish Government was forced, on 24 September 1943, to withdraw the Blue Division (its last act of war was to repel a Soviet attack on 5 October 1943), but it left behind a small contingent of some 2,269 men, under the command of Colonel Antonio García Navarro, in the Blue Legion with the aim of preventing any 'retaliation' on the part of the Germans regarding the repatriation of the Division. On 20 February 1944, the Führer and Franco agreed to the repatriation of the Blue Legion. The repatriation order reached the legion's command on 3 March.

On the 16th, the legionaries handed over the weapons they were carrying, except for pistols and revolvers which would be used for their own defence if necessary.

On the 21st, the last weapons and some of the surplus clothing were handed over, and the legion could be considered disbanded the following day, although it would still take about two weeks to hand over their German uniforms in Stablack-Süd (near Königsberg) in order to receive their own Spanish uniforms in return. The planned withdrawal of the Blue Legion thus took place in practice between 31 March, the first returnees arrived in Irún on the

31st, and April 1944, the last men arrived on either the 11th or the 17th (the exact date depending on the source) among whom was the colonel and the legion's senior officers; with the journey from Königsberg to Irún taking around four days. The repatriation began with the 3rd battalion, followed by the 1st and 2nd battalions; and concluded with the legion's general staff.

For various reasons, some Spaniards decided not to return to Spain despite the risk of losing their Spanish nationality that came with continued collaboration with the German armed forces. These men, largely former divisionaries and legionaries, together with other men who crossed the Spanish border to join the German armed forces of their own accord, plus many Spanish civilians working within the Reich, who had lost their jobs

This photograph, which includes Colonel García Navarro, demonstrates the varied uniforms in terms of footwear, trousers, belts, epaulettes and caps that could be seen throughout the German armed forces in the final years of the conflict. (Courtesy of L. E. Togores)

Colonel García Navarro looking sombre as the *Legión Española de Voluntarios* prepares to depart. (Courtesy of L. E. Togores)

Aerial photograph, taken from a De Havilland Mosquito of the RAF Film and Photography Unit, showing heavily damaged buildings in the area between Friedrichshain and Lichtenberg, Berlin. The Allied bombings had left much of the city in ruins, but the arrival of the Soviets would complete its destruction. (Public Domain)

due to the incessant Allied bombing of factories and German industry, decided to fight as part of the German Army.

Of this group of Spaniards, which according to various sources numbered around 1,000 men, many of them eventually joined, after many vicissitudes, units belonging to the Waffen-SS (such as the *28. SS-Freiwilligen-Panzergrenadier-Division Wallonien* or the *11. SS-Freiwilligen-Panzergrenadier Division Nordland*), while others were assigned to the 3rd Mountain Division or the 357th Infantry Division. Spaniards also fought against the partisan guerrillas in Yugoslavia in August 1944 as part of the 8th Company of the 2nd Battalion of the 3rd Regiment of the *Brandenburg Division*, which would also fight against partisan guerrillas in Italy.

The last unit into which Spaniards were integrated is the subject of this study. It was known as *Einheit* or *Einsatzgruppe* or *Kampfgruppe Ezquerra* (in reference to its commander) and was, in practical terms, integrated into the *11. SS-Grenadier-Division Nordland* (it should be noted that *11. SS-Panzergrenadier-Freiwilligen Division Nordland* is its original designation, although for the sake of simplicity we will refer to it by the former name, as is the case with other divisions called by their own names). As a curious fact, it was actually the only unit that can be considered fully Spanish within the German organisational structure, as until then the Spanish had been put into larger units of other nationalities (German and Belgian, usually). For the sake of simplicity in the text, we will refer to the Spanish unit as the *Einheit Ezquerra* (*Ezquerra Unit*) although some historians prefer to refer to it as the Ghost Battalion[1] or *Kampfgruppe Ezquerra*.

1 Aaron Stephan Hamilton, *Bloody Streets: The Soviet Assault on Berlin* (Warwick: Helion & Co., 2020) for example.

Shoulder badge used by the Blue Division, later by the Blue Legion and finally by some men of the *Einheit Ezquerra* during the Battle of Berlin. (Public Domain)

The unit to which the largest number of Spaniards had been deployed was the *Wallonien*, which, according to some authors, was able to accommodate just over a hundred men, although it is more likely that the number reached 240–350 men by January 1945 (this figure is approximate, as one might expect, given that there are various opinions on the matter; for instance, Sourd states there were around 350, Caballero Jurado puts the figure between 350 and 400; and according to Albert Steiver's testimony, there were around 240). We will briefly recount the engagements in which Spanish soldiers took part, which toughened up many of them even further, since, as discussed below, many of them would end up fighting for Berlin in April and May of 1945, after receiving the order to leave this Walloon SS unit to form a Spanish SS unit. As we shall see, many of the names that appear in this chapter will reappear during the fighting for Berlin, forming the 'hard core' of the *Einheit Ezquerra*.

In the Walloon unit, the Spanish were integrated into the division's sole battalion of the *70. SS-Grenadierregiment*, commanded by *SS-Hauptsturmführer* (Captain) Robert Denie, leading to the formation of a third company within it (3rd Company of the 1st Battalion of the *70. SS-Grenadierregiment* or 3/I/70). The Walloon unit was deployed in various sectors, such as the Rhineland area, where they were prepared for a possible role in the Battle of the Bulge, but in which they did not ultimately take part, although on 24 December 1944 a group of Spaniards under the command of *SS-Untersturmführer* (Second Lieutenant) Ricardo Botet was in the Marmagen (Nettersheim) area as part of *SS-Obersturmführer* Derriks's force. Once they had left the Western Front, they moved to Stettin (now Szczecin) and the Stargard sector (now Stargard Szczeciński) in February. In early February 1945, when the *Wallonien* was already deployed in the Stargard area, near Stettin (Szczecin), it received several contingents of Spaniards from Vienna and Berlin. With these volunteers, the 3rd Company was expanded to three sections, and a fourth section was formed within the 1st Company of the same battalion (an independent section that would later be attached to the company commanded by the Walloon *SS-Untersturmführer* Albert Steiver). The organisational structure of the 3rd Company was:

Commander: *SS-Obersturmführer* Luis García Valdajos/*SS-Untersturmführer* Rudolphe Bal (who took command when Luis García Valdajos was in Berlin for an extended period).

Section Commanders: *SS-Untersturmführer* Ricardo Botet Moro
SS-Oberscharführer Lorenzo Ocañas
SS-Hauptscharführer Manuel de la Fuente
SS-Hauptscharführer Abel Ardos (his section would be independent)

As we can see, both the section and platoon leaders were mostly Spanish and were mostly veterans of the Blue Division. Rudolphe Bal (known as Rudi) was Belgian, but had lived in Argentina for several years, so he spoke Spanish perfectly and acted as a liaison with the rest of the Walloon unit.

Albert Steiver in his memoirs 'Krüssow – 1945 Wallons et espagnols', bears witness to the actions of the Spaniards stationed there.[2]

Another account comes from *SS-Sturmbannführer* Franz Hellebaut, second in command of the Walloon unit, who recorded that the battalion saw the arrival of well over a hundred former combatants from the Blue Division whom Degrelle had discovered in Vienna and whom he had invited to join his unit after having received permission to form a third company.[3] Some of the Spanish volunteers who came forward to join the *Wallonien* were rejected due to a lack of military training.

In the absence of *SS-Hauptsturmführer* Denie, Steiver assumed command of the battalion, as well as the task of making the best possible use of the new Spanish recruits. The recruits had to immediately face a march of some 35 kilometres to reach their position on the front line. According to Steiver's account, he estimated that around 260 men arrived, although the number was likely somewhat lower (possibly between 100 and 150 men).

The Spanish company (the 3rd Company) was initially under the command of *SS-Oberscharführer* Luis García Valdajos, and the section leaders and platoon leaders were, in most cases, veteran officers and non-commissioned officers of the Blue Division. The leaders of each of the three sections that made up the company were *SS-Oberscharführer* (Sergeant First Class) Manuel de la Fuente[4] and Lorenzo Ocañas[5] with *SS- Untersturmführer* Ricardo Botet[6] acting as company commander who combined the role with that of commander of the 1st Section. Other officers and non-commissioned officers in the Company included Pedro Zabala, Juan Pinar, Cabrejas and Van Horembeke, who had returned to 'active' service following his work as a recruiting officer for the *Wallonien*.

To maintain good liaison with the rest of the Walloon unit, *SS-Untersturmführer* Rudi Bal was chosen as liaison officer; he spoke perfect Spanish, having lived for several years in Argentina. It was Rudi Bal who would take command of the Spanish Company in the absence of García Valdajos, who was to move to Berlin before the fighting in which Degrelle's unit took part in Pomerania.

---

2 Steiver's memoirs are unpublished but see Eddy de Bruyn, 'Spanish Volunteers in the 28. SS-Frw.Gr.Div. Wallonien' at https://www.forum-der-wehrmacht.de.

3 Hellebaut's memoirs have not been published but there are several accounts and testimonies from him in different interviews and post-war interrogations. Erik Norling has some info in *Guerreros de Borgoña*. (Granada: García Hispán, 2008) and there is more in Tomasz Borowski, *Last Blood on Pomerania* (Warwick: Helion & Co, 2016).

4 According to Sourd, his rank was *Waffen-Hauptscharführer der SS*.

5 According to Sourd, his rank was *Waffen-Oberscharführer der SS*.

6 According to Sourd, his rank was *Standarten Oberjunker*.

Officers of the *SS Wallonien Division* pose for the photographer at the Kienschlag Officers' School (Botet also attended this school). Among these officers is the Spaniard Lorenzo Ocañas (6), who would go on to fight with the *Einheit Ezquerra* during the Battle of Berlin, where he was captured. The names of some of the SS officers with Ocañas in the photo are known: Serlet (1), Suain (2), Foulon (3), De Goy (4), Hancisse (5). (Courtesy of L. E. Togores)

Steiver stated that, while the Division was at the front, Spaniards continued to join its ranks, some of whom were turned away because they lacked weapons or due to their limited military training. The fourth section, formed from the Spaniards who had arrived, was, as mentioned, attached as a support unit to Steiver's 1st Company, with which it would take part in the Battle of Stargard. This section came under the command of Sergeant Abel Ardoos (whose real surname was Ardos, and whose rank, according to Sourd, was *Waffen-Hauptscharführer der SS*) and was fairly well equipped, having received heavy machine guns and anti-tank weapons, as well as a field kitchen. The choice of Ardos for command of this section was greatly aided by his knowledge of both French and German.

Near Stargard, Sourd recounts that some Spaniards had a run-in with a German officer and his men from an unknown army unit. This altercation was triggered by the summary trial to which three Polish women had been subjected after being accused of stealing potatoes from some German warehouses; as a result, after being arrested, they were sentenced to death. By chance, the Belgian *Hauptsturmführer* Denie and the Spaniard Botet Moro, together with another group of Spaniards whose names we do not have, arrived at the farm where the sentence was to be carried out and firmly opposed its execution. Finally, after a heated argument involving threats from both sides, the Spaniards and Denie managed to free the women, though not without receiving a final threat from the German officer, which amounted to nothing less than a court-martial. Shortly afterwards, as the Spaniards were marching to new positions, Sourd notes that five of them broke away from the column and, allegedly, killed the German officer and some of his men to prevent any revenge for the events that had taken place.

Returning to the general deployment of the men of the *Wallonien*, they were deployed in a sector of the front of the German defensive line where they were alongside forces with numbers of men from the most diverse

Recruitment poster for the SS *Wallonien* unit, in which many Spaniards ended up fighting. (Public Domain)

nationalities. Here they would fight to halt the mighty Soviet 'steamroller', with Norwegians, Swedes, Danes, Flemings, Walloons, Dutch, French, Estonians and Latvians and of course Spaniards, in complete camaraderie, fighting for a common cause. The Soviets were approaching the south-west of Stargard, and the arrival of the two Belgian units – both the Flemish and the Walloon – was urgently needed.

On 28 January, the order to embark was received by the various detachments of the Walloon Division, and they were transported to the front in 10 trains. From the rear of the lines, as well as from Berlin, the transfer of the Spaniards serving in the division to the Pomeranian Front began, arriving between 2 and 4 February at the town of Stettin (now Szczecin in Poland), situated on the west bank of the Oder. Subsequently, after they had approached the front on a thirty-five-kilometre march, they took up their positions on the River Ihna, south-east of Stargard, in the area between Lake Madü and Lake Plone, covering the flank of the main attack. Thus, the area entrusted to the Walloons to defend was situated to the south-east of the town of Stargard, with the sole battalion of the 2nd Regiment – into which the Spaniards were integrated as its 3rd Company – serving as the reserve force.

It was the Soviet 2nd Guards Tank Army and 61st Army, both from 1st Belorussian Front, that would face the Walloon unit. On 7 February, the battle for Arnswalde, some 30 kilometres south of Stargard, reached its climax. On 10 February, Soviet forces renewed their offensive against the town of Stargard; meanwhile, the Spanish carried out various raids into Soviet-occupied territory, demonstrating great courage and ferocity in each of these operations.

On the 11th, the 1st Company of the 1st Battalion of *SS-Freiwilligen-Grenadierregiment 69*, temporarily attached to the *10. SS-Panzer-Division Frundsberg*, attempted to capture the village of Klutzow, supported by some of the increasingly hard-to-obtain air and armoured units. Among the men were some Spaniards – the Ardos section which was assigned to Steiver's 1st Company. The attack stalled and subsequently failed, leaving the Walloons and their Spanish comrades in charge of defending that sector of Krüssow-Stargard (now Kluczewo-Stargard Szczeciński in Poland), following the withdrawal of the air and ground support on which they had relied for the offensive. Control of the town of Krüssow was of vital importance to Degrelle, although the rapid Soviet advance towards it would thwart the wishes of the *Wallonien* battalion's commander. Léon Degrelle himself recounted the events that took place there:

> As night fell, there was a drizzle in the air and a deep chill in our bones. Our company's small radio crackled. It was the general call from Stargard. Their attack had failed, a joint operation was impossible, and the German tanks were supposed to retreat under cover of night. As for us, we were to return quietly to our morning positions that night. We had barely managed to withdraw through those muddy swamps when I received the order to send one of my companies to our right flank, to Krüssow, which was being defended by nothing more than a small group of *Volkssturm*. The town stretched on both sides of the Lindenberg-Stargard Road. We expected the Russians to attack at any moment, as they were quite emboldened by their successful defence the previous day.
>
> Our lads reached Krüssow at exactly the same time as the Soviet tanks. They were forced to retreat to the other side of the River Ihna. Their situation was particularly difficult. The company commander gathered his defences on the right bank, but could do very little, as he had been sent there too late. However, the village was important, and our officers did not give up easily.[7]

Troops of the *Wallonien* advance through Pomerania over terrain littered with Soviet leaflets urging desertion. The uniform seen in the foreground is similar to that which some of the Spanish soldiers who took part in the Battle of Berlin might have worn, as they came from the *Wallonien* Division. (Courtesy of Massimiliano Afiero)

7 Léon Degrelle, *Campaign in Russia* (Newport Beach, CA: Institute for Historical Review, 1985), pp. 282–283.

Inevitably, Krüssow fell into the hands of Soviet troops, which led to the Walloons' retreat on 13 February towards Wittichow (now Witkowo) and Schneidersfelde (now Radziszewo). The 3rd Company (the Spanish Company), together with Rooryck's 6th Company and Lecoq's 1st Company, took up positions south of the village of Streesen (now Strzyżno in Poland).

On 15 February 1945, Operation *Sonnenwende* (Solstice) began, involving, amongst others, the SS divisions *Frundsberg*, *Nordland*, *Langemarck*, *SS Polizei*, *Nederland* and *Wallonien*, all under the joint command of *SS-Obergruppenführer* Felix Steiner. The rationale behind this operation was to capitalise on the fact that the Soviets, following the significant advances they had made during their January 1945 offensive – in which they crossed from the Vistula to the Oder – had left their flanks exposed. With a view to exploiting this situation, the Germans were to launch a pincer movement to encircle these troops and overwhelm them. One of the arms of the pincer would come from Pomerania and the other from Hungary. However, the grim reality of the state of the German armed forces meant that the necessary manpower could not be mustered, so the main objective of the German offensive was to make contact with the besieged troops at Arnswalde (now Choszczno), a feat achieved on 18 February, albeit at the cost of heavy and irreplaceable casualties, without ultimately managing to stabilise the front line.

The main thrust of the attack was led by the *Nordland* Division, with the 11th Panzer Battalion *Hermann von Salza* acting as the battering ram, flanked on both sides by the division's two regiments: the *Norge* to the east

Several German soldiers wait in their trench for the arrival of the Soviets during the fighting in Pomerania in February 1945. Many of the combatants in Pomerania ended up fighting in the Battle of Berlin – Spaniards, integrated into the *28. SS Freiwilligen-Grenadier-Division Wallonien*, Estonians in the *15. Waffen-Grenadier-Division der SS*, French in the *33. Waffen-SS Grenadier-Division* or the *11. SS-Panzergrenadier-Freiwilligen-Division Nordland*. (Courtesy of Massimiliano Afiero)

and the *Danmark* to the west. The men of the *Langemarck* and *Wallonien* covered the western flank; the *Frundsberg* and *Polizei* were positioned in the direction of the River Oder; while the eastern flank was covered by the Dutch of the *Nederland* and the *Führer Grenadier-Division*. The 19th and 20th saw intense fighting in the vicinity of Arnswalde, with the withdrawal of all forces south of the Ihna River beginning on the 21st.

The subsequent reorganisation of the forces still operational in that sector led to the *Wallonien* coming under the control of the more powerful *Nordland*.

On 27 February, the Soviets advanced with the intention of encircling the troops stationed in Stargard, marking the start of the Battle of Stargard. During the battle, the Walloon troops were deployed near Kollin, some 15 kilometres from the town that gave the battle its name. Casualties were once again heavy, to such an extent that the sole battalion of the *SS-Freiwilligen-Grenadier-Regiment 70*, to which the Spaniards belonged, had to be disbanded, and its men distributed among the two battalions of the *SS-Freiwilligen-Grenadier-Regiment 69*. Here, the Spaniards, fighting alongside the Walloons, destroyed Soviet tanks – mainly the well-known T-34 – with their new anti-tank weapons the feared *panzerfausts*, doing everything possible to halt the Soviet advance. There is an account of a battle in which the Spaniards, armed with *panzerfausts*, faced a group of T-34s – destroying one, hitting another and forcing the rest to retreat. The patrols that the Spanish were required to carry out would increasingly wear down the already depleted forces that always remained combat-ready; for, displaying their recklessness, they were on occasions taken by surprise by the deadly responses of their opponents, who were constantly lying in wait for the movements of the Spanish. During this period, Steiver's 1st Company, and therefore the Ardos section, were temporarily assigned to the *Frundsberg* Division.

The Spaniards took part in the offensive, capturing the village of Krüssow, nine kilometres south of Stargard.

Indeed, the few accounts we have of the participation of the Spanish soldiers of the Wallonien come from *SS-Untersturmführer* Albert Steiver, who, as commander of the 1st Company of Battalion 1/70, recounted the fighting ability and courage of the Spanish soldiers. Specifically, during the fighting to defend Sickow, Steiver deployed the Walloons within the town and entrusted external surveillance to patrols from the Spanish section led by Ardos. He recalled it thus:

> One night, a Spanish patrol, guided by a local member of the *Volkssturm*, discovered a Russian anti-tank gun quietly positioned and hidden in a wood. Confident in the additional weaponry provided to the patrols, the Spaniards felt compelled to attempt a surprise attack and return victorious with an enemy anti-tank gun! Although the *Volkssturm* man advised against it, the Spaniards launched their assault that night, believing they would find Ivan asleep; but he, on the contrary, met them with grenades and rifle fire. The result was two dead, whom they

> could barely carry back to their own lines, and three seriously wounded who, after examination in the battalion infirmary, were sent to Stettin.

On 3 March, the remnants of the division's missing 1st Battalion of the *70. SS-Grenadierregiment* covered the *Wallonien Division*'s retreat along the Baltic coast.

On 4 March, Stargard was abandoned for good, with the Walloons and the Spaniards from Ardos being the last to withdraw, as well as the last to cover the civilian population trying to flee westwards and the military units in disarray seeking the rear lines. There were 28 days of almost continuous fighting that caused heavy casualties in the section of Spaniards serving in the 1st Steiver Company. Casualties in the section may have reached up to 90 per cent of its members. Although there are no precise figures to confirm the accuracy of this information, it does give us a very rough idea of the significant attrition suffered by the section. The remaining Spaniards in the 3rd Company also suffered significant casualties, so much so that, as mentioned, they had to be incorporated into the *SS-Freiwilligen-Grenadier-Regiment 69*. Only around 60 Spaniards managed to escape the Siege of Stargard in early March 1945. Rudi Bal, then commander of the Spanish

Ricardo Botet (on the right) while serving in the Spanish Volunteer Division (the Blue Division) in 1941. (Courtesy of L. E. Togores)

Soldiers from an SS unit rest after destroying a Soviet tank. In the battle for Stargard, the Spaniards serving in the *Wallonien* engaged the Soviet tanks with some success thanks to the use of *panzerfausts*. (Courtesy of Massimiliano Afiero)

Company, was killed in action on 6 March while leading his men, leaving the company under the command of Pedro Zabala and Ricardo Botet.

The survivors from Stargard were regrouped at Scheune, south of Stettin, where they initially formed part of a defensive line north of Berlin.

They did not stay there long, as, on 16 March, García Valdajos arrived at the barracks where the Spanish survivors of the *Wallonien* Division were stationed, ordering all Spaniards in the *Wallonien* Division to assemble in the vicinity of Potsdam. This took place in mid-March, taking advantage of the fact that the units of the III SS Corps were retreating towards the capital of the Reich. It was thus in Potsdam that the *Einheit Ezquerra* would be formed, which would defend the centre of the Reich capital alongside a motley crew of defenders of many nationalities against the looming Russian onslaught that was almost at the city gates.

It is possible that some of the Spanish did not retreat to Potsdam and continued until the end of the conflict with the *Wallonien*, scattered amongst its companies. Léon Degrelle himself, in an interview given in 1969 to the Madrid newspaper *Arriba*, stated that he commanded Spanish troops until the end of the war; this may well be true, although we have been unable to confirm it with any documents or specific information from the period. Similarly, Albert Steiver recalled in his memoirs that, due to the chaos caused by the retreat from Pomerania, a few Spanish soldiers scattered among other units within the Division were unable to withdraw to Berlin, remaining with the *Wallonien* until the end of the war.

Both photographs show Léon Degrelle at the head of his Walloon unit in Estonia. His close contact with his men, even on the front line, made him a much-appreciated commander. Many Spaniards ended up joining the *Wallonien* Division and taking part in the fighting at Krüssow-Stargard in Pomerania. (Courtesy of Massimiliano Afiero)

2

The Formation of the Spanish SS Unit Under the Command of Ezquerra

Going back in time, we find ourselves in March 1945, in the town of Potsdam, very close to the German capital. It was here that the Spanish unit that would go down in history as the *Einheit Ezquerra* was formed. The German High Command (influenced by the wishes of the Director of the Ibero-American Institute (*Ibero-Amerikanisches Institut*), *General* Wilhelm Faupel, to raise a Spanish Waffen-SS unit) wanted a unit composed solely of Spaniards, possibly encouraged by their admirable performance in the fighting in Pomerania and, of course, driven by the need for more troops to defend what remained of the German Reich. *SS-Obersturmführer* Luis García Valdajos was considered to command this unit, and he would indeed become its first commander. However, his tenure was very brief, as he himself immediately proposed Miguel Ezquerra Sánchez for the command (although García Valdajos also had extensive experience as a front-line combat officer, he was better suited to organisational tasks due to his extensive experience in this regard, acting as a liaison between the unit and the SS command). Thus, practically from its inception, the Spanish unit came under the command of Miguel Ezquerra, who hastened to recruit Spaniards from 'every nook and cranny' to fill its ranks.

Consequently, Ezquerra and García Valdajos were entrusted with the mission of gathering as many Spaniards as possible, removing them from the various military units in which they might be serving, recruiting Spanish workers in the Reich's industries, or, in general, any Spaniard living in the Reich who met the physical and the age requirements. In this, General Faupel's assistance played a significant role in facilitating the creation of this new Spanish unit.

During this mission, Miguel Ezquerra experienced some friction with the Spanish Embassy in Berlin, as the embassy was, to the best of its ability, attempting to repatriate the Spaniards who were still in the Reich, while the idea of promoting the creation of a unit of Spanish fighters within the SS was not even remotely on the mind of Mr Rodríguez del Castillo, the last representative of the Spanish Embassy in Berlin.

In fact, (as Vadillo recounts), in mid-April, between the 12th and the 16th, Gonzalo Rodríguez del Castillo managed to evacuate some 200 workers of Spanish origin by rail. From the 14th onwards, the Spanish Embassy in Berlin had been without electricity (like so many other buildings in the battered city) and Rodríguez del Castillo moved his operations to the Falange's building on Berlinstrasse. It was from there that he made his final calls to secure the evacuation of all Spaniards in Greater Berlin, using both radio announcements and notices from the embassy in the newspapers for this purpose. But the situation in the Reich capital became critical, and shortly afterwards, on the 19th, it was the Spanish Diplomatic Corps, led by Rodríguez del Castillo, who had to flee the city as quickly as possible.

On the 19th, a small convoy consisting of six cars and a few motorcycles bearing the Diplomatic Corps' pennant and number plates left the capital, taking one of the magnificent motorways that made up the Reich's road network, heading west, before turning north-west towards Hamburg. Throughout their journey, they mingled with thousands of military personnel and civilians heading in one direction or another (both fleeing from the Soviets and marching to meet them) and would be subjected to countless road checks by the police, the army, the SS or other security forces. Their 'legal' status, enabling them to flee the hell that much of Germany had become, and thanks to their papers allowed them to keep moving forward. However, the harshness of the journey would take its toll on two of the vehicles in the Spanish convoy, which were abandoned to their fate along the way. As the Spaniards passed through the town of Wusterhausen on 24 April, they were informed by German security forces of the presence of Russian troops just 20 kilometres from the motorway they were travelling on, where the town of Neuruppin had been taken. They sped up as soon as they could, as their capture by the Soviets, despite belonging to the Diplomatic Corps, would have an uncertain outcome

A Soviet artillery battery shelling German defensive positions. In this instance, the target was the Seelow Heights, although within just a few days they would begin a sustained bombardment of the city of Berlin. (Bundesarchiv Bild183-E0406 0022 012)

and would almost certainly prove fatal. Two days later, on 26 April, they found themselves in the city of Lübeck; from there they moved to Hamburg and, after a two-day stay, set off for what would be their final destination: Copenhagen. Following the German surrender and its coming into effect in the occupied Danish territory on 5 May, the Spaniards led by Rodríguez del Castillo endured days of uncertainty, which would come to an end in the height of summer (on 24 July); through the mediation of British troops, they boarded an RAF aircraft to take them to London, where their difficult and dangerous flight from a German Reich that was crumbling with every passing minute came to an end.

The men of the Spanish unit who were beginning to assemble in Potsdam presented a very diverse picture, and their ranks comprised a motley crew of former legionaries (veterans of the African Wars), veterans of the Spanish Civil War, the Blue Division and the Blue Legion; former members of the *Wallonien* Division and other German military units, as well as workers who, having been employed in the Reich now found themselves unable to continue their work in the destroyed German industries, Spanish members of the Organisation Todt, Falangists recruited from Madrid, and Spaniards who, for various reasons, were being held in German prisons.

Undoubtedly one of the most valuable groups among the Spaniards gathered in Potsdam were the men who had served with the *Wallonien* Division in Pomerania. They had taken part in numerous engagements in addition to their previous combat experience with other units, and had had extensive experience in the use of modern weapons such as the *panzerfaust* and the MP44 assault rifle. Among the men who, after leaving the *Wallonien*, marched to Potsdam was Ricardo Botet, and upon reaching the destination

The luxurious *Adlon* Hotel witnessed numerous deals during the Second World War, one of which led to the incorporation on 1 November 1944 of Luis García Valdajos into the *Wallonien* Division commanded by Léon Degrelle. (Bundesarchiv Bild 102-13848F)

Botet and his comrades were integrated into a new unit which, under the command of Ezquerra, was being formed from the Spaniards arriving from various places. Ricardo Botet recorded:

> We received orders to go to Potsdam, where all the Spanish were being regrouped into a single unit, commanded by Miguel Ezquerra Sánchez. We were sad to leave our comrades in the SS *Wallonien*, with whom we had fought and shed our blood for the same ideal. When we arrived in Potsdam, we were housed in a school for military orphans, and there we found a colossal circus-like spectacle: there were more sergeants than soldiers, quarrelsome legionaries, people of ill repute, clueless individuals who didn't know where to go, and former veterans of the Blue Division and other *Wehrmacht* units; there were between around 100 and 150 of us. Among them all, I remember a legionary who acted as Ezquerra's escort; his face was completely tattooed and he wore a huge '*tercio* belt' with two pistols, one on each side. Years later, I was told that he died buried beneath the ruins of Berlin.[1]

In early April 1945, the unit that Ezquerra had managed to recruit was broadly distributed as follows:

It was made up of survivors from the 3rd Battalion, 1st Regiment, 70th Infantry Regiment of the *Wallonien Division*, and a number of men from other units from which some Spaniards had managed to 'desert' (many of whom had previously served in the Blue Division or the Blue Legion), as well as students, workers from the Organisation Todt, and some individuals

Many of the men in the *Einheit Ezquerra* had good military training from their time in the DEV and the LEV, and in many cases from their participation in the Spanish Civil War. (Museo del Ejército/ Biblioteca Virtual de Defensa)

1 A. Ferrer-Dalmau, 'Españoles en las Waffen SS' in *Eurouniformes*, no. 14, diciembre-enero 2002–2003.

wanted by the German authorities. In the end, the *Einheit Ezquerra* consisted of two companies stationed in Potsdam, where the last volunteers gathered. Naming a unit after its commander was common practice in German troops.

Vadillo mentions that *Unterscharführer* Ramón Baillo Fernández was sent by Miguel Ezquerra from Berlin to recruit Spanish volunteers for the unit commanded by José Ortiz (specifically, a Spanish company designated *5. Kmp./II.Btl* belonging to *SS-Gebirgs-Regiment 59* of the *24. Waffen-SS Gebirgs Division Karstjäger)* to the town of Tolmezzo, near Udine.[2] As we can see, no effort was spared in establishing this final unit of Spaniards, which would soon be sent into combat.

Ezquerra mentions in his book that some survivors from the Belgian and French SS divisions joined his unit. It is not impossible that this happened on occasion (for example, Alphonse Van Horembeke, a Walloon who had

SS soldiers, one armed with a *panzerfaust* 60, in a trench in Pomerania in February 1945. The Spanish company belonging to the *Wallonien* gained extensive combat experience using this weapon during the defence of Pomerania. (Courtesy of Massimiliano Afiero)

2 Fernando Vadillo, *Gran Crónica de la División Azul en los Irreductibles* (Granada: García Hispán, 2008).

Ricardo Botet Moro was one of the most active Spaniards within the German armed forces, having served in the Blue Division, the Blue Legion, the SD (*Sicherheitsdienst* or Security Service), the *28. SS-Freiwilligen-Panzergrenadier-Division Wallonien* and the *Einheit Ezquerra*. (Collection of J. Arráez. Public Domain by ESC 90)

served in the 4th Battalion of the Tercio and later in the 67th Company of the 17th Battalion during the Spanish Civil War and who served in the *Wallonien*, did indeed join the *Einheit Ezquerra*) but the reality is that there is no information in the existing documentation of either the French or Walloon units to suggest that this is true.

To house this recruitment and training centre for the Spanish troops in Potsdam, the German High Command offered (as we learnt from Botet Moro's account) a former military orphanage and which had previously served as an officers' training school. It was there that they were supplied with weapons, mainly light arms; however, this supply of weapons took place in two stages.

The stay in Potsdam enabled Ezquerra's men to receive a variety of supplies, not just weapons. It is worth noting that they were issued with modern M44 camouflage uniforms, which was very welcome as many of the men from other units, such as those from the *Wallonien*, had seen a great deal of fighting in their uniforms. However, the key issue regarding what was expected of this unit in Berlin was its armament, which initially consisted of obsolete French-made Lebel rifles and other weapons of the most varied of origins, but in no case of the highest standard.

Faced with this major drawback, Van Horembeke and Ezquerra himself went to the relevant German command post to demand that they be supplied with better weapons. This meeting must have been quite difficult, as Ezquerra did not speak German, and Van Horembeke spoke it very poorly. However, the visit had the desired effect and, according to Van Horembeke, the following day the Spaniards received at their barracks 'a veritable arsenal of rapid-fire machine guns, submachine guns, grenades, *panzerfausts*, rifles and plenty of ammunition, with which we were well equipped'.[3] Among this armament, we highlight the ubiquitous *panzerfausts*, which put the destruction of an armoured vehicle in the hands of a single infantryman.

3 Alphonse Van Horembeke (as a veteran from Spanish Civil War, and Spanish-speaking, he was the link between Spanish soldiers and the SS Division *Wallonien*). He has no formal published memoirs but accounts from him are published in several works from Tomasz Borowski, *Last Blood on Pomerania* (Warwick: Helion & Co, 2016) or Carlos Caballero Jurado, 'Los últimos de la División Azul: el Batallón Fantasma' in *Revista Defensa*, no. 114, 1987 – see Bibliography.

Shortly afterwards they received more weapons, notably the modern MP44 rifle (also known as StG44) and the Gewehr 43 semi-automatic rifle. These weapons were the best in the German arsenal and allowed a small unit to generate far greater firepower than expected against both infantry and armoured vehicles by employing ambush tactics – precisely what was anticipated during the Battle of Berlin.

Although many of the men in the unit were already experienced in the use of the MP44 or the *panzerfaust* (remember that in the *Wallonien* they had access to them), intensive training was carried out on these weapons, with particular emphasis on theoretical instruction on the use of the various *panzerfausts*, delivered by *SS-Obersturmführer* Zabala. Ezquerra reveals this following a visit to the Faupel couple during the Spanish unit's training process:

> The following morning, I travelled to Potsdam, where my unit's barracks were located, in what had previously been the Officers' School. When I arrived, they were in a theory class: Zabala was explaining how the *panzerfaust* worked. I gathered the officers together: Ocañas, Botet, Martínez, Múgica and Zabala. The non-commissioned officers' roll-call was not complete. Ramón Baillo and Artiaga were corporals; there were two sergeants, one a former civil guard and the other a former carabineros officer. My liaison corporal was Roberto Gracia, whom I promoted to sergeant that very same day. My assistant was a young man from Galicia in the Frente de Juventudes, and among the corporals was Juan Pinar.... I was sent four interpreters: Gerardo Liebert, Juan Klimovich, Jacobo and another whose name I cannot recall. Two belonged to the regular army and the other two to the SS. From the very start, they were my best and most loyal collaborators, devoting themselves body and soul to the task entrusted to them.[4]

The few days the Spaniards were in Potsdam were spent conducting brief training sessions for the men, in theory aimed more at those who had not been in active military service recently, as was the case with the former workers from the Reich's industries. The prevailing atmosphere, despite the complexity of the situation, was one of anticipation and a desire to begin fighting the Soviets. It was not for nothing that they were volunteers, although it is also true that some were more convinced of their reasons for being there than others. Despite the volunteer nature of the unit, it is possible that some men deserted during these days of training, as well as during the Battle of Berlin itself. Thus, although there is no very reliable data, it may be that several dozen men became deserters. Regardless of this, the unit's numbers dwindled because it was while it was in Potsdam that

4 Miguel Ezquerra Sánchez, *Berlín, a vida o muerte* (Granada: García Hispán, 1999) pp.62–66.

the first casualties occurred in the *Einheit Ezquerra* when, following an Allied bombing raid on the town of Potsdam, the Spanish barracks were hit. Twelve Spanish soldiers lost their lives and were buried in the town.

The Spanish unit would once again see its numbers reduced after receiving orders from Ezquerra that the company under the command of *SS-Obersturmführer* Pedro Zabala (totalling 71 men) was to separate from the rest of the unit and join the German forces attempting to regroup in the Alpine stronghold. Ezquerra received these orders while staying at the *Hotel Excelsior* in Berlin, which served as his 'Berlin office'. Among this group that would leave the unit on 18 April was, according to Ezquerra's account, Martín de Arrizubieta, who had been the editor-in-chief of the newspaper *Enlace*.

The destination for the men under Zabala's command was the Rheinigs Camp in the Alps, where they would arrive on 29 April, having passed through Innsbruck the day before. This journey, undertaken by lorry and rail, took them from Berlin to Prague (where they arrived on 21 April), to Munich (23 April), Salzburg (26 April), Innsbruck (28 April) and Rheinigs (29 April). Upon arriving at the 'Alpine Fortress', Zabala's Company found that there was no longer any point in continuing the fighting, as the *SS-Hauptsturmführer* who was awaiting the Spaniards' arrival at their destination informed them. The men of Zabala's Company, disheartened at being unable to fulfil their mission, were ordered to return to Innsbruck to operate behind enemy lines as guerrillas – an idea that did not appeal to them in the slightest. In fact, the men under Zabala's command asked their commander to request of the *SS-Hauptsturmführer* that they be parachuted into Berlin to rejoin their comrades who had remained there (obviously, this idea was rejected).

On 30 April, the Spaniards assembled at the Rheinigs Camp to hear a few words from *SS-Hauptsturmführer* Stenley, who highlighted the assistance the Spaniards had provided to Germany and bid them farewell with honours, after which they set off for Innsbruck. Once in the Austrian city, after the idea of returning to Berlin and that of acting as guerrillas had been rejected, they received orders to head for Italy to try to return to Spain.

This new unit, just as had happened during the Battle of Berlin with the non-German troops belonging to the Waffen-SS, was integrated into the *11. SS-Freiwilligen-Panzergrenadier-Division Nordland*, by the time the front line was already in the vicinity of Berlin.

3

First Days in Berlin

Following its rapid formation, the unit named Ezquerra (in accordance with the practice common among German units of naming certain units after their commanding officer) began its first, and only, deployment in the last third of April 1945. The events recounted below took place between 20 April and 2 May of 1945, and in the narrative we attempt to bring together information on the Spaniards obtained from various sources of the general fighting that took place in Berlin. Although there are not many reports from the *Einheit Ezquerra* regarding its activities during the period between 22 and 26 April, these few largely correspond to the early days of the Spanish presence within Berlin's defensive network. It is reasonable that, across the various sources, some details or facts may not coincide perfectly. In this case, we will opt for the most reliable of the sources, while also providing an overview of the fighting across the rest of the German capital.

But let us return to the events where we left off in the previous chapter, in Potsdam, where the Spanish troops were stationed.

A Polish armoured column advances towards Berlin in April 1945. Note the T-34/85 tanks. These tanks became one of the main targets of the city's defending forces. (Public Domain)

Friday 20 April:

On the day of Adolf Hitler's 56th birthday, which was celebrated in his Berlin bunker, troops from the 1st Belorussian Front were advancing towards the east and north-east of Berlin, while those from the 1st Ukrainian Front were advancing towards the south of the city. The Spanish soldiers' feeling that 'something was about to happen' came true, as, having been stationed in Potsdam, they were to be transferred to Berlin the following day on the orders of *Obergruppenführer* Gottlob Berger, head of recruitment for the Waffen-SS. Because the encirclement of the German capital had not yet been completed, reaching it should not have posed any particular problem for the small Spanish unit.

Soviet soldiers of the 1st Belorussian Front advance through a village near the city of Berlin. Despite German resistance, the attackers' superiority in every respect sealed Germany's fate. (Public Domain)

The soldiers were informed of the orders received, leaving it up to each of them to decide whether to carry out this mission.

The Spaniards comprised two companies, with a third perhaps still in the very early stages of formation, made up of men arriving at the unit's facilities.

With regard to the volunteers gathered in the unit under Ezquerra's command, it must be understood that, as their backgrounds were very different, this likely meant the unit was not homogeneous in terms of combat training. As mentioned earlier, the hard core of the *Einheit Ezquerra* must have consisted of veterans from the *Wallonien*, hardened by the very fierce fighting in Pomerania and generally well-versed in the use of weapons such as the MG42, the MP44 rifle or the *panzerfaust*. Men from other German units or veterans of the Blue Division certainly did not lack combat experience. However, the recruitment of men from other backgrounds, such as industry or, quite possibly, prisons or detention centres, would have given the unit a certain heterogeneity in terms of combat capability. It is therefore reasonable to assume that, due to this mix of greater or lesser, or even no, combat experience among its members, not the entire unit possessed the same combat capability. However, attempts were made to address this through a rapid training programme involving instruction in the handling of available weapons, and by placing veterans of the Eastern Front (primarily from the *Wallonien Division*) in command of the various formations within the *Einheit Ezquerra*.

A German soldier armed with a *Sturmgewehr* 44 with a telescopic sight. This modern and powerful weapon was responsible in many cases for the tenacious resistance of Berlin's defenders. The soldiers of the *Einheit Ezquerra*, as the shock unit that it was, were equipped with this rifle. (Bundesarchiv Bild 146-1979-118-55)

After holding talks at the SS High Command headquarters in Berlin's Fehrbelliner Platz with Gottlob Berger (who was head of all foreign formations integrated into the SS), *Hauptsturmführer* Ezquerra (although another source refers to Ezquerra as a *Sturmbannführer*) set off once again for Potsdam with the intention of briefing his men. He began by informing his non-commissioned officers and trusted men: Pedro Zabala Urrutia, Ricardo Botet Moro, Enrique Lafuente Barros, Cipriano Sastre Fraile and Lorenzo Ocañas Serrano.

Armoured vehicles of the 2nd Guards Tank Army advance through the outskirts of Berlin. In this instance, the two T-34/85s are loaded with infantry to facilitate and speed up their transport in the 'race' to capture Berlin. (Public Domain)

Defense sectors in Berlin April-May 1945. The Spanish soldiers fought mainly in the Z (Zitadelle) sector.

Saturday 21 April to Monday 23 April

Following the final collapse of the German defensive line, the units of the 56th Panzer Corps that were still combat-ready began their retreat towards Berlin, with the first of them reaching the south-eastern outskirts of the capital during the night of 20–21 April. The units comprising this 56th Panzer Corps – the *9. Fallschirmjäger Division*, the *Müncheberg Panzer Division*, the *Nordland Division*, the *20. Panzergrenadier Division* and the *18. Panzergrenadier Division* – were largely depleted and exhausted following the recent fighting on the Oder defensive line. The troops of the 1st Belorussian Front (under the command of Marshal Georgy Konstantinovich Zhukov) from the north and the 1st Ukrainian Front (under the command of Marshal Ivan Stepanovich Konev) from the south were accelerating their advance to encircle the German capital.

The date of the Spanish unit's arrival in Berlin from Potsdam is believed to have been at dusk on the 21st, almost at the last moment before the encirclement of Berlin was completely closed.

Cuff band title of the *Nordland Division*, to which the Spanish unit was nominally attached. From the collections of the Tøjhusmuseet, Copenhagen. (Nationalmuseet, Danmark); CC-BY-SA

Members of the 7th Guards Tank Corps in the suburbs of Berlin. In the foreground, the wreckage of a destroyed German car. To the right of the image, a Soviet soldier aims his pistol at the vehicle. (Georgi Ugrinovich, Public Domain)

Saturday 21 April

In the city, from 11.30, approximately 500 pieces of heavy artillery, mainly 152mm, began to strike not only the capital's suburbs as had been the case before, but now also reached the city centre because of the proximity of the front line. The immense number of shells fired affected most of the city, with the Reichstag, the Brandenburg Gate, the Royal Palace and the wide boulevard Unter den Linden, as well as elsewhere, being hit. Corpses, wrecked vehicles and more rubble littered the streets, which were already badly damaged by the continual bombing that had taken place in the preceding months. The smoke and burning buildings served only to foreshadow what awaited the capital of the Reich: a veritable hell of fire, death and desolation, which would unfold in the days to come.

The point of impact of artillery fire was far less predictable than that of aerial bombardments, to which the people of Berlin, like those in other German towns, had become accustomed (if it is indeed possible to become accustomed to such a situation).

On the 21st, the 2nd Guards Tank Army approached the city from the north-east, occupying the area between the Weissensee (held by the 1st Mechanised Corps) and the vicinity of Hohenschönhausen (held by the 12th Guards Tank Corps). In between them, troops from the 3rd and 5th Shock Armies were deployed, both armies belonging to Zhukov's 1st Belorussian Front.

Helmuth Weidling was appointed commander of the defence of the Reich capital during the Battle of Berlin. (Bundesarchiv, Bild 146-1983-028-05)

From the Rüdersdorf-Erkner area, troops of the 8th Guards Army and the 1st Guards Tank Army also advanced towards the city, carrying out an encircling manoeuvre towards the south-west, with the aim of approaching the city from both the south and the south-east. This sector corresponded to the access route used by the Spanish to reach Berlin.

The 3rd Guards Tank Army reached Königs Wusterhausen, completing the encirclement of the German 9th Army. As a result, the latter would not be able to take part in the fighting to defend Berlin.

Inside *Festung* Berlin, chaos was taking hold; Hitler ordered the arrest of the commander-in-chief of the 56th Panzer Corps, Helmuth Weidling, and sentenced him to death on the (erroneous) suspicion that his troops had withdrawn from the front. After proving his innocence, he was promoted to the post of commander-in-chief of the Berlin defence on 23 April, replacing *Generalleutnant* Hellmuth Reymann. The three anti-aircraft towers responded with their fire to the intense artillery barrage, inflicting casualties on the Soviets in the suburb of Marzahn. These impressive, almost impregnable towers not only fulfilled their anti-aircraft role but also played a part in actions against enemy armoured vehicles.

Panic grew by the minute among senior ministry officials and their agencies' staffs, who began to flee Berlin en masse as the encirclement of the city closed in. This occurred during the final US air raid on the capital, as from that moment onwards Soviet troops would begin fighting in its streets and their Western Allies would not risk their being accidentally targeted.

That morning in Potsdam, the Spanish troops were reviewed, resulting, according to Vadillo,[1] in a muster figure of 359 men, although, as is always the case, this figure is open to debate. According to other historians, this figure should be reduced to some 150–200 men, with 150–180 being considered more likely. When one of the companies of the *Einheit Ezquerra* was called up to be sent to the 'Alpine fortress', existing records put the number at around 70 men; therefore, considering that by this stage of the war the companies numbered around 90 men, the figures add up to the entire unit totalling 150 (bearing in mind that approximately 30 would decide not to move to Berlin). Taking into account the testimonies of Miguel Ezquerra and Pedro Zabala, the figure would correspond to some 80 or 90 men from the Spanish *Einheit* during the fighting for Berlin. It should be remembered that, in these final days of the war, German companies ranged in size from 80 to 120 men, although this number was variable depending on a great many circumstances.

The troops were informed of the new orders, and those who did not wish to take part in the difficult undertaking – defence in the streets of Berlin, 'to the last man' – were allowed, for the last time, to return to Spain, if they could manage it by their own means, with money and a safe-conduct pass for the area still occupied by the Germans.

LEV troops in their Spanish uniforms march past the commander of the *Königsberg* Army Group at the farewell ceremony for the Spanish unit on 31 March 1944. (Museo del Ejército/Biblioteca Virtual de Defensa)

1 Fernando Vadillo, *Gran Crónica de la División Azul en los Irreductibles* (Granada: García Hispán, 2008), pp.183–184.

In his speech, Ezquerra highlighted the causes for which many had been fighting since the days of the Blue Division: anti-Bolshevism, the defence of the West against the Soviet hordes, and loyalty to the German people in that terrible war. Demonstrating what Spanish soldiers are capable of and how they know how to fight both when the light of victory shines and when the darkness of defeat looms on the horizon. To recall the words from his biography:

> I returned to Potsdam, had the companies fall in, and informed them of the situation, without concealing the gravity of the moment: "Comrades: The encirclement of the city of Berlin can be considered imminent. This is the moment for the great decisions that each of us must make, with full awareness and in accordance with it. We have been assigned to the defence of Berlin, which will be long, arduous and perhaps painful. Who wishes to stay? Who wishes to leave? To those who remain, I gratefully give you this news: it will be Russian troops we will have to face in the siege of Berlin. With the strength God grants us, we shall know how to avenge the dead of our war.
>
> The task will be arduous and requires, in addition to courage, physical endurance. I repeat, those who do not feel capable, for whatever reason, of risking their lives in this battle, may return to Spain today. They will receive passports and money, as well as the necessary instructions to join other Spaniards who are in Munich or on the Swiss border. I am not ordering you to leave; what I do not want is for anyone to stay against their will."[2]

Following this impassioned speech, the majority of the men reaffirmed their resolve to continue their 'adventure' in Berlin, with only 34 deciding not to fight on the streets of Berlin, preferring the no less complicated adventure of attempting to return to Spain. Those who remained were thus volunteers amongst volunteers, and for the most part with extensive combat experience.

The men who decided to stay behind travelled into the heart of Berlin on the *U-Bahn* (underground railway), which was still in operation. After boarding the train, the journey began, with various stops at the stations of Krumme Lanke, Onkel Toms Hütte, Oskar- Helene-Heim, Dahlem-Dorf and Hohenzollernplatz on *U-Bahn* line 3; following the route along *U-Bahn* line 1 through the station at Kurfürsten, ending when they reached the vicinity of Anhalter Station. The Spaniards would have alighted from the *U-Bahn* at the station closest to their destination, Gleisdreieck, a few dozen metres from Anhalter Station.

2 Fernando Vadillo, *Gran Crónica de la División Azul en los Irreductibles* (Granada: García Hispán, 2008), pp.218–219.

Anhalter Station must have been one of the first buildings the men of the *Einheit Ezquerra* saw when they arrived in Berlin on Saturday 21 April 1945. (Public Domain)

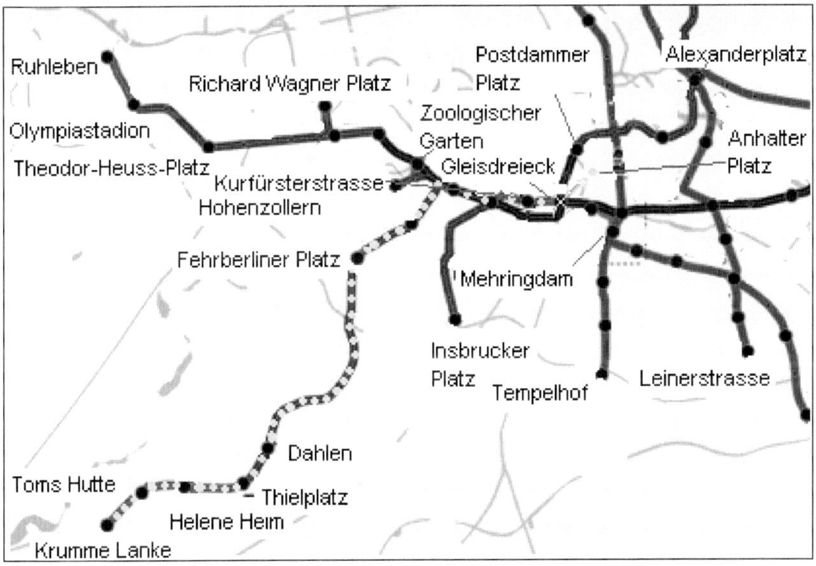

Route taken by the *Einheit Ezquerra* on 21 April 1945 from Krumme Lanke Station in the Potsdam area to close to Anhalter Station. The journey was made by *U-Bahn*. (Image by the author)

Following the departure on 18 April of the 71 men from *SS-Obersturmführer* Pedro Zabala's Company, the Spanish unit known as the *Einheit Ezquerra* was reduced to around 80–90 men, who were divided into two combat units, most likely after orders received by Ezquerra upon his arrival in Berlin. To these would later be added a variable number of men who, in one way or another, came to be temporarily under the command of the *Einheit Ezquerra*.

As for the two groups of *Einheit Ezquerra*, one remained under Ezquerra's own command and the other came under the command of *SS-Untersturmführer* Ricardo Botet Moro. In the subsequent days of fighting in Berlin, existing sources make no distinction between the two groups, although they very likely lost contact during the numerous skirmishes that took place within the city. The fact is that Ezquerra, in his biography, makes no further mention of Ricardo Botet during the fighting in the days that followed.

Upon leaving the station and reaching the surface, the men would see the pitiful state the capital was in; blackened buildings, largely in ruins, some of them still smouldering, wrecked vehicles, rubble, barricades. In a word, it was hell, and yet the worst was still to come.

Once assembled, and after parting ways with Botet, Ezquerra's men were housed in an emergency shelter. This was situated on the ground floor of a half-ruined building, in premises that in better times had been a shoe shop. It was located near the Chancellery and the Ministry District. One of Ezquerra's men recalled these moments:

> Once in Berlin, we were housed, along with other Latvian volunteers, in a house on Jägerstrasse, with the narrator of this story being appointed as the liaison between our temporary quarters and the high command, which was based at that time in the Air Ministry, a short distance away.[3]

It was here that Ezquerra recalled, 'the arrival of 17 Frenchmen wearing the uniforms of Doriot's militias, as well as four Belgians from the SS *Wallonien* Legion'. It is possible that these additional men were incorporated into the *Einheit Ezquerra*, as it had far too few men for the difficult and dangerous tasks for which it had been brought to Berlin, although there are no reports of this other than Ezquerra's account. Another, far less credible version given by Ezquerra in his book states that some 30 Belgians belonging to the *Wallonien* joined his combat force; however, as there is no reference to this in any other source (the *Wallonien* is usually well-documented), it is highly doubtful that this actually happened.

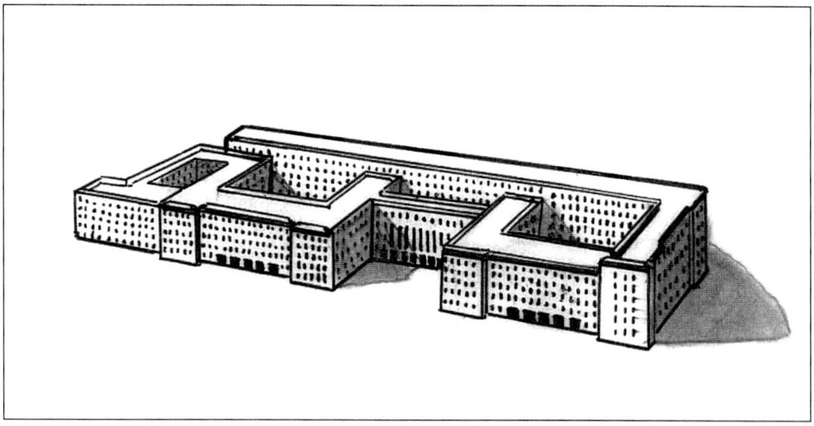

Artistic view of the Air Ministry in Berlin. Many of the units that took part in the city's defence were organised from here, including the one led by Ezquerra. (Image created by the author in collaboration with J. Pérez)

3 S.N., 'Yo estuve prisionero en Rusia' in *Diario Patria*, Granada, 21 de diciembre de 1945, p.3, cited in Ángel González Pinilla, *La Legión Clandestina* (Madrid: Gutiksland, S.L. 2021).

Whether there were 21 or a few more, the French and Belgian men attached to Ezquerra's unit would have been distributed amongst the Spanish soldiers and not as an independent group. This most likely occurred due to the need to increase the unit's numbers to make it fully operational. Furthermore, it is highly likely that, circumstantially, in the heat of the fighting in the German capital, at specific moments, men attached to other units – who may well have included French or Belgian soldiers – were temporarily placed under the command of the Spanish unit, which, as we have noted, needed more men to carry out the missions assigned to them with a better chance of success. In fact, we shall see later that the Spanish unit began to operate alongside the Latvian unit for the same reason: the small number of soldiers in both units.

Vincent Hunt reports the account of a veteran Latvian soldier, Oļģerts Bunga, who refers to the presence of Spaniards at the temporary barracks on Jägerstrasse, specifically mentioning the ruthless attitude of some SS squads tasked with watching them:

> On my return, I saw two cars with machine guns and SS soldiers at the junction of Jägerstrasse. The guns were trained on our quarters. At the next junction, behind our quarters, there was a restaurant with a cellar. Our soldiers had visited it and taken a few bottles of alcohol. They told me this while we were waiting for the remaining soldiers to return from the cellar. Apparently, five soldiers had been shot. I did not see them. I do not know which units they were from. The German soldiers who had arrived at Jägerstrasse were, apparently, not aggressive. Once their commander had left, they had no desire to fight or shoot. Our soldiers considered what to do to save the others. We went across the street, where the soldiers of the Spanish Blue Division were billeted on the upper floors, to ask for advice and act as allies. They were drunk and we realised they would not get involved. No one came out of the cellar and the Germans soon left without entering it. I do not know what our unit commanders were doing. I did not see any civilians in the buildings and streets around Jägerstrasse.[4]

Pre-war image of central Berlin showing Friedrichstrasse and Jägerstrasse towards Unter den Linden. The area where Spanish soldiers were stationed during the Battle of Berlin. (Public Domain)

4 Vincent Hunt, *Sent to Die in Berlin* (Warwick: Helion & Co., 2026). Details from the author; at the time of writing the book is forthcoming.

In this account, the Spanish soldiers (still being referred to as belonging to the Blue Division) are situated on the upper floors of the building on Jägerstrasse. Despite the short time they had been in the city, they had already got hold of alcohol and were making good use of it. In this regard, it should be noted that Faupel was responsible, at least initially, for providing certain supplies in the German capital using funds from the Ibero-American Institute.

Upon arriving in Berlin, the Spanish soldiers, as they did not have enough weapons, nor ones suitable for the mission that awaited them, were supplied with a significant quantity of armament. Among these, the MP40 submachine gun and the MP44 assault rifle stand out, as well as *panzerfausts*, pistols, hand grenades, MG42s, et cetera. Of course, they were also supplied with ample ammunition for the various weapons.

This weaponry would prove extremely useful in close-quarters combat, both against infantry and against armoured vehicles moving through Berlin's largely ruined buildings and shattered streets. The heavy firepower these weapons could provide enabled small groups of men to halt, at least temporarily, the advance of the Soviet troops, who were vastly superior in numbers. In this regard, the MG42 machine gun and the MP44 assault rifle, together with the *panzerfaust*, were the 'stars' of the defence of Berlin.

Close-up of the battle scars on Jägerstrasse as they appear today. The fighting in Berlin's Government District was particularly fierce. (Photograph by Akiko Hada, courtesy of Vincent Hunt)

From the time when the Spanish troops were still quartered on Jägerstrasse, sharing accommodation with the Latvians, we have another account from a Latvian soldier in which he also mentions the Spanish; Uldis Dukurs in an interview said:

> On Jägerstrasse, when they [the Latvian soldiers] are about to go into battle, a Latvian officer lines them up and they sing *'Dievs, Sveti Latvija'* [God bless Latvia]. Some Spanish officers from the Blue Division ask what they are singing. A translator tells them that they are asking for God's help for their homeland. They ask: 'Can you go to your death and

> pray not for yourself, but for your homeland? Do you really love Latvia that much?' 'Yes,' says the translator. 'You can see they are singing from the heart. That is what defines us as Latvians, and if anyone says we are fighting for Germany and on its side, it is the greatest folly, the greatest absurdity. We are fighting against the world's greatest enemy.'[5]

Hunt also notes, 'the historian specialising in the Soviet Army, Aivars Pētersons, wrote that the 10 men from *Kampfgruppe Ezquerra* who were accompanying them watched the Latvians' attitude with amazement.'[6]

View of Jägerstrasse today, photograph taken by Vincent Hunt. The Latvian soldiers were positioned at 4–6 Jägerstrasse (where the headquarters of a coal mining company was located), with the Spaniards on the other side of the street on the upper floors of the building. (Courtesy of Vincent Hunt)

This account shows us how the Latvians, who had been forced to deploy in Berlin, were very clear about what they were fighting for, and it was the same enemy as that of the men of Ezquerra (although the latter had gone to Berlin voluntarily) – the Soviet Army.

The city of Berlin had lost at least two-thirds of its buildings as a result of the relentless pounding by Allied bombers; as well as half of its pre-war population of 4 million (many of whom had not died but had been forced to leave the capital). Those residents who had decided to remain in the capital had to seek shelter in bomb shelters and cellars. Berlin's streets and avenues, once clean and well-maintained, presented a pitiful sight, littered with craters, rubble, barricades, fires, smoke, vehicle wrecks and corpses. As an example of the practical use made of any available material,

5 Vincent Hunt, *Sent to Die in Berlin* (Warwick: Helion & Co., 2026). Details from the author; at the time of writing the book is forthcoming.

6 Vincent Hunt, *Sent to Die in Berlin* (Warwick: Helion & Co., 2026). Details from the author; at the time of writing the book is forthcoming.

it is worth noting how the remains of destroyed or disabled trams were used as barricades; these were partly made with rubble to give them greater stability in their role as obstacles. Similarly, any type of vehicle capable of serving the same purpose was employed as part of the hastily constructed and haphazard defensive network on Berlin's streets.

The rubble of the countless bombed-out buildings sometimes served as genuine 'natural' obstacles, hindering the advance of the Soviet infantry and their supporting armoured vehicles, while creating terrain that was relatively easy to defend for well-trained men determined to hold the ground. But as we shall see, this was not always the case, and the sheer number of Soviet troops had tipped the balance long before the assault on the city began.

A multitude of parapets, strongpoints, barricades, et cetera were created, whose mission was initially to prevent the advance of Soviet troops or at least to delay that advance. These ranged from simple piles of rubble and sandbags to proper fortifications in various buildings (as was the case with the opera house during the Soviet advance towards the Reichstag). There was a particular preference for machine guns and anti-tank weapons in these defences, given the nature of the fighting in the city streets.

A special type of defence fortification involved the use of tank turrets, half-buried in various strategic positions around the city. There are photographs of Panther tank turrets, half-hidden amongst rubble on wide avenues, which allowed for the greater range of their guns.

As part of Berlin's static defensive system, there was strict control of the bridges that had not been blown up. These featured anti-tank barriers and obstacles as their main defensive elements.

The war in Berlin is over, and the winners celebrate victory. The photograph shows a group of Soviet soldiers posing with their armoured vehicles in front of the Siegessäule (victory column). (From waralbum.ru. Photographer unknown)

The Soviet Army would launch an assault on the city with one and a half million men, backed by vast quantities of artillery, tanks and air support. Opposing them were around 45,000 men from the *Wehrmacht* and the SS, some 2,000 men in the Government District, as well as just over 40,000 men from the *Volkssturm*. The armoured component consisted of about 60 tanks for the defence of the entire city. The ratio was at least 10 to 1 in terms of troop numbers in favour of the Soviet attackers.

The defensive deployment in Berlin was roughly as follows: in the south-east was the *SS Nordland Division*; in the south-west, the *20. Panzergrenadier Division* (in relatively good condition), protecting the left flank of the former; to the east were the remnants of the *Müncheberg Division*; to the north, the remnants of the *9. Fallschirmjäger Division*; and in the centre, the *18. Panzergrenadier Division*. Due to the general weakness of these divisions, the density of the defensive lines was increased in all sectors with the addition of the generally ill-prepared and poorly-trained men of the *Volkssturm*, the boys of the Hitler Youth, and the newly formed battalions made up of soldiers back from the front for any number of reasons, as well as rearguard units. SS troops garrisoned in the capital, as well as the *Grossdeutschland Regiment*, also did their bit.

A man from the *Volkssturm* learning to fire the *panzerfaust*. This weapon became a dangerous enemy for Soviet armoured vehicles, even in the hands of children and the elderly. (Bundesarchiv Bild 146-1973-001-36)

In reality, the bulk of the troops holding out in Berlin consisted of the men of the *Volkssturm*, with 69 battalions mobilised and a further 47 ready for mobilisation; the problem being that in many cases they lacked weapons or had very little ammunition. Also present in Berlin were remnants of the 503rd SS Heavy Tank Battalion (SS-*Pz.Abt.503*), with a few Panzer VI *Königstigers*. We should also recall that, like the Spanish unit, there were remnants of the French *33. Waffen-SS Grenadier-Division* (*Französische Nr. 1*) *Charlemagne* and a battalion from the severely depleted *15. Waffen-SS Grenadier-Division* (*Lettische Nr. 1*).

In this regard, an extract from the book *Berlin 1933–45 avec Wilhelm Mohnke* mentions the presence of these units in Berlin:

> When the *Divisionskommandeur*, *SS-Brigadeführer* Dr Gustav Krukenberg, was sent to the Reich capital, Fenet, with the battalion [referring to the French *Sturmbataillon Charlemagne*], and *SS-Obersturmführer* Wilhelm Weber, with the *Divisionskampfschule* (combat school), they set out from Neustrelitz, 100 kilometres north of Berlin. There are also Spanish volunteers from the 'Blue Division' and Latvian SS riflemen, who cannot and will not surrender, and who are fighting at the Zitadelle.[7]

Photograph taken on 5 March 1944 when the members of the LEV received the order to return home – not all of them returned to Spain. (Museo del Ejército/Biblioteca Virtual de Defensa)

Although the Spaniards are erroneously referred to as being from the Blue Division, Fischer does mention the three foreign units that would actively participate in the Battle of Berlin in the same sectors.

In the capital, the army had only 46 field guns and 41 anti-tank guns, but there were also some 270 anti-aircraft guns that could also be used in ground combat, although the majority were situated in static positions with no possibility of tactical movement, as was the case with those in the anti-aircraft towers.

The three gigantic anti-aircraft towers situated within the city provided significant artillery support to the defenders, while also serving as excellent observation posts in the final days of the war, as would become evident during the Soviet assault on the city. The first was situated at the zoo, the second in Friedrichshain, and the third in Humboldthain. These three towers were situated about 3 kilometres apart. This allowed them to support one another and form a triangle around the centre of the city, which was covered by all three. The maximum horizontal range of the guns was about 20–22 kilometres, and about 14,800 metres in vertical fire. The artillery pieces consisted mainly of 12.8cm, 10.5cm, 8.8cm and 2cm guns. The fire control was handled by towers built specifically for that purpose some 350 metres away.

7 Thomas Fischer, *Berlin 1933–45 avec Wilhelm Mohnke* (Paris: Éditions Heimdal, 2013), p.63.

The troops responsible for manning the towers consisted mainly of *Luftwaffe* personnel supported by members of the Hitler Youth.

Some parts of these anti-aircraft towers were used as air-raid shelters for the civilian population.

Their construction was so robust that they remained virtually intact until the end of the war, despite the intense artillery bombardment to which they were subjected.

The order was issued on 6 March 1945 to turn Berlin into *Festung Berlin*, for which *Generalleutnant* Reymann was put in charge of the fortification works, which were based on three defensive rings:

> The first is the suburban ring (which overlaps with the route of the *S-Bahn* circular line) and, with a perimeter of approximately 234 kilometres, would encircle the entire city. It was actually based on natural or pre-existing obstacles (lakes, rivers, canals, et cetera), supplemented by a small number of defensive positions, mainly consisting of trenches, barricades and anti-tank ditches manned by the *Volkssturm*.
>
> The second is the ring situated between the first and the third, which surrounds the Government District and is bounded by the River Spree to the north and the Landwehr Canal to the south. It had a perimeter of some 96 kilometres. It ran through the outermost suburbs of the capital, and within it defensive works similar to those of the first ring had also been carried out, though these too were woefully inadequate for the task at hand.
>
> The third defensive ring, with a perimeter of around 40 kilometres, covered the Berlin districts and was nominally divided into eight defensive sectors (from A to H), plus a central sector (Z), each commanded by an *oberst*. The latter sector is also known as the *Zitadelle*; it housed the most important government buildings, including the Reichstag, the Chancellery and the various ministries, and would be the last part of Berlin to fall into Soviet hands.

The main units defending Berlin were those belonging to Weidling's 56th Panzer Corps, which had been stationed just a few days earlier on the Oder River line. Following the fighting on the hills of Seelow, this Panzer Corps was overwhelmed by the Soviet advance and was ultimately tasked with defending the capital of the Reich.

Based on the assumption that the main Soviet attack would be launched from the south and the east, the troops of the 56th Panzer Corps were initially deployed as follows.

> The *9. Fallschirmjäger Division* in Sector A (in the north-east of Greater Berlin).
> The *Müncheberg Panzer Division* in Sector B (in the north).
> The *Nordland Division* in Sector C (in the south-east, in the districts of Neukölln and Treptow).

The *20. Panzergrenadier Division* in Sector E (in the south-west, in the districts of Steglitz-Zehlendorf).
The *18. Panzergrenadier Division* remained in reserve near Tempelhof Airport, which was part of Sector D (in the south).

The rest of the city's defensive forces consisted mainly of *Volkssturm*, Hitler Youth, elements of the RAD, the *Grossdeutschland Regiment*, SS police detachments and remnants of various *Luftwaffe* units.

Sunday 22 April to Thursday 26 April

During this period, there is almost a complete absence of data or reports indicating the activities of the men of the Spanish unit.

General Helmuth Weidling took charge of the defence of the German capital on 23 April by the direct order of Adolf Hitler and replacing *Generalleutnant* Hellmuth Reymann.

Although the regular troops in the defence were for the most part severely understrength, being mere shadows of their former selves, the civilians contributed quantity rather than quality. After the deployment of the troops in anticipation of the main Soviet attack from the south and east as outlined above, the entire defensive force had to be redeployed in the face of a Soviet assault from all directions. Consequently, the defence was reorganised:

Sectors A and B (north-east and east of Berlin): the *Müncheberg Panzer Division*, consisting of about 3,000 men and around 30 armoured vehicles.
Sector C (southeast of Berlin, including the districts of Neukölln and Treptow): *SS Division Nordland*, comprising some 1,500 men and around 20 armoured vehicles (mainly *Sturmgeschütz III* assault guns and Panzer V, Panther, tanks), supported by some 2,000 men of the *Volkssturm*, to whom were added the remnants of the *33. Waffen-SS Grenadier-Division* (*Französische Nr. 1*) *Charlemagne* after they managed to enter Berlin on 24 April.
Sector D (south of Berlin, including the districts of Tempelhof and Schöneberg): *Volkssturm* and SS police detachments.
Sector E (south-west Berlin, including the districts of Steglitz-Zehlendorf): *20. Panzergrenadier Division.*
Sector F (west of Berlin, including the districts of Spandau and Charlottenburg): around 3,000 boys from the Hitler Youth and elements of the RAD, of the *Volkssturm* and of SS police detachments.
Sectors G and H (in northern Berlin, including the Frankfurter Allee axis): *9. Fallschirmjäger Division* with around 4,000 men.

Sector Z (*zitadelle*): *18. Panzergrenadier Division*, comprising some 3,000 men and an unknown number of tanks, and *Kampfgruppe Mohnke*. This was the sector in which the small Spanish unit was deployed.

Sunday 22 April

While the German troops were retreating, on Sunday 22 April the Soviet troops, after fierce fighting, managed to penetrate the north-east of the German capital towards the suburbs of Blankenburg, Heinersdorf, Buchholz, Malchow and Biesdorf; the front reaching the districts of Weissensee, Lichtenberg and Pankow. The 3rd and 5th Shock Armies, having taken up their positions in the northern (the 3rd attacked Berlin from Reinickendorf) and eastern districts of Berlin (the 5th from Friedrichsfelde and Karlshorst), slowed their advance to reorganise before the final assault. The persistent rain, combined with the fires, smoke and dust, gave the great city a hellish appearance, which would persist for several more days.

From this day onwards, as Norling recounts, the *Nordland* (the unit to which the Spanish formation was nominally attached) could no longer be considered a military unit in the strict sense. Its men were distributed into various *kampfgruppen*, each comprising around 35–45 men (as previously noted, upon arriving in Berlin, the Spanish unit was divided into two such groups, which fully corresponds to the number of members in these small combat groups).[8] These men were forced to fall back to positions in the Tiergarten, due to the mounting pressure of the Soviet steamroller continuing its slow but determined advance on the battered city of Berlin.

Monday 23 April

Despite the adverse weather conditions and the intense Soviet pressure, some small reinforcements for the defence arrived in the city on this day. Many of them were simply men who had been on the move for days, retreating from the east. Among them, the *Grossadmiral Dönitz* naval battalion, commanded by Franz Kuhlmann, stands out; it arrived by air! This only served to further increase the heterogeneity of Berlin's defending troops.

Fearing that Russian troops might infiltrate via the *U-Bahn* and *S-Bahn* tunnels, traffic on these lines was halted and barricades were erected in many of them.

On 23 April, *General* Weidling took command of the Berlin defence area on Hitler's orders. The Russians occupied the Berlin suburbs, where

8 Erik Norling, *Raza De Vikingos. La División SS Norland (1943–1945) Waffen SS Norland* (Granada: García Hispán, 2007), pp.153–154.

Lesen und weitergeben!

Der Panzerbär

23. April 1945

KAMPFBLATT FÜR DIE VERTEIDIGER GROSS-BERLINS

Vor der äusseren Verteidigungszone

Erfolgreiche Gegenangriffe an der südlichen und mittleren Ostfront

Volk und Führung

Eine ernste Mahnung des Führers: Merkt Euch!

WESTFRONT

Lebensmittel für 12 Wochen

Front page of the *Panzerbär* for 23 April 1945. (Collection of J. Arráez)

the defensive ring was weakest, with the districts of Britz, Lichterfelde, Marienfelde, Lichtenberg and Prenzlauer Berg falling one after another.

In the south, the Teltow Canal served as a 'frontier line', while in the north the Hohenzollern and Schiffahrts Canals (the latter only partially) fulfilled the same role.

The 56th Panzer Corps established its headquarters in the suburb of Rudow during the night of 22/23 April after crossing the Spree and part of the Teltow Canal. Once there, they managed to re-establish contact (after just over 30 hours of being cut off) with the 9th Army. Following some disagreements between Weidling and the OKH, the 56th Panzer Corps was finally ordered to take up positions within the city.

The Red Army was closing the ring ever tighter that would strangle Berlin, almost entirely achieving this by the 24th, but only at the cost of suffering severe losses at the hands of the capital's defenders.

On the 23rd, they received news that the Russians had entered Potsdam,

A column of Soviet IS-2 tanks advancing along a German road. These armoured monsters proved a formidable foe for Berlin's defenders, who had few tanks or assault vehicles at their disposal. (Public Domain)

where a group of Spanish under the command of a *sergeant* named Cerezo were still stationed. And although they fought with extreme bravery, even engaging in hand-to-hand combat, most of them were killed. It appears that only Cerezo and a few other men managed to survive and break through the Russian lines. However, all trace of these men was lost in the chaos of the final days of the Reich. This news only served to heighten the desire of Ezquerra and his men to confront the Soviets.

Tuesday 24 April

The *20. Panzergrenadier Division* was forced back towards the island of Wannsee, with its position in the defensive lines being covered by the *18. Panzergrenadier Division*, which left its previous position to the reserve troops. The *9. Fallschirmjäger Division* prepared to defend the northernmost sectors, based in the area of the Humboldthain anti-aircraft tower; the *Müncheberg Panzer Division* would defend the Tempelhof Airport area and the *11. SS Panzergrenadier Division* was to be responsible for defending the Neukölln-Kreuzberg area. The Spanish troops had been attached to this latter unit, and were therefore positioned in the south-central area of the capital.

On the Soviet side, the 3rd Guards Tank Army crossed the Teltow Canal, which had until then served as the line between the two enemies. The 12th Guards Rifle Corps was already engaged with the men defending the Wedding *S-Bahn* Station and the Humboldthain anti-aircraft tower. The 7th Rifle Corps reached Alexanderplatz. The 5th Shock Army, together with the 26th Guards Rifle Corps and the 32nd Rifle Corps, reached the Schlachthof complex, now within the inner defence ring. The 9th Rifle Corps crossed the Spree, driving back the elements of the *11. SS Panzergrenadier Division* tasked with defending the area.

In the south, the 3rd Guards Tank Army linked up with the 1st Ukrainian Front.

The 3rd Guards Tank Corps crossed the Teltow Canal, against some strong defences. The Corps was supported by the 6th and 7th Guards Tank Corps. The German resistance was led by the *18.* and *20. Panzergrenadier Divisions*, supported by a small armoured force consisting mainly of PzKw IVs.

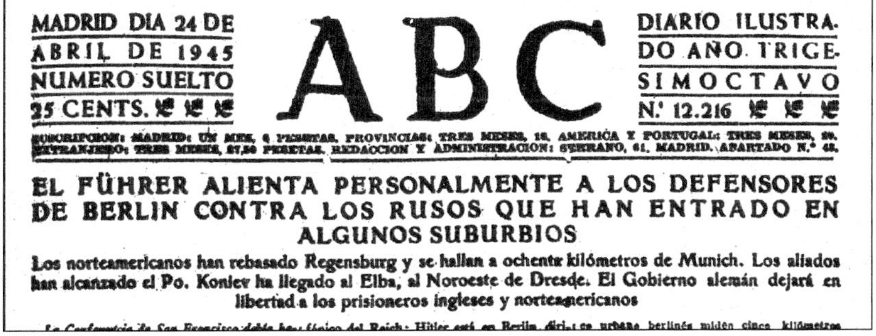

MADRID DIA 24 DE ABRIL DE 1945
NUMERO SUELTO 25 CENTS.

ABC

DIARIO ILUSTRADO AÑO TRIGESIMOCTAVO
N.º 12.216

SUSCRIPCION: MADRID: UN MES, 6 PESETAS. PROVINCIAS: TRES MESES, 18. AMERICA Y PORTUGAL: TRES MESES, 20. EXTRANJERO: TRES MESES, 27,50 PESETAS. REDACCION Y ADMINISTRACION: SERRANO, 61, MADRID. APARTADO N.º 43.

EL FÜHRER ALIENTA PERSONALMENTE A LOS DEFENSORES DE BERLIN CONTRA LOS RUSOS QUE HAN ENTRADO EN ALGUNOS SUBURBIOS

Los norteamericanos han rebasado Regensburg y se hallan a ochenta kilómetros de Munich. Los aliados han alcanzado el Po. Koniev ha llegado al Elba, al Noroeste de Dresde. El Gobierno alemán dejará en libertad a los prisioneros ingleses y norteamericanos

Front page of the *ABC* newspaper dated 24 April 1945, where the arrival of the Soviets in the suburbs of the capital Berlin is mentioned for the first time. (Public Domain)

It was raining on 24 April, which made the already difficult German defensive and Soviet offensive tasks even more challenging.

The Spanish unit was not engaged in any combat and was deployed in Sector Z. Given the nature of the Spanish formation, together with the Latvian unit, they will have been deployed as a rapid reaction force to counter any enemy advance that managed to breach or seriously threaten the defences in that sector.

Wednesday 25 April

At last, the grey weather gave way to a sunny day, but despite this, a thick cloud of smoke hung over the city, caused by the numerous fires and explosions that had been going on for days.

Soviet troops were consolidating their positions in the various suburbs of the capital, with fighting intensifying against the defenders, mainly in the streets of the eastern and northern districts. Specifically, the 47th Army and the 4th Guards Tank Army were advancing towards Ketzin; the 125th Rifle Corps was attacking Spandau and Gatow airfield, although encountering strong German resistance. The 2nd Guards Tank Army was in the vicinity of the Siemensstadt suburb and the 3rd Shock Army crossed the Hohenzollern Canal. The 12th Guards Rifle Corps advanced towards Moabit, while the 7th Rifle Corps was in the vicinity of Alexanderplatz. The 5th Shock Army advanced slightly towards the city centre, while the 9th Rifle Corps forced its way across the Landwehr Canal to reach the vicinity of Görlitzer Station. The 8th Guards Army managed to force the Teltow Canal and headed towards the vicinity of Tempelhof Airport, where it encountered fanatical resistance. Not surprisingly, the defenders had to hold the airport to keep alive the hope of receiving reinforcements and supplies by air. The 3rd Guards Tank Army advanced towards the *S-Bahn* defensive ring, moving from the south towards the city centre.

In *Der Panzerbär*, Wilhelm Mohnke, as commander of Sector Z, issued this proclamation:

> The *Freikorps* Mohnke calls!
>
> Men of Berlin!
> At the hour of the final great decision in the Battle of Berlin, there are, as always in German history, fanatical individual fighters who want to do more than their duty, who want to throw themselves at the hated enemy with all the means at their disposal to take revenge for all the suffering, death, misfortune and destruction he has brought upon our people and our city
>
> You, too, are one of them!
>
> You too have the irrepressible will to be on the front line in the final decisive counter-attack against the Bolsheviks who have invaded our Berlin! Your place is in the Freikorps Mohnke!

The Freikorps Mohnke is currently recruiting men who are ready and determined to fight!

Now, in the face of the greatest danger, show who is a decent bloke with his heart in the right place, who shies away from no challenge and remains loyal to the flag he himself has chosen.

Never have we felt closer to the Führer than at this hour when he has decided to remain among us, to fight with us and to defeat the enemy.

Long live the Führer!

Reporting points:

1. East–West axis, Kleiner Stern
2. Halle Gate
3. Castle Bridge near Zeughaus.

Also bring weapons and bicycles.

Signed Mohnke
SS-Brigadeführer and *Generalmajor der Waffen-SS*,
hitherto Commander of the *Leibstandarte-SS Adolf Hitler*.[9]

Soviet tanks in a suburb of Berlin during the last week of April 1945. (Bundesarchiv Bild 183-R83903)

Also on 25 April, Joachim Ziegler, commander of the *Nordland Division* (or, more accurately, of the remnants of the division that were still in action), was summoned to the Chancellery, and was replaced in his post by *SS-Brigadeführer* Gustav Krukenberg. The latter had only arrived in the capital of the Reich a few days earlier, commanding a French combat group from

9 *Der Panzerbär*, 26 April 1945. This and other quotations from *Der Panzerbär* are taken from, Felipe Anguiano III, *The Panzer Bear and the fall of Berlin 1945: An English Translation of all 8 Panzerbär Newspapers from April 22 to April 29, 1945* (Location unknown: Privately published, 2023).

the *33. Waffen-SS Grenadier-Division (Französische Nr. 1) Charlemagne*, which, according to Norling, possibly consisted of just over three hundred men, although it is thought that the number could have been between 400 and 500 men (a significant reinforcement to the city's depleted defences, as they would demonstrate over the following days).

Thousands of leaflets, in German, produced by the Soviets and aimed at both the soldiers and the civilian population holding out in Berlin, were raining down on the city. The literal translation of the leaflet is as follows:

> To the German soldiers and officers and to the people of the city of Berlin. – The Red Army is concentrating its forces around Berlin. Tens of thousands of guns are being transported towards the capital. Thousands of heavy bombers are waiting at the airfields. We have thousands of tanks at our disposal. The Red Army has the military might of its allies to deploy these powerful forces. Decisive days are approaching. The Red Army troops are ready for the final assault. If you ignore our warnings and do not cease your resistance, we shall send a terrifying cloud of fire and shrapnel upon Berlin. We are prepared to annihilate and raze any pocket of resistance. - Berliners, come to your senses! Do you wish to die for a cause that has nothing to do with you, to sacrifice yourselves for a handful of Nazi leaders? Disobey their orders! Stop digging trenches and abandon your work in the arms factories! Take shelter in the air-raid shelters! Give shelter to the soldiers and officers who no longer wish to fight and admit that the war is lost! – Soldiers and officers of the German armies, men of the *Volkssturm*, cease all resistance, surrender, return home as civilians, go to the air-raid shelters! If you disregard our recommendations, you will be guilty of the deaths of your fathers, wives and children, and of the loss of all their possessions.
>
> The Red Army command guarantees that the lives and property of all those (including members of the National Socialist Party) who cease to offer resistance and surrender to the Red Army will be spared.
>
> The Command of the First Belorussian Front of the Red Army.

Thursday 26 April

The noose around the Reich capital was gradually tightening. *SS-Brigadeführer* and *Generalmajor der Waffen-SS* Mohnke, in command of the *Zitadelle* (Z) sector and his *kampfgruppe*, gradually incorporated into his command all the units operating in this combat sector, along with the troops who had been thrown back from other sectors and were fleeing towards the city centre.

Weidling, as commander-in-chief of Berlin, realised that the arrival of reinforcements in the German capital was becoming virtually impossible and believed that German troops could only continue to defend the capital for a couple of days more. This was why he prepared an escape plan for the German units defending Berlin, with the intention of implementing it if necessary due to the shortage of ammunition. The plan was presented to the German High Command (to Krebs) but would never be carried out. The specific proposal was that:

> A first echelon would comprise troops from the *18. Panzergrenadier Division* and part of the *9. Fallschirmjäger Division*, reinforced by all the armoured vehicles (tanks, assault guns and other support vehicles) still available in Berlin.
>
> A second echelon would consist of the *Kampfgruppe Mohnke* (the troops used in the defence of Sector Z) and a *Kriegsmarine* battalion to protect the German High Command stationed in Adolf Hitler's bunker.
>
> A third echelon would comprise the remnants of the *Müncheberg Panzer Division*, the *11. SS Panzergrenadier Division Nordland*, the *Bärenfänger Kampfgruppe*
>
> And, finally, in the rear, another group made up of the reinforced remainder of *9. Fallschirmjäger Division*.

Lesen und weitergeben!

Der Panzerbär

26. April 1945

KAMPFBLATT FÜR DIE VERTEIDIGER GROSS-BERLINS

Die Schlacht auf dem Höhepunkt

Deutsche Reserven im Eilmarsch auf Berlin

Seit 2½ Monaten rennen die Sowjets gegen Breslau an

„Und wenn die Welt voll Teufel wär'..."

Ein Hundsfott, wer in dieser Stunde die schimpfliche Feigheit dem männlichen Kampfe vorzieht

Front page of the *Panzerbär*, 26 April 1945. (Collection of J. Arráez)

During the afternoon, the increasingly intense Soviet attacks forced the German troops defending the north of the capital to retreat as far as the main railway lines in northern Berlin. In fact, in the city from this day, regular operations of both the elevated railway and the underground, which were still in service, were suspended as a result of the proximity of the front line to the capital.

The Soviet attacks were temporarily held, largely thanks to the support received by the defenders from the three anti-aircraft defence towers equipped with heavy-calibre guns (which covered Sector Z from Humboldthain, the zoo and Friedrichshain, in the northern and central parts of the city). In addition to their anti-aircraft functions, these towers also served as anti-tank gun emplacements, shelters, warehouses and hospitals, amongst other purposes.

The 79th Rifle Corps advanced along the Westhafen Canal, with only the Beusselstrasse *S-Bahn* station holding out against the advance. The Corps advanced towards Görlitzer Station and pressed on towards Kreuzberg. Zhukov's forces stormed Tempelhof Airport, while other units advanced towards the Landwehr Canal.

Destroyed Soviet tanks in front of one of the imposing anti-aircraft defence towers (in this case, the one at the Zoo), whose guns temporarily halted the Soviet advance in some areas of Berlin. (Photograph taken in May 1945. Public Domain)

By the end of the day, the 8th Guards Army and the 1st Guards Tank Army had Potsdamerstrasse to their left and Heinrich von Kleist Park ahead of them.

Georgy Konstantinovich Zhukov, Marshal of the Soviet Union, the most famous and considered the most successful of the Soviet Army's commanders during the Second World War and the victor of the Battle of Berlin. (Public Domain)

The *18. Panzergrenadier Division* sent a combat group supported by six tanks and 15 armoured vehicles to try to re-establish contact with the *20. Panzergrenadier Division*, although they encountered strong Soviet resistance. Meanwhile, the *Müncheberg Division* took up positions in the area of Tempelhof Airport, some 6 kilometres from the Chancellery.

Many of the wounded soldiers remained on the front line despite their condition, because of the ever-present fear that a roving court-martial composed of SS firing squads would arrest them and hang or shoot them for desertion.

The streets of Berlin, where graffiti could be seen on many walls with slogans intended to rally the city's defence – such as 'It is darkest before the dawn', 'Berlin remains German' or 'We are retreating, but we shall prevail' – began to fill with corpses, both military and civilian, and bodies lay in the street, wherever they were struck down by a grenade, a bullet or the explosion of a rocket.

The city was being strangled; gas and water supplies were conspicuous by their absence. Newspapers were ceasing publication; specifically, the party's official newspaper, the *Völkischer Beobachter*, ceased publication on 26 April 1945 (Vadillo says that it was on the 24th), being replaced by a new newspaper called *Der Panzerbär*, which would serve as the mouthpiece for the defenders of Berlin. The contents of this mere four-page newspaper, intended for the defenders of Greater Berlin, were directed by the propaganda machinery of the NSDAP (*Nationalsozialistische Deutsche Arbeiterpartei*). In addition to encouraging the city's defenders, its content highlighted the ties linking the NSDAP's cause to European civilisation, in the face of the 'Asian' enemy. *Der Panzerbär* was only published for six days, due to the extreme situation in Berlin during those days of late April and early May.

On the same day, 26 April, the Western Allies dropped a propaganda newspaper over the capital called *Nachrichten für die Truppe* (News for the Troops), whose headline read 'Berlin has been surrounded', and on its front page were phrases such as:

> Two-thirds of the city have been taken. – Berlin is now surrounded. – Fierce fighting at the underground stations. – Since late yesterday, Berlin has been cut off from the rest of the world. Soviet armies have closed their encirclement around the Reich capital and Potsdam. Tank units from the north-west are attacking Ketzin via Nauen, to link up with Soviet forces approaching the encirclement from the south-west, between Potsdam and Brandenburg. In the late hours of yesterday, Berlin was surrounded by a wide belt of troops. All traces of fronts in northern and central Germany have now been wiped out, and the men and equipment that were there can be deployed to the siege of Berlin. Reports of the encirclement of Berlin emerged shortly after the party's remaining propaganda outlets informed the world that the Führer himself was directing the decisive battle around Berlin, thereby seeking to perpetuate the myth that National Socialism was heroically meeting its end. But the people of Berlin have seen no sign of the Führer and are awaiting no message... – Theatre of operations. The 11th Army has been annihilated. – Its commander-in-chief was General of Artillery Walter Lucht; together with his entire senior staff, he has surrendered to the Anglo-American forces. – The Russians are crossing the Elbe.

During these first days of 'contact' with the German capital, the Spanish troops spent their time patrolling the areas designated in their sector, corresponding to the south-eastern part of Sector Z, taking up strategic positions for its defence. Life became, despite the continual bombing to which the city was subjected, relatively routine between their quarters and the defensive posts. Although there was still time, as was the case in the days of the Blue Division, to fraternise with the civilian population. News of the Soviets' advance reaches them, and they sensed the long-awaited moment approaching when they would finally be able to face the Russians and remind them how Spanish soldiers fight! Faithful to their ideals, without fear of death, and with the firmest intention of not yielding a single inch of the ground entrusted to them to defend.

General Muñoz Grandes (first commander of the Blue Division, or Spanish Volunteer Division) smokes a cigarette as he goes to see off the first group of repatriates from the DEV. The cold Soviet climate is evident in the Spaniards' attire. (Courtesy of L. E. Togores)

During these days, as the siege tightened its grip on Berlin with increasing intensity, some of the conscripted men may have deserted before they were completely besieged. Although there is no evidence to confirm or refute such desertions, it is understandable that this might have occurred in such an extreme situation.

The *Einheit* Ezquerra in Combat

During the first few days, the Spaniards were integrated into the defensive system of Sector Z, while remaining nominally attached to the *Nordland Division*. As the front line had not yet reached their vicinity, there are no records of them having taken part in any combat. It was from 27 April onwards that the Spanish began to fight, almost without respite, until the unit had finally practically disintegrated.

Friday 27 April

On 27 April, the OKW issued a radio broadcast:

> The enemy has penetrated the inner defence ring from the north at Charlottenburg and from the south at Tempelhofer Feld. Fighting for the city centre has begun at Hallesches Tor, Schlesischer Bahnhof and Alexanderplatz. The east–west axis is under heavy fire. West of Berlin, the Brandenburg-Rathenow-Kremmen area was successfully defended against enemy attacks.

Soviet troops were advancing through the rubble-strewn streets, with their objectives in the southern part of Sector Z towards Potsdamer Platz and Alexanderplatz, where the fiercest fighting of the Battle of Berlin was likely to take place. The *Einheit* Ezquerra would fight for the former, which was under attack from vast numbers of infantry, armoured vehicles and artillery of all kinds, notably including Stalin's dreaded rocket artillery.

This area was adjacent to the Government District and was defended fiercely, building by building, doorway by doorway, metre by metre, but this did not prevent an unknown number of key positions from being lost. The intervention of several *Königstiger* tanks from *SS-Pz. Abt.503* managed to temporarily halt the Soviet advance. Although the defenders in Berlin did not have many armoured vehicles, the few that they did have took a heavy toll on Soviet armoured units and infantry. To a large extent, the deployment of several of these behemoths in defensive positions, at a safe distance from enemy shells, allowed the defenders to hold out until the very last moment; they were even used as the spearhead for attempts to break out of the city.

Lesen und weitergeben!

Der Panzerbär

27. April 1945

KAMPFBLATT FÜR DIE VERTEIDIGER GROSS-BERLINS

Bollwerk gegen den Bolschewismus

Berlin: Massengrab für Sowjetpanzer

Rundfunkansprache von Staatssekretär Dr. Naumann

Berlin kämpft für das Reich und Europa

Berlin, 26. April. Der Staatssekretär im Reichsministerium für Volksaufklärung und Propaganda, Stabsleiter Dr. Naumann hielt am Donnerstag folgende Rundfunkansprache:

Deutsche Volksgenossen!

Der Kampf um Berlin tobt nun seit Tagen mit äußerster Härte. Alle Stadtteile tragen schon Spuren dieser großen Schlacht, und unsere weltbekannten Straßen und Plätze sind zu Wahrzeichen eines heroischen Ringens geworden.

Die sowjetischen Befehlshaber, die Stalin die versprochene Morgengabe der eroberten Reichshauptstadt nicht fristgerecht auf den Tisch der Konferenz von San Franzisko legen konnten, treiben zur Stunde ihre Panzerkeile und ihre Schützendivisionen immer rücksichtsloser in verlustreiche Straßenkämpfe. Für sie handelt es sich dabei aber nicht um einen kurzfristigen, außenpolitischen Prestigeerfolg: Der Bolschewismus sieht in der Eroberung Berlins den Schlüssel zur Beherrschung Europas und damit zur Diktatur über die abendländische Welt.

Gegenüber diesem Ansturm der Steppe haben die Verteidiger Berlins einen schweren Stand, aber ihre Haltung entspricht der Größe der Gefahr. Sie sind sich der Bedeutung ihrer Aufgabe bewußt. Sie wissen, daß ihrer Tapferkeit und ihrem Kampfwillen nicht nur das Leben und die Freiheit von Millionen Kindern, Frauen und Männern und die politische Zukunft des Reiches anvertraut ist, sondern auch die zukünftige Gestaltung des Abendlandes. Sie wissen auch, daß der Ansturm des Feindes um so wilder werden wird, je mehr er spürt, daß ein militärischer Entsatz von draußen sich nähert und im Begriffe ist, ihm den Sieg im letzten Augenblick aus den Händen zu winden.

An der Spitze der Führer

An der Spitze der Verteidigung Berlins steht der Führer. Diese Tatsache allein schon gibt dem Kampf um Berlin sein einmaliges und entscheidendes Gesicht. Wie in der Kampfzeit, wie immer in seinem ganzen Leben, weicht der Führer der letzten Entscheidung nicht aus, sondern stellt sich unter Einsatz seiner ganzen Person an die Spitze des Kampfes. Er, der tausend Gründe anführen könnte, die seine Anwesenheit an anderer Stelle als angeblich wichtiger oder nützlicher erscheinen lassen würden, verzichtet auf diese Umwege und gibt damit ein anspornendes Vorbild eines sich selber in jeder Lage treu bleibenden Kämpfers. Niemals hat er dem Herzen seiner Soldaten so nahe gestanden wie in dieser schweren Stunde. Niemals war er in der Liebe der Männer und Frauen von Berlin fester verankert als jetzt, wo er seine geschichtliche Aufgabe mit der seiner Hauptstadt unlösbar verbunden hat.

Gegenüber den haßerfüllten Verkündigungen der Feindpresse, die es nicht zugeben möchte, daß der Führer des Großdeutschen Reiches in jeder Lage zu seinem Volke steht, wissen die Männer und Frauen von Berlin, daß der Führer bei ihnen ist, um die Gefahr des Bolschewismus für die Reichshauptstadt zu bannen.

Während in diesen bewegten Tagen die Staatsmänner der Westmächte in San Franzisko mit den Sowjets in scheinbarer Freundschaft zusammensitzen und versuchen, durch Kompromisse den bolschewistischen Imperialismus aufzuhalten, der sich noch niemals an Konferenzbeschlüsse gebunden gefühlt hat, tritt der Führer in eigener Person tapfer der bolschewistischen Flut aus dem Osten mit dem letzten Aufgebot seiner besten Kräfte entgegen, fest entschlossen, diesen Ansturm aus der Steppe aufzuhalten und zu brechen. Er kannt die Gefahr des Bolschewismus nicht erst seit heute, wo die unverhohlene Machtgier Moskaus auch in London und Washington mit immer stärkerem Mißtrauen vermerkt wird. Sein Kampf hatte seinen Ursprung in der Notwehr des deutschen Volkes gegen den Bolschewismus. Wenn heute Deutschland und Europa noch nicht sowjetisch sind, so ist dies allein sein Verdienst.

Die großen Probleme des 20. Jahrhunderts, die durch das Maschinenzeitalter hervorgerufenen sozialen Fragen, konnten nur auf dem Wege über den Nationalsozialismus gelöst werden. Nach den Absichten und Plänen des Führers stände heute schon ein unzerstörtes und glückliches Europa als unüberwindbares Bollwerk dem Bolschewismus gegenüber. An der Durchführung dieses Planes, der allen Völkern Europas und der ganzen Kulturwelt nur Segen bringen konnte, wurde der Führer durch Mächte verhindert, die in unglückseliger Verkennung ihrer eigenen Interessen und getäuscht über unser wahres Wollen die Helfer des Bolschewismus wurden. Statt, wie versprochen, den kleinen Völkern Selbständigkeit und Freiheit zu garantieren, wurden diese gerade von ihnen dem Bolschewismus ausgeliefert. Auch ihre Terrorangriffe in Europa waren nicht nur kulturzerstörende Vernichtungsorgien in eigener Sache, sondern vor allem Hilfsdienste zugunsten des Bolschewismus.

Roosevelts Verrat

Für immer wird mit dem Namen Roosevelt die Schuld verbunden sein, daß er mit dem Einsatz seines ganzen Einflusses den Kampf Europas gegen den Bolschewismus in den Rücken gefallen ist.

Jahrelang ist es uns gelungen, aus eigener Kraft dem Ansturm dreier Weltmächte siegreich Widerstand zu leisten und

Front page of the *Panzerbär*, 27 April 1945. (Collection of J. Arráez)

View of an anti-tank barrier at Potsdamer Platz in Berlin in early April 1945. These fortifications became important strongholds against the advance of Soviet armoured vehicles and soldiers. (Bundesarchiv Bild 183-R71639)

Line of combat on April 27 and location of areas where the Spaniards were that day.
A Hotel Excelsior (in Saarlandstrasse)
B Reichsluftfahrtministerium (RLM) or Air Ministry. Accommodation on the ground floor of the building.

In an effort to slow the advance of the Russian troops into the city centre as much as possible, at least 120 of Berlin's 248 bridges were blown up. The aim of this manoeuvre was to force the Soviets to attempt to advance along routes where they would face fierce resistance.

Units of the 2nd Guards Tank Army occupied Siemensstadt, advancing to the banks of the Spree where it joins the Havel. The 35th Mechanised Brigade crossed the Spree at Ruhleben.

The 79th Rifle Corps of the 3rd Shock Army continued its advance through Moabit towards the Spree and the Reichstag.

Leipziger Platz came under heavy artillery fire. The 55th Guards Tank Brigade advanced through the area of the Olympic Stadium and the Reich Sports Academy. The zoo, Spandau, Gatow and Tempelhof Airfield had fallen to the Soviet onslaught, the latter dashing hopes of receiving supplies by air. The 8th Guards Army consolidated its positions in the vicinity of the Landwehr Canal (in the southern part of Sector Z). The story, true that it was, circulated that the Russians had blown up the Landwehr locks, causing water to begin flowing through the railway and underground tunnels. As these tunnels were a refuge for many people, a scene of utter horror unfolded. Huge masses of water swept away people who could not flee; and those who managed to escape did so only by stepping over others less fortunate, who ultimately perished in those underground passages.

The 3rd Shock Army attacked Stettiner Station, engaging units of the *9. Fallschirmjäger Division.*

At 17.00, following heavy shelling supported by air strikes, the Soviets of the 3rd Guards Tank Army broke through on both sides of the Hohenzollerndamm.

The air was thick with dust and smoke; grenades were exploding everywhere, making it extremely dangerous to wander the streets, which thus appeared deserted. They were littered with rubble and craters that

Soviet tanks advance through the streets of Berlin. All German resistance was eventually doomed to failure due to the Soviets' immense superiority in manpower and equipment. (From mil.ru.)

would later serve as positions for the defenders to take cover in as they faced the advance of Soviet troops.

The 5th Shock Army was advancing slowly towards the area of the Schlesischer Station and the Friedrichshain anti-aircraft tower.

As is apparent, in practically all of the city's defensive sectors, the German defensive line was retreating, not without inflicting heavy casualties on the attackers, although at the cost of a significant number of their own casualties (casualties that could no longer be replaced, unlike in the case of the Soviets).

After spending a day in position there, the Spaniards left the old shoe shop following orders from an *Oberstleutnant* of the *Luftwaffe* who had arrived there, instructing them to move to their new operations centre. This was situated in a spacious, old military police barracks (the Reich Security Service, RSD or *Reichssicherheitsdienst*), quite close to their previous quarters, and much more suitable for housing troops. A Latvian battalion of SS troops under the command of *SS-Hauptsturmführer* Balli was also stationed there; he was absent at the time as he was on duty at the Air Ministry.

Shortly afterwards, a Latvian liaison officer arrived at the barracks where the Spanish troops were quartered, bearing orders for Ezquerra to report to *SS-Hauptsturmführer* Eldon Walli at the Air Ministry. This is how Ezquerra recalls their meeting:

> We were standing next to a large table on which a detailed map of the city of Berlin lay open and spread out. Some red marks indicated the points on the outskirts where the Russians had managed to make their first breakthroughs. I bent over it and was able to get a clear picture of the military situation, which was undoubtedly quite serious. To confirm my assessment and dispel any remaining doubts, a heavy artillery shell struck the upper part of the Ministry at that very moment, knocking down a section of the cornice.
>
> This meant that the Russians already had targets for a heavy concentration of fire in that area of the Ministries; even so, we continued to examine the map of the city.
>
> Balli was to receive the order to take up position on Unter den Linden and was noting down details of the city's topography so that he could act with a degree of confidence. With a red pencil in his hand, he was explaining his plan of attack and defence to me when an officer from headquarters entered the office, tasked with escorting me personally to the sector assigned to me.[10]

10 Miguel Ezquerra Sánchez, *Luché Hasta El Fin: Memorias de un voluntario español en la guerra 1939–1945, Berlin a vida o muerte* (Granada: García Hispán, 1999), pp.100–101.

On 27 April, the Spanish soldiers had to rush to Belle-Alliance-Platz to defend it against enemy attacks. To reach it, they had to travel part of the way from their base through the streets of Berlin and part through the underground tunnels. (Public Domain)

This Balli or Willi, in *Luché Hasta El Fin*[11], or Willi in *David contra Goliat* by Carlos Caballero,[12] was in fact *SS-Hauptsturmführer* Eldon Walli, who by the end of March 1945 had taken command of the 15th Latvian Rifle Battalion (known as the Reconnaissance Battalion).

Walli was an Austrian Nazi born in the United States and was assigned to the Latvian unit. He was a broadcaster at the *Wiener Hauptrundfunksender* and, when the war broke out, left this profession to enlist. He was eventually assigned to the section where they were to contribute their part to the city's defensive network, initially for purely defensive duties. It was in the second of the three defensive rings; the one situated between the outer ring and the *Zitadelle*. Although, as we shall see, this was clearly not the role the Spaniards were to play in the defence of Berlin.

Ezquerra immediately set off for the barracks where his men were stationed to convey the orders he had received. After a brief rest, the Spaniards' first mission was imminent. They were aware that some of them would soon be casualties, but even so, their determination to do their bit in the defence of the Reich's capital could be seen in the steely resolve in their eyes and their urgent desire to face the enemy as soon as possible.

11 Miguel Ezquerra Sánchez, *Luché Hasta El Fin: Memorias de un voluntario español en la guerra 1939–1945, Berlin a vida o muerte* (Granada: García Hispán, 1999).

12 Carlos Caballero, *David contra Goliat: voluntarios letones en las Waffen SS (1941–1945)* (Granada: García Hispán, 2003).

Unter den Linden in 1950, still bearing the 'scars' of the war. (Trümmer. Bundesarchiv Bild 183-05876-0050)

After inspecting the weapons and getting them ready, Ezquerra led his unit to the designated point, where he reported to the sector commander. This was an *oberstleutnant* of artillery, holder of the Knight Cross, and whose headquarters were situated in a nearby square which, along with the surrounding buildings, was under constant bombardment from Russian artillery. Ignoring the intense enemy fire, the commander explained to Ezquerra the mission to be entrusted to the Spanish troops, which would consist of repelling the Soviet advance near the area where Moritzplatz is located.

On 27 April, Ezquerra's men had to repel the Soviet advance near the area where Moritzplatz is located. Here they destroyed four or five IS-2 tanks. (Public Domain)

Ezquerra gave the order to the 1st Company to advance, commanded by the *sergeant* (formerly *Leutnant* Ocañas, although according to *Yo, muerto en Rusia* he held the rank of *SS-Untersturmführer*).[13] They advanced from the area of the Air Ministry, taking cover behind the walls of the dilapidated buildings lining the streets, as well as any feature that might serve as shelter from Russian fire. The distance to Moritzplatz to the south-east was about two kilometres, so they opted for the quickest route, as the urgency of the situation demanded. This involved going from Wilhelmstrasse towards Stadtmitte *U-Bahn* interchange and then cutting through the narrower streets until they reached Oranienstrasse, at the eastern end of which lay the square.

The destruction in Berlin caused by the Western Allies' air raids was merely the beginning of the city's devastation following the Soviet attack. The photograph, taken in February 1945, shows Oranienstrasse near Moritzplatz. (Bundesarchiv, Bild 183-J31327)

Making their way through the piles of rubble littering the streets of central Berlin, it took them around two hours to reach the vicinity of Moritzplatz. Although the sound of heavy fighting in the area – between German forces and combined Soviet armoured and infantry units – could already be heard.

There, the Spaniards would have been able to see the boys of the Hitler Youth going head-to-head with the Soviets, as they defended the underground station. The Hitler Youth would never cease to amaze Ezquerra and his men as these mere children, still of school age, armed mainly with anti-tank weapons, harassed the invaders, managing to reduce several T-34s to scrap and a burning mess. Their attitude further heightened the Spaniards' euphoria; if a bunch of near-children could hold their ground, what cannot they achieve? Especially as many of the men had several years of combat experience.

13 Moisés Puente, *Yo, Muerto en Rusia*: *Memorias del Alférez Ocañas de la División Azul* (Arantzazu: Ediciones Franciscanas Arantzazu, 2003).

Photograph of Moritzplatz in 1914. This square would witness fierce fighting by the *Einheit Ezquerra* on 27 April 1945. (Public Domain)

On Wilhelmstrasse, at least three Soviet tanks were destroyed by Spaniards armed with *panzerfausts* during the fighting on 27 April. The *panzerfaust* was responsible for the destruction of many Soviet armoured vehicles on the streets of Berlin. (Bundesarchiv Bild 183-R92317)

As they neared the combat zone, by chance, they came across another Spaniard who was serving in a German regiment, but who would eventually be attached to the *Einheit*. This man was Ismael Múgica, who would become one of Ezquerra's trusted men, both for his extensive knowledge of street fighting and for his knowledge of the German language, as Ezquerra himself recalled in his account.

At the end of the street, the Spanish unit finally spotted the small Moritzplatz, across which Soviet armoured vehicles were advancing under the cover of their infantry.

According to *SS-Untersturmführer* Hans Böttger, who commanded the special operation at Moritzplatz, in *Berlin 1933–45 avec Wilhelm Mohnke*, he recounted these fierce battles, mentioning the Spaniards:

At Moritzplatz, the anti-tank barrier stretches out. The front line is no more than 100 metres from my command post. The proud men took up their positions and begin firing at the Soviets. To the right of the anti-tank barrier towards Oranienstrasse were the Spanish volunteers. As we were only a stone's throw away from the Soviet, commands were constantly being shouted back and forth from both sides.[14]

The city of Berlin was already largely in ruins because of the Allied bombing before the Soviet attack. This photograph shows the state of Oranienstrasse following one such attack that had destroyed the water pipes. Passers-by are building an emergency footbridge from the rubble to a wrecked tram. (Bundesarchiv Bild 183-J31346)

To the left of the Spanish positions, German troops were taking cover in some ruins. Unaware of the presence of Ezquerra's men, they opened fire on them; this caused the Spaniards to throw themselves to the ground and return the friendly fire. When both groups finally recognised each other as allies and on the same side, the shooting ceased. The reason for the confusion was that the Germans heard voices in a language unknown to them and mistook the Spanish for Russian troops; the result for the unit was the death of three men and two others with severe injuries.

Following this incident, the unit continued its advance until it made contact with the enemy, storming the first barricades behind which the Russians were taking cover, while the continuous fire from the tanks echoed across the entire disputed area.

There the unit waited for the new horde of men and Soviet tanks approaching from the south of the square. Crouching low and having taken up defensive positions, they awaited their commander's order to unleash the full fury of their weapons on the Soviets. The latter advanced cautiously, though they could not avoid falling into constant ambushes. Such as one carried out by the Spaniards following Ezquerra's plan. Shots came from all sides onto the Russian infantry who took cover and then fell back, leaving the field open to the tank hunters, who made short work of four or five of

14 Thomas Fischer, *Berlin 1933–45 avec Wilhelm Mohnke* (Paris: Éditions Heimdal, 2013), p.55.

the immense IS-2s. Casualties among the men of the *Einheit* were inevitable, but they had managed to halt the advance and force the Russians to retreat. The numbers of the Spanish unit were already low to begin with, and the constant casualties were reducing it to a mere shell of what it once was.

Three of the advancing tanks were heading towards the Spanish positions, firing continuously. A trio of men, Sastre, Vázquez and Múgica, advanced hugging the walls of the buildings. Following this, another group of men, including Ezquerra, advanced. During this exchange of fire, as he approached the tanks with his *panzerfaust*, Vázquez was wounded. His comrades managed to rescue him, risking their own lives to save their comrade under the continuous crackle of Russian automatic weapons.

The end result was that, one of the *panzerfaust* rockets struck the first armoured vehicle, causing an explosion that destroyed it and killed its crew. Three more Russian tanks followed the same fate, also being put out of action thanks to the powerful effect of the *panzerfausts*. The remaining tanks, finding themselves without infantry support, opted for a strategic retreat.

Following that clash, the men, on Ezquerra's orders, withdrew slightly to reinforce their positions and evacuate the wounded. During the engagement, they were reinforced by the addition of some Latvian troops, as well as possibly some other stray soldiers who were temporarily attached to the unit. It is highly likely that this 'convenient' union of the Spanish and Latvian units was intended, as mentioned above, to improve the operational effectiveness of both units, given their small numbers. But in less than a quarter of an hour, the Russians attacked again and so the inferno of fire was unleashed once more. Once again, the defenders managed to take a heavy toll on the Soviet armoured vehicles, which proved defenceless when not accompanied by infantry to take out the crouching men with their anti-tank weapons lying in wait in any pile of rubble, gaps between or in buildings, windows, doorways or even, at times, in the open.

The façade of the elegant *Hotel Excelsior* near Anhalter Station. It was here that Ezquerra was treated for his ankle injuries on 27 April. It was also here that *SS-Obersturmführer* Ocañas was interrogated by the Soviets following his capture in the early hours of 28 April. (Bundesarchiv Bild 146-1998-020-07A)

During this fighting, and according to his biography, Ezquerra injured his ankle (a sprain) when he fell through a hole into a cellar, which was still smouldering from a recent grenade explosion. After being pulled out with the help of his comrades, he was evacuated to receive appropriate treatment, as far as circumstances allowed, at the medical facilities located in the *Hotel Excelsior* on Saarlandstrasse. In Ezquerra's absence, *SS-Untersturmführer* Múgica took command of the Spanish troops, although the Spanish unit remained temporarily under the command of 'the Latvian' Walli.

While Ezquerra was being treated at the field hospital, the rest of the men in the unit held their positions, engaging in hand-to-hand combat on several occasions. Yet hundreds upon hundreds of Soviet soldiers continued their advance despite the heavy casualties they suffered, which were replaced by ever-increasing numbers of reinforcements. However, the German, Latvian and Spanish resistance was fierce and managed to halt this new assault, albeit after losing a significant amount of ground with each Russian attack. Due to this back and forth movement of the front line, a small number of German troops were left behind enemy lines, including some Spaniards and some members of the Hitler Youth. Making the most of their weaponry, avoiding falling victim to the increasingly intense enemy fire or of being captured by the Russian troops, whose numbers grew with every passing minute, after intense hand-to-hand combat, and with a fair bit of luck, these men, and boys, managed to return to German-held territory.

Following the violent clashes, the survivors were withdrawn from the front line and replaced by other units. Exhausted from a full day of fighting, as well as by the constant strain of being subjected to unceasing Soviet fire (which turned the Berlin sky into a gloomy, smoke-filled expanse with its air at times almost unbreathable), they set off on the return journey to their new barracks on the ground floor of the Air Ministry. This was a large Prussian-style building situated on the corner of Leipzig and Wilhelm Strassen, near Leipziger Platz, once a hub of social life but now reduced to a

A Soviet M4A2 Sherman tank from the Lend-Lease programme. It was not only Soviet-made tanks that took part in the Battle of Berlin. (Public Domain)

wasteland by the continuous bombing, with many half-collapsed buildings and rubble strewn everywhere. To prevent the civilian population from being exposed to the hardships of war, efforts were made to house them in the numerous shelters, among which the Ministry's own shelter stands out for its sheer size, capable of accommodating thousands of people.

Their position was near the elegant *Hotel Excelsior*, between the Army Ministry and the Chancellery, close to Potsdamer Platz and the other ministries. The hotel was connected by underground passages to Potsdamer Station, which facilitated movement from one side to the other, avoiding the constant enemy fire that the streets of Berlin were enduring. The scene at Potsdamer Platz was harrowing; it was littered with wrecked vehicles, mutilated bodies and the wounded scrambling to seek shelter in the nearby station.

Interior view of Potsdamer Bahnhof in the nineteenth century. Berlin's railway stations became shelters for civilians, medical aid stations and military command posts during the final days of the Reich. (Public Domain)

After receiving treatment for his foot injury, Ezquerra was discharged from hospital and left after spending the entire night there, and headed towards where his exhausted soldiers were resting. This is how the Spanish commander described his return: 'I made my way there, limping slightly on my leg. When they saw me enter, everyone's joy was evident; at the same time, they were eager to tell me of the exploits the company had carried out in my absence.'[15]

15 Miguel Ezquerra Sánchez, *Luché Hasta El Fin: Memorias de un voluntario español en la guerra 1939–1945, Berlin a vida o muerte* (Granada: García Hispán, 1999), pp.73–74.

Once again, *SS-Untersturmführer* Hans Böttger recounts the ferocity of the fighting at Moritzplatz:

> The chocolate supplied by Father Philipp, together with the stimulant Pervitin, keeps us awake. Three times the square was taken by the Russians, with heavy losses, and three times our troops recaptured it, also with incredible losses. The ferocity is almost beyond imagination. Our young Hitler Youth are desperate to fight.

Several hours had passed since the Spanish had arrived at Moritzplatz and they had already been able to witness with their own eyes the ferocity of the fighting against the enormous Russian Army, which attacked again and again with seemingly endless numbers of troops. Exhaustion was evident among all the defenders, so once the area had been stabilised, they would be replaced by German SS troops. The defensive actions at Moritzplatz completely halted the Soviet advance in that sector, and it was not until around 28 April 1945 that Red Army soldiers were able to continue their advance towards the Government District via Kreuzberg.

Back in their new barracks at the Air Ministry, the Spanish soldiers awaited further orders. This had been their first direct encounter with the Russian enemy on the streets of Berlin; merely a prelude to what would become a constant shuttling back and forth between one area and another, wherever the danger arose. The situation in the *Zitadelle* sector was deteriorating with every passing second, and men were needed to fill every gap the Russians were making in the defensive line. And, naturally, every available soldier would be called upon from one part of Berlin's streets or another to try to halt the enemy's advance; and, among other veteran troops, the Spaniards would be called upon once again.

Lesen und weitergeben!

Der Panzerbär

28. April 1945

KAMPFBLATT FÜR DIE VERTEIDIGER GROSS-BERLINS

Wir halten durch!

Die Stunde der Freiheit wird kommen

Heiliges Wort:

Berlin

Die Hauptstadt des Reiches ist zur Hauptstadt des Kampfes geworden. In Berlin ergingen die Führerbefehle, die aus der inneren deutschen Zerrissenheit ein einiges Großdeutschland machten und dem Volk die Grundlagen einer mustergültigen sozialen Ordnung gaben. Aus Berlin kamen die Führerbefehle, die Europa Zug um Zug befriedeten. Aus Berlin kamen die Führerbefehle, die während des Krieges trotz aller Schwierigkeiten jahrelang dem von uns besetzten Europa Ruhe und Ordnung, Arbeit und Brot gaben. Berlin war die Hauptstadt der inneren deutschen Ordnung, Berlin war die Hauptstadt der europäischen Ordnung.

Heute schlägt der Bolschewismus auf das verhaßte Berlin ein. Er will das Haupt der deutschen Ordnung, der europäischen Ordnung, tödlich treffen. Wir bekennen uns zu diesem Kampf. Darum ist der Führer in Berlin. Er trägt mit uns alle Belastungen der hart umkämpften Frontstadt. Er steht mit uns im schweren Kampf. Von Berlin aus ergehen wieder seine Befehle zum Freiheitskampf, der Weltgeschichte macht. In Berlin wird es sich entscheiden, ob in Zukunft der Bolschewismus alle Völker unterjochen darf oder ob die Völker ihr Selbstbestimmungsrecht behalten. In Berlin werden wir den Bolschewismus entscheidend schlagen. Darum ist der Führer in Berlin. Er steht auf dem heißesten Schlachtfeld, das die Geschichte kennt. Es scharen sich um ihn die fanatischsten Soldaten, von denen man weiß.

In Berlin wurde der bolschewistischen Weltgefahr der Heilige Krieg erklärt. In Berlin wird dieser Krieg entschieden. Alle Völker, die unter der bolschewistischen Geißel zusammenbrechen, sehen auf Berlin. Alle Staaten, die von der bolschewistischen Weltherrschaft bedroht werden, ahnen die Tragweite dieses Entscheidungskampfes. Die Haltung der Berliner und der unbeugsame Kampfgeist seiner Verteidiger werden den Bolschewismus schlagen und die Furcht vor dieser Weltgefahr aus den Herzen der Menschen verjagen.

Der Führer ist in Berlin. Der Welt[illegible] wird hier geschlagen.

Heldischer Kampf um Berlin
Anmarsch der Reserven von allen Seiten

Aus dem Führerhauptquartier, 27. April

Das Oberkommando der Wehrmacht gibt bekannt:

Der Schwerpunkt der Kampfhandlungen in Nordwestdeutschland lag auch gestern in Bremen. In schweren und verlustreichen Straßenkämpfen konnten die Engländer ihre Einbrüche im Stadtgebiet erweitern.

Elbefront im wesentlichen ruhig

An der Elbefront verhielten sich die Anglo-Amerikaner weiterhin ruhig. Lediglich südlich Tangermünde setzten schwächere feindliche Abteilungen über den Fluß.

Im Mittelpunkt der Kämpfe stand auch gestern die Schlacht im Raum Berlin. Schulter an Schulter mit allen waffenfähigen Männern führten unsere Truppen einen heldischen Kampf gegen den bolschewistischen Massenansturm, verteidigten jedes Haus und warfen den Feind durch Gegenangriffe aus dem inneren Verteidigungsring der Stadt wieder zurück.

Die Schlacht im Raum Berlin

Aus dem Raum südlich Fürstenwalde stießen unsere Verbände im Angriff nach Westen in die tiefe Flanke der im Süden von Berlin operierenden Bolschewisten und durchbrachen deren Hauptnachschubverbindung auf der Straße Baruth — Zossen. Unsere im Westen schwungvoll angreifenden jungen Divisionen erreichten den Raum von Beelitz und stehen dort in schweren Waldkämpfen mit den Sowjets. Angriffe auf Brandenburg und Rathenow wurden verlustreich abgewiesen. Beiderseits Oranienburg brachen Uebersetzversuche der Bolschewisten über den Rhin und Hohenzollernkanal verlustreich für den Feind zusammen. Dagegen konnten die Sowjets südwestlich Stettin auf Prenzlau hin weiter Boden gewinnen.

In Süddeutschland

In Süddeutschland hielt der starke feindliche Druck gegen die Donaulinie von Deggendorf bis Ulm an. Bei Dillingen konnten die Amerikaner ihren Brückenkopf nach Südwesten erweitern und nach heftigen Kämpfen in den Nordteil von Ulm eindringen. In der Schwäbischen Alb und nordwestlich des Bodensees kämpfen sich eigene Kampfgruppen durch die feindlichen

Front page of the *Panzerbär*, 28 April 1945. (Collection of J. Arráez)

Saturday 28 April

With each passing day, the fighting became more constant and the intervals between engagements shorter. Exhaustion was taking its toll on the combatants, although the defenders were at a disadvantage, as there are no reinforcements or relief for them, unlike for the Red Army troops. Although the fighting has been intense in

Line of combat on April 28 and location of areas where the Spaniards were that day.
A Anhalter Platz-Cinema Europa; B Hotel Kaiserhof; C Calle Kronen; D Ministries area (between streets Hermann Göring y Unter den Linden)

the preceding days, from the morning of 28 April the battle would reach its peak and would remain at this intensity until the end.

The 79th Rifle Corps continued its advance towards Alt Moabit and had the Reichstag in sight, facing the mined and barricaded Moltke Bridge as an obstacle. The 2nd Guards Tank Army was positioned alongside the Landwehr Canal in the Moabit area. The 5th Shock Army was advancing through the Frankfurter Allee and Lansberger Chaussee areas, but had been unable to take the anti-aircraft tower in Friedrichshain.

The 26th Guards Rifle Corps attacked Alexanderplatz again, while the 32nd Rifle Corps crushed the last pockets of resistance at Schlesischer Railway Station.

The 9th Rifle Corps captured Spittelmarkt, just over a kilometre from the Reich Chancellery.

The 3rd Guards Tank Army, together with the 8th Guards Army, launched an attack to cross the Landwehr Canal.

Resistance within Berlin intensified as the defenders were forced into a smaller and smaller area. In Sector Z, where the Spanish troops were deployed, fierce resistance was offered at Spittelmarkt, Anhalter Bahnhof and Leipziger Platz. Despite the desperate nature of the situation, the defenders continued their fierce fighting in every ruined building in the hope that Wenck's 12th Army was heading towards Berlin to rescue them from the encirclement they were within.

In the early hours of 28 April, the Spanish unit was called upon to halt the Soviet advance in the Saarlandstrasse area, as the Soviets had managed to make headway in the sector. After making the necessary preparations, Ezquerra's men set off towards the designated area in the southern sector of Sector Z, specifically the Anhalterplatz area. Upon arrival, the same old story of the past few days was repeated. The defenders were clearly outnumbered, but they fought like wild boars, knowing that there was less and less space to fall back to. On the other hand, the Soviets persisted in their relentless harassment, aided by the vast quantities of equipment they had available. Although, after days of fighting in the streets of Berlin, they had realised the grave danger posed by a single platoon, a single man,

The fighting in Berlin during the last days of April and the first days of May 1945 was fierce and resulted in the destruction of much of the city. The ultimate symbol of German power, the Reichstag, was badly damaged following enemy bombing. (Public Domain)

Aerial photograph of Anhalter Station in 1945. The destruction wrought on most of the city's major buildings, caused by both Allied air raids and Soviet artillery, is clearly visible. (Public Domain)

well-positioned and determined to defend the capital to the last drop of his blood. The Soviet soldiers also realised how little time remained before the war ended; they knew that the fighting would not last much longer and did not want to risk dying now that victory was so close. After all, when the war ended, it was better to be among those celebrating victory than to be just another number on the casualty lists.

This account is corroborated by Lorenzo Ocañas' memoirs, as it was on this day that he was captured by the Soviets. In the early hours of the 28th (according to the account of its protagonist, Lorenzo Ocañas), in conditions of extreme cold, a small group of Spaniards, led by Ezquerra, were resting for a few minutes in the ruins of the once-majestic *Europa* Cinema. This cinema had a corridor leading out onto Anhalterplatz, which needed to be reconnoitred. Ezquerra ordered *SS-Obersturmführer* Lorenzo Ocañas to send one of his men to carry out the reconnaissance mission. The man chosen was Macario Vallejo, who made his way towards the passageway in the darkness. Minutes passed that felt like hours, and in the distance they could hear shouts in Russian and the rattling of machine guns. Fearing the worst, Ocañas rushed down the passageway, following in the footsteps of the stricken Vallejo. Upon reaching the outside, he too fell into the Soviet ambush, and they captured him. The toll on the unit was four dead and one missing (Ocañas). Following his capture, Ocañas was taken to the cellars of the *Excelsior Hotel*, which was in Russian hands and which they used as their command post. After intense interrogation, Ocañas managed to save his life, only to spend nearly nine years in captivity in appalling conditions in prisoner-of-war camps in the Soviet Union, until he was finally repatriated on the *Semíramis* in 1954.[16]

16 Moisés Puente, *Yo, Muerto en Rusia: Memorias del Alférez Ocañas de la División*

The deck and bridge of the *Semíramis* with the impatient Spaniards, eager to set foot on home soil once more after years of captivity. (Courtesy of L. E. Togores)

In the photograph, *Hauptmann* Palacios is seen in the centre. On the right is *Leutnant* Rosaleny. On the left is *SS-Obersturmführer* Lorenzo Ocañas Serrano, captured on 28 April 1945 in Berlin while serving in the *Einheit Ezquerra*. (Courtesy of L. E. Togores)

Ocañas recounted this event in his memoirs:

In the early hours of the morning, I found myself at the head of my section with the rank of *Obersturmführer*. The front line stretched out as follows: the Russians held their position at the *Hotel Excelsior* and mine was on the opposite pavement, in the ruins of what had once been the *Europa* Cinema. We held the area around the auditorium, and the corridor leading to the street was no man's land. All in all, about 10

Azul (Arantzazu: Ediciones Franciscanas Arantzazu, 2003).

Photograph of the façade of the *Hotel Excelsior* in Berlin during the interwar years. Numerous skirmishes and clashes between the defenders and the Russians took place in and around the building. A tunnel connected the hotel to Anhalter Station. (Public Domain)

metres! As I approached the street door, I came across a group of soldiers who looked to me like Latvian SS. But when I was among them, I realised, in the moonlight, that they were wearing the five-pointed star on their field caps. My reaction was immediate. Pretending to be as calm as possible, I tried to turn around to escape and open fire on the group of Russians. But it was impossible, for they had spotted my SS officer's uniform and shouted, 'The SS are here!' Like a catapult, they all threw themselves at me.[17]

Ezquerra's men, exhausted after long hours of virtually uninterrupted duty, returned to their base at the Air Ministry, where, worn out by the effort, they tried to rest for a few hours. They had endured many battles, and although fatigue was setting in, the troops' morale and their determination to persevere in their resistance against the Soviets remained intact.

At dawn, the liaison sergeant and interpreter from the *Einheit* briefed Ezquerra on the latest developments.

Once Ezquerra had re-joined his men and after a brief rest, they were tasked, alongside a Latvian battalion, under the command of the abovementioned Walli, with the mission of halting the Soviet advance wherever they appeared.

The *Hotel Kaiserhof* on Wilhelmplatz, through which the Spanish soldiers passed during the Battle of Berlin. (Bundesarchiv Bild 183-R99514)

17 Moisés Puente, *Yo, Muerto en Rusia: Memorias del Alférez Ocañas de la División Azul* (Arantzazu: Ediciones Franciscanas Arantzazu, 2003), pp.22–24.

The sector commander, in telephone contact with *SS-Hauptsturmführer* Walli, ordered that Ezquerra's men should move to the area of the *Hotel Kaiserhof*. As the distance to the hotel was quite short (a few hundred metres), despite the intense fire falling on the *Zitadelle*, it was not a difficult task. Once they reached the area, the men took up positions throughout the hotel grounds, as well as inside the building itself.

The *Hotel Kaiserhof* had been one of the finest in all of Berlin, and due to its proximity to the Government District, as well as to various foreign embassies and, of course, a short distance from the Chancellery, anyone of any importance in the Third Reich wanted to stay there or at least make an appearance within its walls. It was for this reason that, in its heyday, it was common to see Germany's elite there. Even Hitler, before becoming Chancellor, had stayed there, and later (once in power) had an apartment in the building.

On Saturday 28 April, the men of the *Einheit Ezquerra* received orders to deploy in the vicinity of the *Kaiserhof Hotel*, where they engaged in several skirmishes with Soviet troops. (Bundesarchiv Bild 183-J31330)

Upon reaching their destination, Ezquerra stationed men at strategic points around the area, awaiting the imminent arrival of the Russian advance parties coming from the south-east. The atmosphere in the hotel was utterly dreamlike. Here, life continued to be lived with the same luxury and artificiality as in the now distant era of peace. Not surprisingly, it was still frequented by high-ranking officials, diplomats, journalists and civilians of high social standing, as well as senior military officers. Of course, there was an abundance of elegantly dressed women, artists, cabaret girls and high-class prostitutes, as well as foodstuffs that were no longer – or had never been – found in the pantries of the Berlin public, among which were the finest French wines and champagnes.

In that microcosm that was the hotel, realising what the future held in store for them, they seized every moment as if it were their last; thus, orgies were a frequent occurrence in the hotel basement, as the danger increased exponentially on the upper floors. It was a realm of depravity and lust, in which some of the men responsible for defending the sector would also take part. As seems to have happened to one of the men from the *Einheit*, tempted by a beautiful woman.

Outside those walls, the Russians were closing in on the area, this time advancing from Kronenstrasse. These were reconnaissance groups, followed by tanks, mainly T-34s and the mighty IS-2s. The Spanish, French and Belgian soldiers in that area once again rushed to the site of the Soviet incursion, taking up positions in nearby houses with their anti-tank weapons, MG42s, assault rifles, and every weapon at their disposal. From positions that were sometimes impossible for the Soviets to locate, due to the vast amount of rubble littering the streets, they were dealing with them effectively.

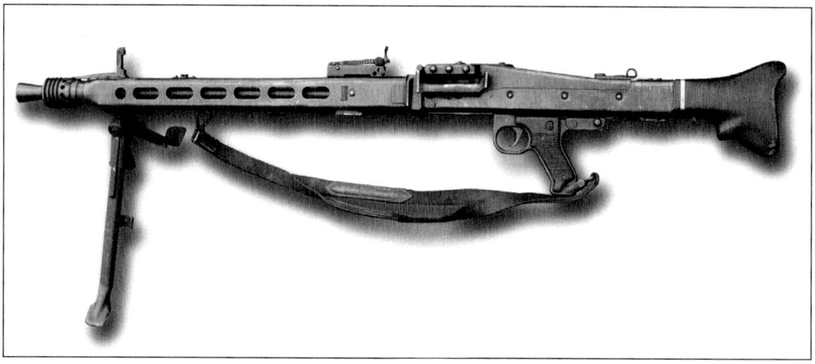

The MG42 or *Maschinengewehr 42* was an ideal weapon for defensive combat. It was another of the weapons with which the Spanish unit was equipped for the Battle of Berlin. (By Phanatic. Public Domain)

After laying down heavy fire against the Russian infantry, a few men – possessing both the courage and a complete disregard for their own lives – were bold enough to approach each tank as closely as possible with their *panzerfausts*, in order to deliver a decisive blow to the most vital parts. They had already been thoroughly briefed that these vulnerable areas were located at the base of the turret, and in the section near the tank's driver. With the T-34 it was difficult, but the task was multiplied when facing that 46-tonne armoured monster that was the IS-2. Despite this, after a battle that lasted at least two hours, the result was five tanks put out of action, as well as dozens of men killed and wounded on both sides.

One of the Spaniards in the *Einheit*, nicknamed 'El Chato', single-handedly reduced three tanks to scrap; Múgica destroyed another, and the fifth was taken out by *Sergeant* Ferrer.

An IS-2 in front of the Brandenburg Gate following the Soviet victory in Berlin. In this area of Sector Z, the remnants of the *Nordland* fought until the very end. (Public Domain)

Following this engagement, the Russians withdrew once more, though not without having advanced a few metres from their original starting position, tightening the pincer grip that was 'strangling' Berlin. Once the positions had been handed over to fresh troops, the men of Ezquerra carried out a reconnaissance advance as far as Hausvogteiplatz.

During this advance, no enemy movement was observed, so strategic positions were taken in anticipation of probable new Soviet attacks. This was carried out by elements of the 11th Tank Corps advancing towards Hausvogteiplatz following the penetration of Spittelmarkt. Hours later, once the 'Soviet fire' had been 'put out', the Spanish troops were once again relieved by a fresh German battalion – if there were any fresh troops left on the German side in Berlin. The constant changes across the entire defensive perimeter that still held required a continuous shuffling of troops from one street to another, or in other words, from one front to another. In reality, being on the front line required moving from anywhere within the German territory of Berlin, in some cases just a few hundred metres.

The roar of howitzers, the pounding fire of heavy mortars, the rattling of machine guns, the bombs from tactical bombers, and the screams of wounded men and women and those seized by panic were the constant sounds that could be heard on any Berlin street.

On this day, once again, Spaniards and Latvians found themselves united in the fight against the Soviet advance in the eastern part of the *Zitadelle* sector. As Vincent Hunt records, as the Soviets drew nearer, the Latvian Jānis Tilmanis positioned himself near the opera house with his men, and:

> A group of Spaniards was by our side, cheerful musicians playing harmonicas. They'd obviously got hold of some wine from somewhere and were in high spirits. Then the Russian tanks appeared. Two of the Spaniards took out three Russian tanks and lived to tell the tale!
>
> We all knew we couldn't do much against the Russians, but we had to save our own lives. As a reminder, there were many bodies decorated with all sorts of crosses hanging from the lampposts. We had to keep fighting. If you didn't shoot, they'd shoot you. Chaos reigned and there was no way to fight. Even the commanders were thinking in broad strokes. The small details were impossible.
>
> In the *U-Bahn* they tried to bring some semblance of order. They looked for the highest-ranking soldier to lead the groups. He had a Danish accent that we couldn't understand. Once an order was carried out, everyone scattered, as there was no command structure whatsoever.
>
> I ended up at the Air Ministry and was sent to the zoo bunker for ammunition or something like that. It was under constant bombardment, near the [Landwehr] canal and the zoo, and it was very well built and strong.[18]

---

18 Vincent Hunt, *Sent to Die in Berlin* (Warwick: Helion & Co., 2026). Details from

A few hundred metres further south, the fighting intensified along Wilhelmstrasse (which leads directly to the Air Ministry, among other important official buildings in the area) and Saarlandstrasse (which leads directly to Potsdamer Platz via the Anhalter and Potsdam Railway Stations), although it had already been subjected to heavy aerial and ground bombardment for days. The constant fire from mortars, artillery and tanks, combined with the vast number of troops the Russians were fielding in combat, forced the defending troops in many cases to carry out strategic retreats and take up new defensive positions.

The nature of urban warfare imposes very specific constraints on the tactics employed by both defending and attacking troops. This fact, combined with Hitler's decision to turn Berlin into a fortress to be defended to the last metre, led to a bloody battle in which the mighty Soviet Army could still be held back momentarily for a few days, despite the 'theoretical' lack of fighting spirit among most of the defending troops.

After the final skirmish, the Spaniards returned under Ezquerra's command to the Air Ministry. There, Ezquerra attempted to locate *SS-Hauptsturmführer* Walli to report on the events that had occurred hours earlier, but was told that he was in the bunker located in the Ministry's garden. Ezquerra, Carranchas, *Sergeant* García and the unit's interpreter made their way to the bunker entrance, where, after passing through rigorous security checks, they were granted access. They were escorted by a sentry to an inner room, where Walli appeared and after a brief chat with Ezquerra, he ushered him into another room. In this room was the sector commander, as well as several generals and other senior military officers gathered around a table with a map of Berlin on which lines of different colours could be seen, representing – or at least attempting to represent – the various points of advance of the Soviet troops. Ezquerra was introduced to the military officers and was warmly received by the sector commander. They discussed the events of the skirmish that took place in the area of Kronenstrasse. Afterwards, Ezquerra was given new orders, which were to defend the entire Ministry District, situated between Hermann Göringstrasse and Friedrichstrasse, all the way to Unter den Linden.

It would not be difficult to get there (at least in terms of distance), as movements were increasingly limited to a few hundred metres. Nevertheless, due to the rubble, ruins, fires and continuous attacks by Russian artillery, it was not going to be a comfortable journey.

As Ezquerra recounts in his book, at that meeting he was promoted to *SS-Obersturmbannführer*, due to his success in combat (a fact that is very likely fictional, or at least there is no other source to corroborate it).

The chaos reigning in the city, particularly in the increasingly shrinking sector controlled by the Germans, meant that many men were already beginning to think more about fleeing and not remaining in the fight. In this regard, González Pinilla refers to a letter shown by Vázquez Enciso,

---

the author; at the time of writing the book is forthcoming.

Line of combat on April 29 and location of areas where the Spaniards were that day.
A Extension north towards Brandenburg Gate and Reichstag; B Hermann Göring Strasse; C Potsdam train station
D Reichsluftfahrtministerium (RLM) or Air Ministry; E Saarlandstrasse; F Europahaus; G Anhalter train station / Anhalterplatz

dated 28 April in Berlin and which must have been written by a soldier from the *Einheit Ezquerra*:

> ...tomorrow night, with a group of SS soldiers, Belgians and Germans, we are going to try to get out of here, because our Captain von Craim has advised us that, as we are not all Germans, we should try to flee and not fall into the hands of the Russians. Many have tried and we know of some who have reached other areas and escaped or have been taken prisoner by the British or by American troops, which is better than the French.... The truth is that they are very close and have the city surrounded on practically all sides except the north-west, and that is where we are going to try .... I hope you receive what may be my last letter from this great country, Germany...[19]

Sunday 29 April

Throughout the night, Berlin was nothing short of a living hell. The stench of decomposing corpses hung over vast areas of the city. The screams of raped women could be heard beyond the front line.

On 29 April, the Russians advanced from the Grunewald (west of the capital), near the Reichssportfeld; from Anhalter Bahnhof through the tunnels; from the Tiergarten (where fighting raged for the strip occupied by the embassies and the area west of the zoo down to the Havel) and from Potsdamer Platz (the underground levels of the combined metro and railway station were the scene of unspeakable fighting for hours on end, with both sides battling in the darkness of the tunnels using hand grenades and in hand-to-hand combat).

At dawn, the 1st Mechanised Corps broke through the blockades on the Spree. The 12th Guards Tank Corps advanced towards the western part of Moabit. Somewhat further north of the Spanish deployment, the 79th Rifle Corps attacked the Moltke Bridge following intensive preparations the previous night, and encountered significant pockets of resistance in the adjacent buildings. The first attack was repelled, but a second followed, which succeeded in establishing a bridgehead in a corner of the diplomatic quarter. Little by little, the Soviets advanced along Herwarthstrasse. This advance was temporarily halted by the *SS Regiment 1. Anhalt* in cooperation with some men from the *9. Fallschirmjäger Division*. Thus, during the night of 28/29, the Soviets attempted to consolidate their positions in the buildings in the northern part of Königsplatz. At around 07.00, heavy artillery fire supplemented by rockets attempted to crush all resistance in

19 Manuel Vázquez Enciso, *Historia postal de la División Azul. Españoles en Rusia* (Madrid: Lindner Filatélica Ibérica, 1995), pp.281–283.

Der Panzerbär

Lesen und weitergeben!

29. April 1945

KAMPFBLATT FÜR DIE VERTEIDIGER GROSS-BERLINS

Heroisches Ringen

Bei Tag und Nacht neue Eingreifkräfte herangeführt

Der Kampf um den Stadtkern entbrannt

Entlastungsangriffe laufen

Aus dem Führerhauptquartier, 28. April.

Das Oberkommando der Wehrmacht gibt bekannt:

In dem heroischen Kampf der Stadt Berlin kommt noch einmal vor aller Welt der Schicksalskampf des deutschen Volkes gegen den Bolschewismus zum Ausdruck.

Während in einem in der Geschichte einmaligen grandiosen Ringen die Hauptstadt verteidigt wird, haben unsere Truppen an der Elbe den Amerikanern den Rücken gekehrt, um von außen her im Angriff die Verteidiger von Berlin zu entlasten.

In dem inneren Verteidigungsring ist der Feind von Norden her in Charlottenburg und von Süden her über das Tempelhofer Feld eingedrungen. Am Halleschen Tor und am Alexanderplatz hat der Kampf um den Stadtkern begonnen. Die Ost-West-Achse liegt unter schwerem Feuer.

Fliegende Verbände unterstützen die Kämpfe unter aufopferndem Einsatz der Besatzungen. Trotz stärkster Jagd- und Flakabwehr wurden bei Tag und Nacht Eingreifreserven gelandet und Munition abgeworfen. Unsere Jagd- und Schlachtfliegerverbände vernichteten in den letzten vier Tagen 143 Flugzeuge, 58 Panzer und über 300 Fahrzeuge.

Im Raum südlich Königs Wusterhausen setzten Divisionen der 9. Armee ihre Angriffe nach Nordwesten fort und erwehrten sich während des ganzen Tages konzentrischer Angriffe der Sowjets gegen die Flanken. Die vom Westen angesetzten Divisionen warfen den Feind in erbittertem Ringen auf breiter Front zurück und haben Ferch erreicht.

Westlich Berlin wurde die Linie Brandenburg—Rathenau—Kremmen gegen alle feindlichen Angriffe behauptet.

Im Raume von Prenzlau warfen die Sowjets neue Panzer- und Infanterieverbände in den Kampf und erzwangen unter starkem Schlachtfliegereinsatz tiefe Einbrüche.

Im nordwestdeutschen Raum kam es gestern nur zu örtlichen Kämpfen. In Bremen hält der Kampfkommandant mit dem Rest der tapferen Besatzung den Nordostteil der Stadt.

An der Donau brach der Feind in Regensburg und Ingolstadt ein. Zwischen Dillingen und Ulm setzten die Amerikaner ihren Vorstoß nach Süden fort. Kämpfe sind in Mindel und im Guenztal im Gange.

Die Armeen in Italien setzten sich hinter dem Po und Tessin ab.

Während die Sowjets im Südabschnitt der Ostfront sich auf starke örtliche Vorstöße beschränkten, setzten sie ihre Angriffe im Raum Brünn mit starken Kräften fort und konnten trotz zäher Gegenwehr der Besatzung in die Stadt eindringen.

Nordwestlich Bautzen, wo bei Meißen die Verbindung mit der Westfront an der Elbe hergestellt wurde, sind unsere Truppen zum Angriff nach Norden angetreten.

Sicherungsfahrzeuge der Kriegsmarine versenkten östlich Gotenhafen ein sowjetisches Schnellboot und schossen ein weiteres in Brand.

Schwächere amerikanische Kampfverbände führten am Tage Angriffe gegen Orte in Süddeutschland. In der Nacht herrschte über dem Reichsgebiet nur geringe feindliche Kampftätigkeit.

Kleinstunterseeboote versenkten aus dem stark bewachten feindlichen Nachschubverkehr zwischen Themse und Schelde zwei vollbeladene Schiffe mit 8000 BRT.

Der längere Atem

Seit fünfeinhalb Jahren lodert die Fackel des Krieges in Europa. Ihr verzehrendes Feuer hat nach Polen ganz Europa, nach diesem Erdteil schließlich noch zwei weitere erfaßt, Asien und Amerika.

Deutschland mußte einerseits die Ketten abzustreifen versuchen, die ihm in Versailles auferlegt waren und ihm jede Lebensmöglichkeit nahmen. Es hat dies seit 1933 in dem denkbar engsten Rahmen getan und peinlichst vermieden, dabei den Kreis der unmittelbar betroffenen Gebiete, d. h. die deutsche Lebens- und Interessenzone zu überschreiten.

Wenn unsere Feinde behaupteten, Deutschland habe eigennützige Machtziele verfolgt und die Unabhängigkeit und Freiheit der kleinen Nationen bedroht, so haben England und Amerika sehr bald durch ihr Verhalten bewiesen, daß ihnen in Wirklichkeit nicht nur nichts an der Freiheit dieser kleinen Nationen gelegen ist, sondern daß sie selbst bereit waren und sind, diese an Stalin zu verkaufen, ja, sie für ihre eigenen imperialistischen Ziele auszubeuten.

Mehr noch! Während die von Deutschland besetzten Feindländer durchaus auskömmlich leben konnten, zum Teil sogar einen fühlbaren wirtschaftlichen und sozialen Aufschwung nahmen, ächzen die „befreiten" Bundesgenossen unter der Hungersnot, Desorganisation und Ausbeutung durch die Engländer und Amerikaner. Besonders groß aber sind die Leiden der Neutralen und jener Völker, die sich den jüdisch-plutokratischen und bolschewistischen Drahtziehern auf Gedeih und Verderb unterwarfen.

Deutschland ist durch den Verrat klug geworden, dem es 1918 zum Opfer fiel. Es weiß, daß alle Versprechungen der Feindseite nichts anderes bedeuten als den Versuch, unser Volk wiederum völlig wehrlos zu machen und es damit der wirtschaftlichen Ausbeutung, persönlichen Versklavung und völkischen Vernichtung auszuliefern.

Zu verlieren haben wir nichts mehr. Wir haben alles verloren und würden durch Kapitulation uns selbst, unsere Zukunft, Frau und Kind preisgeben. Wohl aber haben wir die Chance, uns zu behaupten und einst dann Existenz, Familienleben und unseren sozialen Staat wieder aufzubauen, in dem wir einen noch größeren Wohlstand erreichen werden, als wir ihn vor diesem Kriege bereits genießen konnten.

Dies ist ein fernes, aber ein reales Ziel. Wir wollen es stets vor Augen behalten, wenn die Gegenwart heute Anforderungen an uns stellt, die uns fast unerträglich erscheinen mögen, wenn unser Todfeind uns Wunden schlägt, aus denen das Blut unserer Besten fließt.

In Berlin, in den rauchenden Ruinen der Reichshauptstadt

Front page of the *Panzerbär*, 29 April 1945. (Collection of J. Arráez.)

some of the buildings still in German hands, including the Kroll Opera House and the Ministry of the Interior.

The 3rd Shock Army advanced slowly towards Stettiner Station; the 5th Shock Army was advancing towards the Börse *S-Bahn* Station and the *Rotes Rathaus*, which were located in the area defended by units of the *Nordland Division*.

The 32nd Rifle Corps captured the Jannowitzbrücke *S-Bahn* Station, drawing closer to the Spree. The 8th Guards Army begins its assault on the Landwehr Canal.

As the Soviets approached Sector Z, the German defence became more compact as men retreating from the various sectors regrouped. From true bastions created within the sturdy brick and stone buildings, they sought to hinder, as much as possible, the advance of the enemy armoured vehicles, which were increasingly closely protected by their infantry.

The Spanish troops, scattered after so many vicissitudes, found themselves in the vicinity of Saarlandstrasse, which was the 'artery' linking Anhalterplatz (where they fought side by side with other men, including the remaining troops of the *Müncheberg* and *Nordland Divisions*), the Alexanderplatz area, and the Anhalter and Potsdam Stations. They were also deployed on Hermann Göringstrasse, the extension of Saarlandstrasse towards the Brandenburg Gate and the Reichstag. In all these locations, they held their ground using their automatic weapons and *panzerfausts*. In the streets near Alexanderplatz, fierce fighting took place, with the defenders inflicting heavy losses on the Soviets. The Soviet advance became extremely difficult, as they had to take and destroy every single house.

Faced with the Soviet advance and their incursion into the Gestapo headquarters at Prinz-Albrecht-Strasse, carried out by two regiments of the 301st Rifle Division, the commander of the *Zitadelle* sector, *Oberstleutnant* Seifert, sent a group to drive out the Soviets (Sector Z had been divided into two sub-sectors; the western sub-sector was commanded by *Oberstleutnant* Seifert, with the command post in the Air Ministry building, and the eastern sub-sector was commanded by *SS-Brigadeführer* Krukenberg, with most of the *Nordland Division* troops and the French from the *Charlemagne Division*, the dividing line between both sub-sectors being Wilhelmstrasse). The Latvian and Spanish soldiers would once again share trenches here.

The Brandenburg Gate and Pariser Platz following the fighting in Sector Z of Berlin. The extensive destruction suffered by the city is evident. (Bundesarchiv B 145 Bild P054320)

The Gestapo building on Prinz-Albrecht-Strasse in Berlin following the fierce fighting in the city. (Bundesarchiv Bild 183-S85918)

For Ezquerra and his men, the next mission was not long in coming. This would be to head immediately, alongside the Latvian SS soldiers, to repel an incursion carried out by two infantry battalions accompanied by several tanks that were approaching Potsdamer Platz. At that moment, the forces resisting the Soviet onslaught there were mainly made up of military police personnel and did not appear sufficient to withstand that powerful enemy advance.

The Latvian *SS-Obersturmführer* Liepnieks gathered some of his men who had been covering Wilhelmstrasse with machine guns and joined forces with Laiviņš's Latvian company, half a company from a *Nordland* sapper battalion and a handful of Spanish volunteers to drive back the Red Army and take control of the nearby *Europahaus* (a large 11-storey office block with a roof garden, on Saarlandstrasse near Potsdamer Platz).

The remains of the *Europahaus* after the fighting. Here, Spanish soldiers alongside their Latvian comrades engaged in fierce fighting to take control of the building. (Abraham Pisarek. Deutsche Fotothek)

Ezquerra's men, alongside the Latvians, began to advance towards the square, but their progress was slowed by the continuous explosions of shells of all types and calibres. Having overcome this danger, although not without suffering at least five casualties, they managed to reach the vicinity of the square, where they began to take up positions, mainly in partially ruined buildings.

Once the enemy advance had been halted; at 15.00, Latvian troops launched a counter-attack supported by Ezquerra's men and forced the Soviets to withdraw from the ruins surrounding the *Europahaus*. One of the Latvian soldiers, regarding the ferocity of these battles recorded:

> Our final counter-attack was dramatic. It was only after the war that we discovered that on the opposite [southern] side of the small block on Anhalterstrasse, the three battalions of the Red Army's 1050th Rifle Regiment had concentrated their forces, and they were apparently not short of ammunition. The counter-attack was successful and the Russians were pushed back behind the *Europahaus* and *Anhalter Bahnhof*, but it cost us dearly. Those with minor injuries

Potsdamer Platz after the end of the war. In the last days of April 1945, it looked very different, as it was littered with wrecked vehicles, mutilated bodies and wounded soldiers. (Public Domain)

> withdrew; we, the seriously wounded, withdrew later under intense enemy fire. The Russian soldiers who lost the battle and were pushed back onto Anhalterstrasse replenished their ammunition, reloaded their weapons and subsequently fired without remorse.[20]

Ezquerra recounted these events:

> From this moment on, we will have no respite; we will rush to every threatened location, we will fight for every building, for every floor, for every square, for every street, for every inch of ground, leaping through the ruins, subjected to relentless shelling from guns and mortars, accompanied by a group of Latvians just like us, we managed to reach Potsdamer Platz and occupy a building of which only the skeleton remains standing. Before reaching it, we lost five comrades forever.
>
> No sooner have we taken cover behind the piles of rubble than I see a group of tanks (I count up to 15) advancing relentlessly, protecting the infantry following behind them. Fortunately, we have plenty of iron fists. I give the order for no one to fire. I set my submachine gun down on the ground and readied my iron fist. When the first of the tanks reached a suitable distance, I fired a projectile at it while shouting: 'Fire! Fire!' The lead tanks, hit squarely, were rendered useless; one of them exploded, sending a column of greasy smoke into the sky. It smells of burnt flesh. The T-34s bringing up the rear attempt to manoeuvre to escape this deadly trap, but the lack of space prevents them from doing so. The infantrymen try to take refuge in the adjacent buildings, but our automatic weapons and the concentrated fire from Walli's men cut them down. They fall one after another, without having fired a single shot.

Anhalterplatz and, on the right, the battered *Europahaus* after the fighting in Berlin had finally ended. The destruction and desolation of Berlin's streets is clearly visible. (Abraham Pisarek. Deutsche Fotothek)

20 Vincent Hunt, *Sent to Die in Berlin* (Warwick: Helion & Co., 2026). Details from the author; at the time of writing the book is forthcoming.

> We have captured several Russian soldiers. None of them offered the slightest resistance. I got the impression they were drugged... or drunk. A German reinforcement battalion arrives, but the fighting has ended. The new arrivals take up our positions and we move back to the Air Ministry.[21]

With thanks to Vincent Hunt, is an account of that battle from the Latvian soldier Peteris Krievs:

> We received the order to prepare for an attack. It was led by the battalion commander himself, *SS-Hauptsturmführer* Walli. The starting point was the *Europahaus* hotel [*sic*], located behind the security agency to the right of the garden. Moving around this area was dangerous as it was constantly under fire. On the way to this building, on a small concrete bridge in the garden, beneath which there was a cobbled path, I stood for a moment beside *SS-Hauptsturmführer* Walli. He wasn't wearing a helmet, just a standard military cap, and was armed with a submachine gun. From there we reached the 10-storey hotel (if I remember correctly), of which only the burnt walls remained, and on whose ground floor lay burnt corpses. Without the support of any heavy weaponry, we began the attack from the garden. It was no longer a garden, as it had been torn apart by shells and the trees were a ragged grey. Another man and I were armed with an MG42 machine gun. We were on the right flank. When we reached the centre of the garden, our machine gun stopped working. A bloke called Tams, from Jelgava, ran alongside us with a bullet wound in his arm. My comrade and I kept further to the right, reaching the last building in the garden before the

The tall *Europahaus* building was the 'battlefield' for Latvians and Spaniards on 29 April 1945. Photograph from 1936. (Bundesarchiv Bild 146-1987-031-28)

21 Miguel Ezquerra Sánchez, *Luché Hasta El Fin: Memorias de un voluntario español en la guerra 1939–1945, Berlin a vida o muerte* (Granada: García Hispán, 1999), pp.119–121.

> street. It reminded us of a ruined cinema with a projection room on the ground floor, the ceiling having collapsed and the window openings broken. The rest of us ran into the wall and could go no further.[22]

During this clash, a number of prisoners were taken, from whom information could be extracted with little difficulty. Although there was really little need for it by then, because simply by looking at the next street, corner or square, one could already guess the movements of the main body of Russian troops.

As is customary for the Spaniards, after the storm came the calm; so, once the sector has been secured, they were relieved by German troops which took over their positions.

Having put out this new 'fire', the men, visibly exhausted after a long day of constant tension, returned to their base at the Air Ministry. Night was already falling and they deserved a rest and something hot to eat. But the return journey was once again under intense artillery fire, to which the men were so accustomed that they barely took notice of it, merely taking cover as close as possible to the walls of the buildings.

After this, and again according to what Ezquerra recounts in his book (another account, which is not entirely implausible but for which there is no evidence whatsoever that the events took place) he was taken by Walli, an *SS-Standartenführer* in Hitler's personal guard, and an SS non-commissioned officer, to the basement of the Air Ministry and led through electrical conduits that connect to underground tunnels, and these to further basements. They continued along these paths, sometimes lit by the light of their own torches, until they finally arrived at a larger basement where a garrison belonging to the SS was stationed. They had finally reached their destination – none other than the Führer's bunker. There Ezquerra was able to see the leading figures of the German Government, such as Goebbels, Axmann, Burgdorf, et cetera; as well as being introduced to Adolf Hitler himself, who awarded him the Knight Cross (there is an important observation regarding this decoration below). This entire story is based solely on Ezquerra's account, and there are no other witnesses. However, while it is true that there is no evidence to support this story, there is equally no evidence to the contrary. Despite our disbelief regarding this event, we must bear in mind that as all this took place at a time when Berlin was literally being crushed by the Soviets, nothing that happened there at this time was normal.

According to Ezquerra, four hours after abandoning his men, and following this mysterious encounter, he returned to the Air Ministry, where he conferred with his non-commissioned officers.

---

22 Vincent Hunt, *Sent to Die in Berlin* (Warwick: Helion & Co., 2026). Details from the author; at the time of writing the book is forthcoming.

The Russians were advancing inexorably, arriving with their armoured vehicles accompanied by infantry troops along Wilhelmstrasse and Saarlandstrasse, right up to the vicinity of the Air Ministry itself and Potsdam Station respectively.

Defenders were gathering in this area, along with troops retreating from various points along the front line. A front line that was just a few metres ahead and behind them.

Despite the diverse nature of the defending troops and the relentless bombardment to which they were subjected, they were still able, thanks to their anti-tank guns, their *panzerfausts* and, above all, the desperate resolve of each and every one of the men, to make the Russians pay a heavy price for every metre they advanced.

By the end of the day, numerous bomb craters had rendered the roads on Friedrichstrasse impassable. Just as night fell, the Latvian soldier, Peteris Krievs, was among a small group of men taking refuge in a ruined cinema and recounted the events thus:

> There we recognised the Spaniards with whom we had been on the Jägerstrasse. We decided to return to the Ministry. We withdrew one by one in single file, and suddenly a Spanish lieutenant blocked the way with his arm and ordered the rest of us to stay with them. He gave me a friendly pat on the shoulder and said: 'Du Kamerad aus Lettland und ich Kamerad aus Spanien' ['You, comrade from Latvia, and I, comrade from Spain'] and gave me a cigarette.
>
> In the darkness, through the empty window frames, snipers were firing at us with automatic weapons. They were firing explosive bullets that were easily visible in the dark, as they ricocheted off the wall and sent sparks flying as they exploded.

View of Jägerstrasse in Berlin today. On this street, Spanish and Latvian soldiers shared barracks during the final days of the city's defence. (Courtesy of Vincent Hunt)

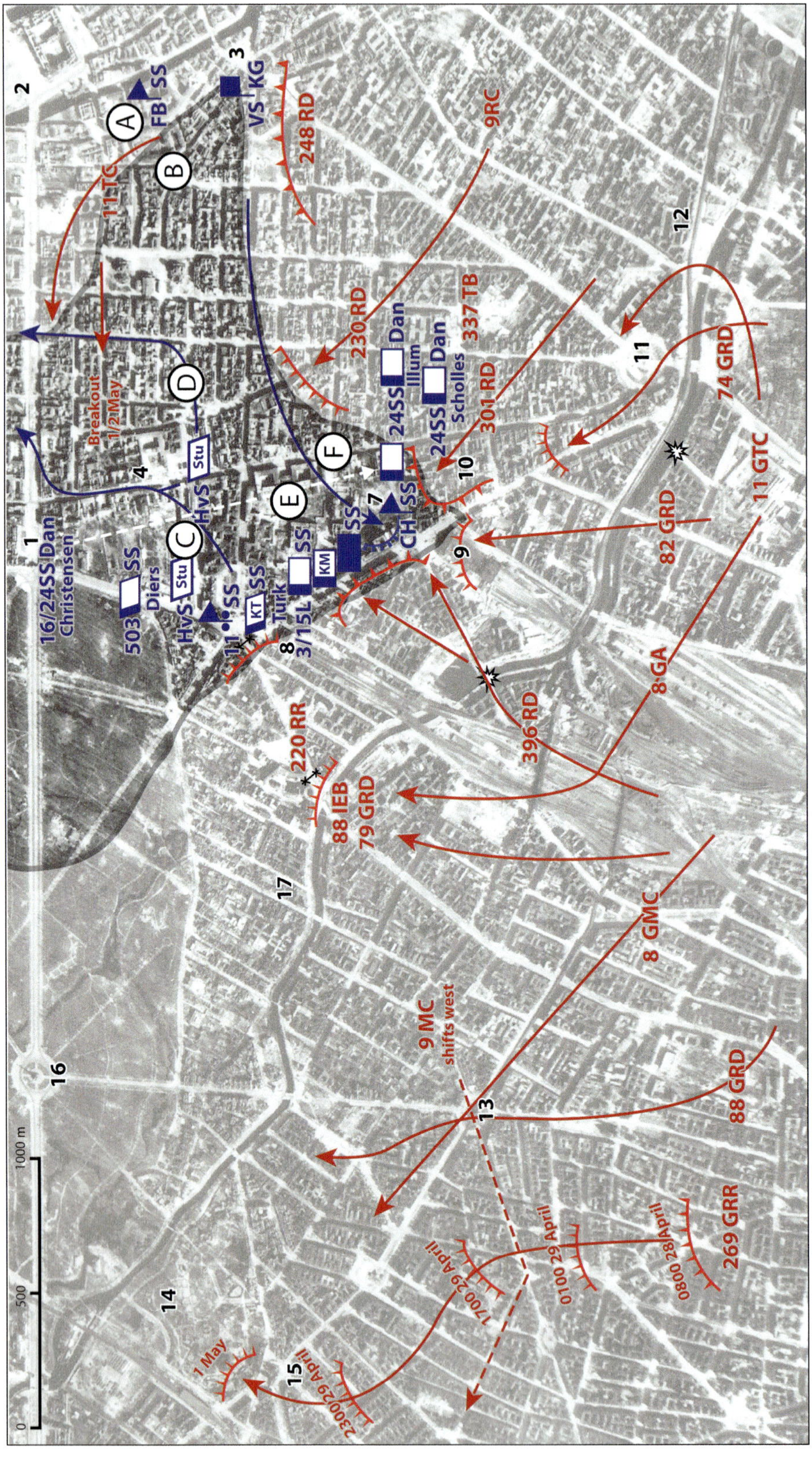

Line of combat on April 30 and location of areas where the Spaniards were that day.
A Reichbank; B Hausvogteiplatz (the Spanish were here on 28 April); C Reich Chancellery; D Vicinity of the Chancellery towards Friedrichstrasse; E Reichsluftfahrtministerium (RLM) or Air Ministry; F Sector from Prinz-Albert-Strasse to Wilhelmstrasse

> On the road, on the other side of the building, the roar of tanks could be heard. It was said that the Spaniards had just fired on a tank. I took charge of our split group. Later, the Spaniards let us go, and we re-joined the rest of our men at the Air Ministry.[23]

As is apparent, there was no order whatsoever; they simply fought and held their ground at a single point until they were finally driven out of it by the incessant fire of guns and mortars that literally crushed the defenders' positions. And again at the next corner, the same operation: wait for the enemy armoured vehicles behind some ruined wall without firing until the very last second. Although each time with less and less space to fall back into.

Whenever possible, the city's defenders used the scarce German armoured vehicles to move from one place to another. On this, Spanish *SS-Sturmmann* Horacio E. relates:

> Whenever we could, we'd climb onto the tanks so we wouldn't have to walk; we'd be crammed in there, clinging to one another so we wouldn't fall off in the potholes. I remember a man we called 'the Asturian' who had a large Spanish coat of arms sewn onto his arm and who, on one of those bumps, slipped down the right side of the tank and had the misfortune of getting caught in the tracks. He let out terrible screams as his leg was torn from his body at the groin; it happened in a matter of seconds, but to me it seemed like an eternity; there was nothing we could do for him; he bled to death shortly afterwards.[24]

Monday 30 April

On 30 April the OKW made the following radio broadcast:

> The heroic struggle for the central districts of the capital continues with unrelenting fury. In fierce local and street fighting, troops from all branches of the *Wehrmacht*, the Hitler Youth and the *Volkssturm* are defending the central districts of the city, a shining symbol of German heroism. At Anhalter Bahnhof, along Potsdamerstrasse and in Schöneberg, the enemy has been halted by our brave defenders. The self-sacrificing pilots of the *Luftwaffe* dropped supplies for the Berlin Garrison. To the south of the city, our relief units are fighting against the strong Bolshevik units, which are suffering heavy, bloody losses. Between Berlin and the Baltic Sea, the front line now stretches from Kremmen-Neustrelitz-Neubrandenburg-Anklam.[25]

---

23 Information from Vincent Hunt.

24 Augusto Ferrer-Dalmau, 'Españoles en las Waffen SS' in *Eurouniformes*, no. 14, diciembre-enero 2002-2003.

25 Aaron Stephan Hamilton, *Bloody Streets: The Soviet Assault on Berlin* (Warwick:

A member of the *Volkssturm* stationed in a trench on the outskirts of Berlin with his *panzerschreck*. The photograph is from late April 1945, with the Soviet offensive already well underway. (Bundesarchiv Bild 146-1985-092-29)

In Berlin, from the early hours of dawn, the Russians saturated the German defences with intense artillery fire. The *Katyushas* (colloquially known as a Stalin Organ) launched salvo after salvo of rockets, causing the destruction of large areas of the reduced defensive perimeter. The noise became deafening, which, combined with the dust clouds and the smoke from the numerous fires, gave Berlin a ghostly appearance, and it was under these conditions that the fighting took place in the streets of the capital.

Several Soviet soldiers are busy loading a Soviet BM-31-12 rocket battery – a modification of the *Katyusha* with M-31 rockets – onto the chassis of an American Studebaker truck. The firepower of these vehicles, together with conventional artillery, was responsible for the destruction of the German defences in Berlin. (Georgi Ugrinovich. Public Domain)

Helion & Co., 2020), p.358.

The Soviets were positioned 300-400 metres from the Chancellery. The 79th Rifle Corps occupied the Ministry of the Interior and the western sector of the diplomatic quarter, facing fierce resistance. The 207th Rifle Division advanced towards the Kroll Opera House, where they encountered a large body of German defenders.

The first direct attack on the Reichstag took place, followed by a second; both were repulsed, partly thanks to the support of the guns positioned in the zoo's anti-aircraft tower.

The 26th Guards Rifle Corps relentlessly attacked the Börse *S-Bahn* Station and the telegraph office.

On the outskirts, only the District of Pichelsdorf continued to resist the fierce Soviet onslaught.

In the Government District under the command of *SS-Brigadeführer* Mohnke, the aim was to gather the last remaining troops for the further defence of the city's government sector, where Spaniards, French and Latvians, together with their 'parent' unit, the *Nordland*, were regrouping.

It was no coincidence that, just as had happened to the Spanish contingent, the command post of the *15. Waffen-SS Grenadier-Division* was moved to the Air Ministry. What remained of its companies covered a sector from Prinz-Albrecht-Strasse to Wilhelmstrasse (possibly, in some cases, in conjunction with the Spaniards). The commander of the 2nd Company, Laiviņš, established his forward positions in the gardens along Prinz-Albrechtstrasse and Anhalterstrasse. These positions were held by the Latvians until the end of the battle for the Berlin Ministry District.

As the Spanish and Latvian contingents were so depleted, it was decided to place them under the sole command of the Latvian *SS-Obersturmführer* Neilands, who recorded,

> Having returned to the Reich Chancellery, I reported to *General* Mohnke on what had happened. Having heard my report, he ordered me to take charge of the defence of the Air Ministry building. My *kampfgruppe* would include units of the French and Spanish SS and a company of naval infantry. I knew that the commanders of the French and Spanish units were both captains, so they outranked me, and furthermore, both had been awarded the Knight Cross of the Iron Cross. Noticing my surprise, Mohnke replied that I had more combat experience. Returning to the security headquarters, I thought about my new order of battle. I had never seen the naval infantry before, and, as it turned out, I never saw them afterwards either.[26]

(This detail regarding the Knight Crosses awarded to both the Spanish and French commanders is discussed below.)

26 Vincent Hunt, *Sent to Die in Berlin* (Warwick: Helion & Co., 2026). Details from the author; at the time of writing the book is forthcoming.

SS-Hauptsturmführer Walli, in command of his own unit (comprising approximately 10 Latvian and German officers, as well as some other members of the Latvian Battalion), with the attached Spanish reserve (mostly officers and non-commissioned officers), carried out a series of attacks from his position at the Air Ministry. These small-scale, close-quarters skirmishes took place mainly in the Friedrichstrasse area.[27]

The destruction evident in the city was absolute. Collapsed houses, ruins in every street, and the dead – large numbers, both civilians and military personnel, who had found themselves caught up in a spiral of blood and death that seemed to have no end. On this, there is an account by Ricardo Botet's liaison officer, *SS-Schütze* Julio Lobo Varela:

> I felt hatred and rage, pity for myself and pleasure when I killed, but above all I felt an excruciating panic at the thought of losing any limb of my body; the whole of Berlin was a dumping ground of human limbs torn apart by bombs and shrapnel.
>
> I remember that a German from another unit – I think he was from the *Luftwaffe* – and I were stationed very close to the underground entrance when we saw a woman on the other side of the street with a child in her arms who was about to cross. The German shouted at her not to move as we were in a shelling zone; either she didn't understand us or she ignored us. The point is, she ran towards us. She hadn't taken more than three steps when a grenade exploded in front of her; the blast threw her towards us as if she were a rag doll. She sat up, dazed, almost naked and bleeding from all over. The child had been decapitated and what remained of his body was a mass of flesh. The poor woman, between moans and sobs, began the macabre task of searching for the child's head. We remained indifferent; by then, we didn't care about anything anymore.[28]

Following his four-hour absence (to receive the Knight Cross, as related above), Ezquerra recounts his return thus:

> I was talking to my officers, telling them what had happened, when a messenger arrived to inform us of what was taking place at the Reichsbank: the Russians were already dangerously close to the building and we had to go to the aid of the men engaged in its defence.

Following this, he relayed the new orders to his men, which consisted of taking up positions in the area where the Reichsbank was located, a

27 Information provided by Vincent Hunt.

28 Augusto Ferrer-Dalmau, 'Españoles en las Waffen SS' in *Eurouniformes*, no. 14, diciembre-enero 2002-2003.

Berlin *U-Bahn's* Inselbrücke Station in 1913. The *U-Bahn* and its tunnels served as shelters, field hospitals, barracks and communication routes for those under siege, offering protection from the enemy fire on the surface. (Public Domain)

building being defended by members of the Hitler Youth. The journey itself was not very long, although, it would require the utmost care to carry it out, as they had to travel over open ground. There, the roar of the hail of shells resounded continuously, it was still dark but it was illuminated by a reddish-yellow light from the numerous fires breaking out everywhere.

The unit advanced slowly along the sides of the streets, taking cover behind the remains of the smoking buildings. Finally, they reached the vicinity of the Reichsbank, where they observed a company of Russian infantry attempting to encircle it without the support of tanks. Inside the bank, amidst a motley crew of defending troops, members of the Hitler Youth stood out, continuing to display a steadfastness and loyalty to the Führer that many had lost after so many years of combat.

The men of the *Einheit Ezquerra*, although already reduced in number by casualties from the intense fighting, still maintained a high fighting spirit. Despite having had only a few hours' rest over the last three days, they attacked the Russians from the flank, managing to break their line of advance and forcing them to retreat with heavy casualties.

Hamilton describes this clash in his book as follows:

> While elements of the 60th Guards Rifle Division and the 416th Rifle Division advanced towards the Reichsbank, they came under intense fire from the Spaniards (*Unidad Ezquerra*), positioned in buildings on the other side of the Kupfergraben canal, which formed the new German front line.[29]

29 Aaron Stephan Hamilton, *Bloody Streets: The Soviet assault on Berlin* (Warwick: Helion & Co., 2020), p.362.

In his account, Ezquerra recalls his time at the Reichsbank:

> Seeking cover amongst the ruins of the buildings, we advanced slowly, defying death at every turn, until we came within sight of the Reichsbank, defended by the ever-present Hitler Youth. There weren't too many Russians – two companies, perhaps – without tanks, but with flamethrowers. Our attack on one of their flanks took them by surprise, and those who did not die instantly retreated in haste.... only to be mowed down by a group of German submariners covering the other flank.[30]

The Reichsbank headquarters in Berlin in a photograph taken in 1903. This building was defended by the men of the *Einheit Ezquerra* on 29 and 30 April 1945. (Public Domain)

We also have information regarding the presence of Spaniards at the Reichsbank from Vincent Hunt in his study of the Latvians in Berlin:

> With his 24 men and two mortars, Uldis Dukurs was immediately sent to the reserve of Defence Sector B. Together with a platoon of Spanish SS volunteers, they were deployed on the left bank of the Spree Canal to defend the Reichsbank building on the Kupfergraben, behind Berlin Castle. Here, Dukurs possibly saved the lives of many of his men by

30 Miguel Ezquerra Sánchez, *Luché Hasta El Fin: Memorias de un voluntario español en la guerra 1939–1945, Berlin a vida o muerte* (Granada: García Hispán, 1999), p.81.

> winning an argument over how they would be deployed with the highly decorated but fanatical Nazi defence sector commander Erich Bärenfänger.
>
> We entered the bank. There were banknotes everywhere and of every denomination: pounds, dollars, crowns, francs, et cetera. A fine haul for a collector! However, I completely forgot about the banknotes when I saw two tins of Portuguese sardines, which I grabbed without hesitation. How little value money has at certain moments![31]

Chaos took hold of the last areas defended by the German Army, and as Ezquerra records: 'The fighting is becoming increasingly difficult; there are no longer any fixed positions, and no one knows where their own forces or the enemy's are.'[32]

General Weidling ordered the broadcast of a communiqué granting permission, given the extreme nature of the situation, to break through the encirclement in which the troops found themselves. This order would lead, in the hours that followed, to numerous and varied attempts to break through the encirclement that was tightening more with every passing minute. Some attempted to escape through the capital's many tunnels, others preferred to swim to safety via the waterways surrounding the *Zitadelle*, and still others opted for direct confrontations with the Soviets; all with varying degrees of success.

Whenever a German unit managed to break through the encirclement, hundreds of people waiting in cover – including civilians and soldiers – would immediately rush through the breach to try to capitalise on the effort made by their compatriots.

Although the image does not depict the streets of Berlin, it shows a small German assault squad, equipped with a flamethrower and at least one MP44, moving through a landscape of ruins. (Public Domain)

31 Vincent Hunt, *Sent to Die in Berlin* (Warwick: Helion & Co., 2026). Details from the author; at the time of writing the book is forthcoming.

32 Miguel Ezquerra Sánchez, *Luché Hasta El Fin: Memorias de un voluntario español en la guerra 1939–1945, Berlin a vida o muerte* (Granada: García Hispán, 1999), p.81.

What remained of the *Einheit Ezquerra*, which was no longer a unit but a group of stragglers, was holding out in the vicinity of Potsdam Square, taking cover in any hollow, pile of rubble, abandoned vehicle or anything else that might serve the purpose. With the motto of not taking 'a single step back', they held their ground against the onslaught. A good example of this is a final account of the Spanish presence in the Battle of Berlin, which González Pinilla recorded, quoting the words of Erich Bodenstein of the *18. Panzergrenadier Division*:

> ...The remnants of the Spanish Company, made up of seasoned volunteer fighters from the former Blue Division and the Spanish Tercio, under the command of their resolute leader Captain Roca, stand out particularly for the superhuman courage and recklessness of their men. French and Spanish soldiers, fighting in staggering numbers, are being killed amidst piles of ruins rather than give up a single inch of street. Truly, there has been no troop in the world that has fought with greater courage than this brave handful of men fighting in the heart of Europe for a square kilometre of ruins. There will not be a single soldier who, as a soldier, does not owe them a tribute. There will not be a single man who has defended his ideals with his life who does not owe them respect .... of the Company of Spanish Volunteers, only 12 legionaries managed to survive. When these indomitable Spanish fighters fell into the hands of the Reds, they were all, without exception, wounded...[33]

The man known as 'Captain Roca' was *Sergeant* Pinar, who during his years of captivity at the hands of the Soviets became known as 'Captain Roca'.

The resistance was fierce, but when it no longer made sense to stay in a position – and only then – Ezquerra authorised the retreat through the underground tunnels, following the remnants of the *Müncheberg Division*, who had used them shortly before to flee the area.

They fled in a hurry through the tunnels, which, despite the darkness within them, could at least afford them a few minutes without being exposed to the continuous Soviet fire. There they encountered thousands of civilians seeking refuge from the Russians, as well as bodies and a motley mix of troops trying to flee towards the nearest station. Although by this stage, few places, if indeed any, would serve to escape the relentless onslaught of the Russian bear.

Some of the Spaniards, retreating with Soviet troops at their heels, withdrew along Friedrichstrasse, taking up positions near the Chancellery, in whose bunker Adolf Hitler would commit suicide that day at 15.30 hours. His body was burnt alongside that of Eva Braun in the Chancellery garden. A few hours later, *Reichsleiter* Bormann and *General* Krebs sent a

---

33 Erich Bodenstein, 'Recordando a mi regimiento y a mis camaradas' in *Memorial del ejército de Chile*, 1979, pp.154–157.

radio message from the Armed Forces High Command to the head of the northern sector, *Grossadmiral* Dönitz, stating:

> *Grossadmiral* Dönitz. In place of the former *Reichsmarschall* Göring, the Führer has appointed you, *Grossadmiral*, as his successor.
>
> Written authorisation is on its way.
>
> Furthermore, *Feldmarschall* Schörner will be the Supreme Chief of the Army and *Generaloberst* Jodl, Chief of the General Staff of the *Wehrmacht*.

In the bunker of the Chancellery, according to Ezquerra, Adolf Hitler himself awarded him the Knight Cross. No document has been found to corroborate this fact, which may be an 'exaggeration' on Ezquerra's part. (Bundesarchiv Bild 146-1988-092-32)

Two German soldiers walk along a destroyed street in a German town. The soldier in the foreground is armed with an StG44 assault rifle. (Public Domain)

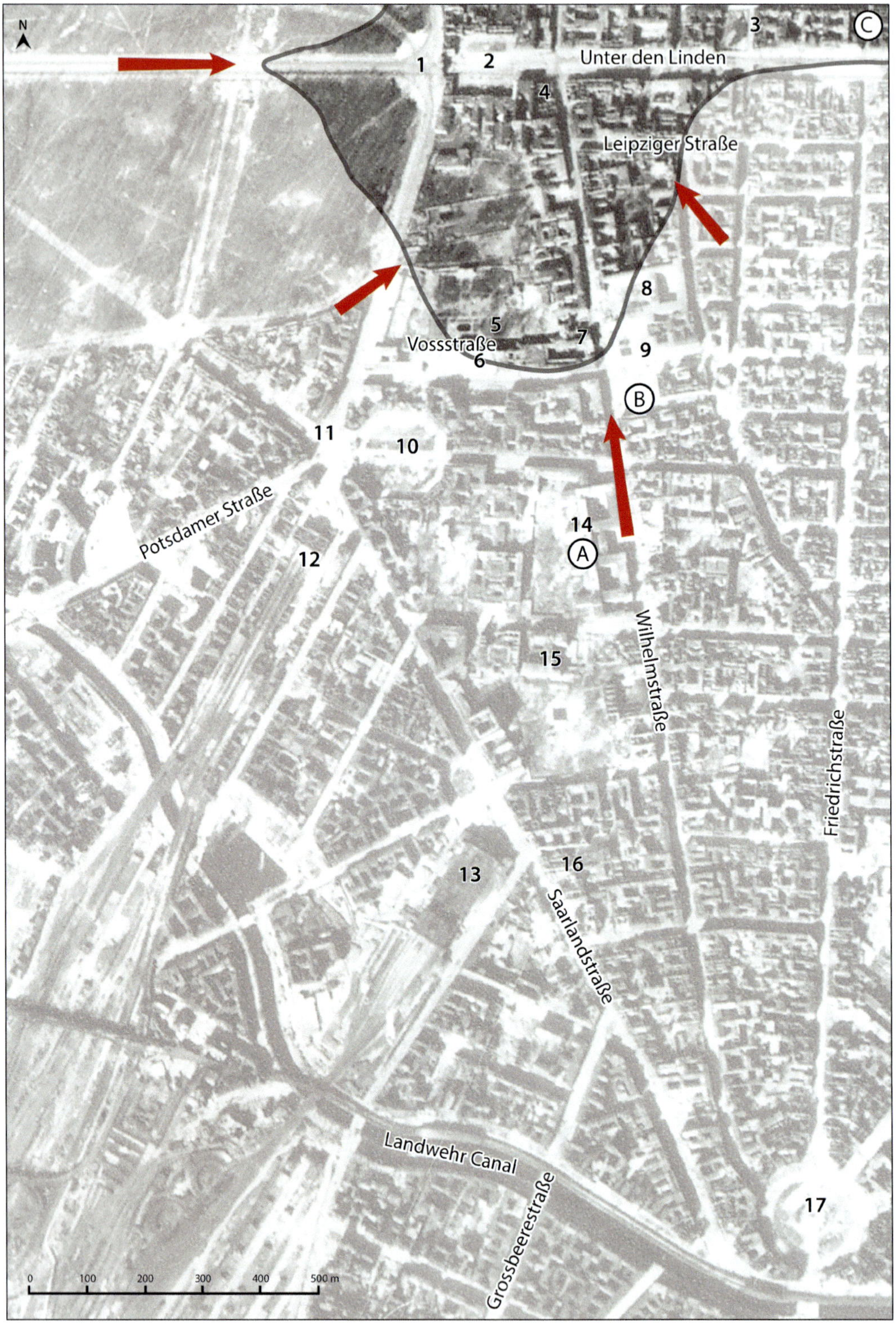

Line of combat on May 1 and location of areas where the Spaniards were that day.
A Reichsluftfahrtministerium (RLM) or Air Ministry; B Wilhelmplatz; C Towards Weidendamm Bridge, Friedrichstrasse train station, Elsastrasse and Stettiner train station.

Seeing victory within reach, the Soviets were not prepared to allow themselves to die unnecessarily at that stage of the war, which was almost over; so they continually sought to demoralise the defenders, urging them to surrender.

As González Pinilla notes, drawing on the work of Ferrer-Dalmau, *Scharführer* Julio Antonio Lobo Varela, a member of the *Einheit Ezquerra*, recounted the harshness of some of the events he experienced in Berlin during the final hours of resistance:

> ...they shouted over the loudspeakers that we should hand over our weapons, that Hitler was dead and that nothing would happen to us. I was stationed at a window watching as some Germans raise their arms and surrender to the Russians. My first reaction was to contact my superiors to receive orders; when I reached the basement where my group was, I found only Felipe Vilches and the two families living in the house; he had taken off his uniform and was getting dressed in civilian clothes. Without saying a word, I did the same and put on a Hitler Youth jacket I found on the floor. At that very moment, the Russians burst in, trampling over everyone as they shouted and shoved. One of them grabbed a little girl and began to assault her in front of her parents. The girl wouldn't stop crying and screaming while the Russians searched us, beating us as they went. I was scared to death, thinking they were going to kill me right there, when suddenly I saw Felipe pull out a pistol and start firing wildly. Taking advantage of the confusion, I ran out and managed to slip away through the ruins. Hours later, I was captured along with some Germans by a Russian patrol who treated us with a little more consideration. I never heard anything more of Felipe Vilches. I suppose he must have died in that cellar. Though certainly not without putting up a fierce fight first...[34]

Tuesday 1 May

During the morning, the Spandau Citadel surrendered to the 47th Army; fighting continued for the Reichstag, which had been heavily damaged and where the defenders had taken up defensive positions. The 5th Shock Army moved to capture the Ministry of Justice, the Reich Security Main Office, the Chancellery and the Reich Postal Ministry; in all of these, they faced a desperate defence by men who knew they had no way out. All these clashes took a heavy toll on the defenders, and an even greater one on the Soviets.

34 Augusto Ferrer-Dalmau, 'Españoles en las Waffen SS' in *Eurouniformes*, no. 14, diciembre-enero 2002-2003, pp.57–58.

The 8th Guards Army crossed Bellevuestrasse towards Siegesallee, until it finally captured Potsdamer Station, and then continued to the vicinity of the Saarlandstrasse *U-Bahn* Station.

The 3rd Guards Tank Army advanced along the Kurfürstendamm, where it engaged the remnants of the *Müncheberg Division*. Under these circumstances, the 'pocket' where the last defenders still held out was no more than 800 metres wide at any point, although it still almost reached the *S-Bahn* ring on both the northern and western sides.

Ezquerra, and the few who were with him, as well as other scattered groups of Spanish soldiers, began the defence of the Ministry District, fighting for every building in the limited Berlin territory still held by the Germans.

It is important to note that, on 1 May, the German delegation was sent to negotiate the surrender of Berlin with Soviet General Vasili Chuikov. The delegation comprised *General* Hans Krebs (Chief of the Army General Staff), accompanied by *Oberstleutnant* von Dufving, a couple of escort soldiers and the Latvian *SS-Obersturmführer* Atis Neilands, who would return after the meeting to take command of his unit. Ezquerra recounts his participation in these negotiations in his memoirs as follows:

> Through loudspeakers, the order for a ceasefire is given and the Russians are informed of our desire to parley. A white flag is placed on a pole, carried by a Latvian *sergeant* accompanied by two soldiers, all three unarmed. Behind them, to their left, were *Oberstleutnant* Weis, *General* Krebs and myself.... Along the way, the rank-and-file soldiers glared at us with hatred, clearly eager to finish us off, but our escorts would not tolerate us being insulted in any way. I realise that most of the soldiers have had too much to drink. One of them, perhaps under the influence of alcohol, tries to snatch my watch; the political commissar intervenes and with a shove sends him rolling across the ground; his comrades pick him up to take him away, and we resume our march without further complications.... I seem to recall, though I cannot be certain, that that meeting took place in the Schöneberg area.[35]

Once again, Ezquerra 'attributes' himself to an event that did indeed take place; he even correctly mentions some of the members of the German delegation, but there is no evidence whatsoever of his presence.

But just as the German delegation was returning, accompanied by two Soviet soldiers, they came under fire from their own lines, which killed the two Soviets and wounded Neilands in the hand. This critical situation prompted Dufving to send Neilands back to the Soviet lines, after his

35 Miguel Ezquerra Sánchez, *Luché Hasta El Fin: Memorias de un voluntario español en la guerra 1939–1945, Berlin a vida o muerte* (Granada: García Hispán, 1999), pp.82–83.

hand had been bandaged for the injuries he had sustained, to apologise. Evidently, his reception was not a friendly one, as he was reproached for having committed a flagrant violation of international law. When Chuikov himself addressed Neilands, the Latvian told him that the cause of this misunderstanding was a lack of communication, because the Russian mortar battery had continued to fire on his command post, even though there should have been a ceasefire during the negotiations.

This incident was recalled by Neilands in a 1982 interview with a Latvian-Australian newspaper, as Vincent Hunt recounts in his book. But what is interesting about this research carried out by Hunt is that the commander of the Latvian Company, Valdemārs Laiviņš, believed that the men who opened fire as the Soviets approached were from Ezquerra's Spanish unit: 'About halfway to the Ministry of Security, they suddenly started shooting from there, wounding a Russian soldier. The shooters, it seems, were Spanish.'[36] We cannot know for certain whether it was indeed the Spaniards who fired, but it is certainly worth noting that the Latvian commander again mentions Spanish soldiers who were deployed in the vicinity, so Ezquerra was fully aware of the existence of this delegation about a ceasefire, and we can now at least confirm that some of the men from his unit were also there.

The negotiators left after about an hour and the battle resumed.

During the ceasefire for the negotiations, the Soviets shouted from their positions over loudspeakers: '*Hitler kaput, voyna kaput!*', and, as was to be expected, the failure of these negotiations meant that the Soviet attack recommenced, and they advanced from Wilhelmstrasse and Friedrichstrasse. The defenders clung to every defensive position they could find, though due to the intense pressure exerted by the Soviets, they were

Wilhelmstrasse, the scene of many defensive battles in Sector Z, was still showing signs of the heavy damage when this photograph was taken in 1946. (Bundesarchiv Bild 183-U0731-506)

36 Information from Vincent Hunt.

forced into a continuous retreat. That said, this retreat involved fighting to the point of exhaustion for every doorway. Several tanks were destroyed and hundreds of Russian infantry were killed, but the sheer volume of men and weapons at the Soviets' disposal would not allow the defenders a single second's respite.

For every tank destroyed, more would appear, and although the Spanish had no shortage of ammunition, it was impossible to fully regroup once they had been shaken once again by the Soviet advance.

Despite Adolf Hitler's suicide on 30 April, the fighting continued, and the defenders continued to make their defeat costly for an enemy who, already feeling victorious, did not wish to increase its casualty figures against small groups of soldiers who did not see surrender as an option. Like the other units defending Berlin, the Spaniards continued to fight until the very last moment before the surrender, taking casualties on 1 and 2 May.

The remnants of the Spanish unit continued to defend the area around the Ministry of the Interior, alongside the remnants of many other units such as the *Nordland* and the *Müncheberg Divisions*. The building was defended, as had become customary, metre by metre. Every room was a death-trap for the Soviets, but serving only to delay the inevitable for a few more hours.

We have an account of these final battles in the German capital from the Latvian, Liepnieks, who was one of the soldiers defending the Wilhelmstrasse area and its surroundings, a key junction in the heart of Berlin and one of the main access routes to the *Führerbunker*. Liepnieks had positioned machine guns to cover the roads leading to the Reich Chancellery (these positions were held by the Latvians until the attempted escape from central Berlin on 1 May). Liepnieks' account of the events runs thus:

> We were assigned to the *Nordland Division*. There were French, Danes and Spaniards. It was a unit that defended to the very end. Those who had nowhere to go, nowhere to retreat to, surrendered. We had no one to surrender to. We knew we couldn't be captured by the Bolsheviks: we had to fight as long as there was something to shoot at and something to shoot with. I'm reading in books about how others have written about their experiences in the war, but we weren't able to write. For example, the French SS unit at that time; the commander of *Nordland* was Krukenberg.[37]

The remnants of the *Einheit* gathered at the Air Ministry, following a day of continuous fighting and retreats. There, *SS-Hauptsturmführer* Walli conveyed to Ezquerra an order of great importance that he had received shortly before from the *Führerbunker* itself (according to Ezquerra in his memoirs, from Hitler himself, although as Hitler had committed suicide, it

37 Information from Vincent Hunt.

is unlikely that the order was given by him). This ordered the forming, with his men and the remnants of Latvian troops still fit for combat, of a group that would attempt to break through the Soviet encirclement. Ezquerra recorded it in his memoirs: 'We must gather our comrades here, and the marching orders will be as follows: head north; in the event of accidental or forced straying due to circumstances, the assembly point is Stettiner Bahnhof.'[38] As we have seen, given that this was a secret mission, it had to be carried out with the utmost discretion.

Realising the difficulty, not to say the desperation of the situation, Ezquerra, together with his non-commissioned officers, decided to inform all the men of his unit, including those who were wounded. It was likely that those unable to leave Berlin would die or be taken captive by the Soviets without hope of escape, so it was necessary to warn all those still fit to attempt the escape. The order was passed from one man to another, so that within a short time all the men still with Ezquerra fully understood. A final attempt by the defenders to flee the small area in which they were surrounded by the Soviets in Sector Z of the city began to take shape.

Ezquerra recounted the decisions taken for this escape attempt:

> So I took Gracia, Carranchas and Vázquez aside and said to them: 'You, Roberto, will go to the garage where the Latvians are so that they can immediately take up the positions defended by our comrades. You, Carranchas, bring Juanito 'the Belgian' and his men to me, and make sure none of our men remain in position. And you, Vázquez, go to the room serving as a hospital and, very discreetly, speak to our wounded to inform them of the situation and tell them to use whatever means they have to camouflage themselves.'
>
> Walli had gone personally to fetch the Latvians. When he returned with a group of about 15 men, my men were already there and had received specific orders regarding their mission.[39]

For this escape attempt, it had been decided that on the night of 1/2 May, the men willing to attempt this dangerous move to force their way through enemy lines – primarily by crossing the Weidendammer Bridge – would gather in the vicinity.

The Latvian Valters Krūmiņš recounts part of these events:

---

38 Miguel Ezquerra Sánchez, *Luché Hasta El Fin: Memorias de un voluntario español en la guerra 1939–1945, Berlin a vida o muerte* (Granada: García Hispán, 1999), pp.85–86.

39 Miguel Ezquerra Sánchez, *Luché Hasta El Fin: Memorias de un voluntario español en la guerra 1939–1945, Berlin a vida o muerte* (Granada: García Hispán, 1999), p.86.

> We had destroyed several tanks – I can't tell you how many – and [*SS-Hauptsturmführer*] Walli wanted me to attend a meeting at the command post. Why did he invite me? Later I thought that perhaps I was a witness to the battles taking place without water, smoke, rubble, dust, and fighting non-stop. He was the commander of the battle; I was to be the human witness. We went to the command post. It seemed there were far more important matters concerning the people there when we gave our reports. Walli waited and told me to return to our unit. Amidst the surrounding chaos and rubble, I don't know how we got there and now I didn't know how to get back, and I didn't return to the starting point. I came across a Latvian group while seeking respite in a hospital. If you went into the hospital you had to leave your weapons outside and I didn't want to hand over my weapon. The Latvian group gave me the first indication that Hitler had shot himself and we were preparing for an escape from Berlin. I don't know who told me that we would try to get out through the underground tunnels, and perhaps once outside the city we could make our way into the forest. It was all nonsense.[40]

After receiving these orders, they quietly began to abandon their positions and made their way towards the Air Ministry, the assembly point for them. There, the Spaniards agreed on a password that would allow them to recognise each other as friendly troops in the event of being separated from the main body of men. The word chosen, as Ezquerra tells us, was '*carajo*', which would leave no doubt whatsoever that those shouting it amid the din of battle were Spanish soldiers.

The Stettiner Bahnhof (pictured as it appeared in 1875). Like Berlin's other railway stations, this became a place of refuge for many civilians, as well as for military personnel and medical services. Ezquerra was captured by the Soviets in the station's bunker on Wednesday 2 May. (Public Domain)

40 Vincent Hunt, *Sent to Die in Berlin* (Warwick: Helion & Co., 2026). Details from the author; at the time of writing the book is forthcoming.

A Soviet soldier looks out from a position beside the River Spree. The rivers and canals that abounded in the German capital became good defensive positions for the Germans. (Public Domain)

In the Air Ministry's communications room, Ezquerra briefed his men on the route they must take to reach their destination at the Stettiner Bahnhof, which lay to the north, beyond the Spree.

Although this mission was secret, it would not only involve Latvians and Spaniards, as other troops with a proven track record in the Berlin defences also joined the call to arms. All of them, like the Spaniards, had the primary objective of crossing the Spree – the opposite bank of which was partially occupied by the Soviets – and reaching Stettiner Bahnhof.

Once well equipped with rifles, pistols and *panzerfausts*, they left the Air Ministry via the garage and headed outwards, making their way along Wilhelmstrasse. There, taking cover amongst the rubble and the walls of the adjoining buildings, they advanced towards the nearby station, which is a short distance from the Ministry. From there, protected by the underground tunnels, they managed to reach the nearby Wilhelmplatz Station. Here, Ezquerra's men regrouped, gradually arriving and mingling with their Latvian comrades.

The station had been badly damaged by the continuous bombing to which the whole city was being subjected. Its interior was completely packed with civilians who had found refuge there, as well as various groups of soldiers who were also using it as a place of shelter.

A soldier with a *panzerfaust*. In many cases, this was the only defence the Germans could muster against the endless columns of Soviet tanks. (Public Domain)

Image of Wilhelmplatz in 1937 with the *Hotel Kaiserhof* on the right. This square was one of the points on the escape route for some of the Spanish soldiers at the end of the Battle of Berlin. (Bundesarchiv Bild 183-C10805)

Finally, an *SS-Hauptsturmführer* managed to organise the various groups of soldiers arriving at the station and informed them of the next meeting point: Friedrichstrasse Station, next to the Spree.

The journey would once again take place through the underground tunnels (this fact was confirmed to me some years ago by a relative of one of the Spanish soldiers in Berlin, who had been told about it), in order to avoid the many dangers above ground. Due to the darkness, they had to rely once again on their torches as they made their way in single file, to avoid losing contact with one another. After a long walk in which they navigated various obstacles in the tunnels, as well as the bodies of the unfortunate souls who met their end there, they finally reached Friedrichstrasse Station.

The destroyed Ministry of Public Enlightenment and Propaganda (*Reichsministerium für Volksaufklärung und Propaganda*) in Berlin on Wilhelmplatz, damaged by British night-time bombing and subsequently destroyed by Soviet attacks. (Bundesarchiv Bild 183-J313336)

There, scenes very similar to those they had experienced at the station they had come from were repeated. That is to say, thousands of people crammed together with their meagre belongings, as well as many injured people, some of whom were undergoing surgery right there in conditions that were more than a little precarious. Once again, the men had to be be regrouped; they were arriving little by little through the tunnels and, without wasting any more time, were preparing to head back outside after leaving the safety of the underground tracks. On the street, the roar of the thousands of bombs pounding the centre of Berlin was deafening, even more so, if that is possible, due to the station's proximity to the Weidendammer Bridge. The north bank of this bridge was currently the northern front line of Berlin in this part of the city and had to be be crossed in order to reach the destination the Spanish had set their sights on: the Stettiner Bahnhof. As the Soviets knew that this bridge was one of the possible escape routes for the encircled German troops, they had stationed infantry and tanks on the north bank of the Spree.

The Weidendammer Bridge was blocked by anti-tank barriers set up there by the defenders themselves, as well as by the numerous bodies – in many cases completely mutilated – of people who had attempted to cross it under heavy enemy fire during previous unsuccessful attempts. Ezquerra recounted it thus: 'On the other side, three tanks were firing incessantly, blocking the way, but we had to cross it if we did not want to be left in that graveyard. I had never seen so many dead piled up nor trodden on so much human flesh…'[41]

The Soviet troops were firing at anyone who tried to cross, as well as at any groups of enemy troops that might form on the south bank, so the German troops opted to attempt to approach the bridge under cover of darkness. The remaining men under Ezquerra, as well as the Latvians accompanying him, also assessed the situation to determine the best way to cross the bridge. According to Ezquerra, both the Spaniards and the Latvians had scattered to such an extent that the group was growing ever smaller: 'We had to force our way across. Amidst all that confusion, Walli's Latvians had vanished. Walli repeated the order over and over, trying to locate them, but to no avail: they had vanished as if by magic. Consequently, Walli joined our group.'[42]

In an attempt to improve the defending troops' chances of breaking through the encirclement, the remnants of the very few German armoured units still operational were deployed.

---

41 Miguel Ezquerra Sánchez, *Luché Hasta El Fin: Memorias de un voluntario español en la guerra 1939–1945, Berlin a vida o muerte* (Granada: García Hispán, 1999), p.87.

42 Miguel Ezquerra Sánchez, *Luché Hasta El Fin: Memorias de un voluntario español en la guerra 1939–1945, Berlin a vida o muerte* (Granada: García Hispán, 1999), p.87.

Postcard of the *Hotel Kaiserhof* practically in ruins after the war. Here, both Latvian and Spanish troops would fight the Soviets. (By Sludge. Public Domain)

At dusk on 1 May, the troops defending the Reichstag and the surrounding area received orders to assemble at Friedrichstrasse Station in order to cross the Weidendammer Bridge within a few hours, despite both locations being under continuous Soviet artillery fire. In reality, this was not a single attempt to break the encirclement, as the first attempt began at around midnight on 2 May and was followed by four more attempts over the next two hours. The reason was the large number of troops and civilians who preferred to attempt an escape rather than wait to be captured or killed by the Soviets; and the significant response from Soviet artillery and riflemen directed at the troops crowding the German side of the bridge and, of course, at all those who were trying – or, to a lesser extent, managing – to cross it.

Faced with this flood of disorganised troops crossing the Spree, the Soviets were forced to fall back a few metres, while continuing to harass them. Although they had the option of advancing along Friedrichstrasse, the Germans found themselves under constant fire from the surrounding streets, where a significant number of Soviet troops were stationed.

After managing, thanks to the support of the *Königstiger*, to keep the Soviets 'at bay' – who nonetheless continued to fire all manner of weapons at the Weidendammer Bridge – the Germans began their northwards movement in an attempt to break through the Soviet encirclement and escape the city.

In this climate of 'every man for himself', we can see how the Spaniards accounts align with the facts outlined above. Ezquerra warned that the only feasible way to succeed was to advance with the utmost caution and speed, and above all with a great deal of luck – the luck that, up to that point, had not deserted them throughout all the days of combat they had endured. Possibly during one of the German troops' attempts to cross, and on the orders given by Walli and Ezquerra to their men, they began to cross the bridge. The Dantesque scene that the men saw before their eyes caused most of them to back down and they could not bring themselves to follow their leaders. Of the Spaniards, only the seasoned *Sergeants* Roberto Gracia and Juan Pinar, as well as *Korporal* Carranchas, followed them. The rest of the men, who did not have the strength to attempt it, remained on that bank of the river, possibly fighting to the end.

The four Spaniards and the Latvian, Walli, miraculously – and not without a good dose of luck – managed to cross the bridge and immediately took shelter in the first houses on the left. They made their way into the ruins of these houses to take shelter and rest for at least a few seconds. An unsurprising reaction as many men had lost their lives attempting the deadly crossing of the Spree under enemy fire.

According to Ezquerra, he and the *korporal*, armed with *panzerfausts*, attempted to take out the tanks guarding the Weidendammer Bridge, while the two *sergeants* and Walli provided cover with their automatic weapons from the heights of the building. They advanced crouched low amongst the rubble after leaving the building's entrance, closing in on two of the three armoured vehicles in their vicinity. When within firing range, they fired their weapons, managing to hit both armoured vehicles. The third rapidly approached them with its roaring engine revving to eliminate the threat that had taken out their two comrades, only to be met by another well-aimed shot from a third *panzerfaust*.

The Russian infantry riddled the area where the two men were positioned with a hail of fire and shrapnel. Faced with this situation, and taking cover behind whatever objects might be of use, they ran at full speed towards the protection of the building from which their comrades were doing their utmost to protect them. They succeeded, but the Russians concentrated their fire on the house into which they had taken shelter. Although they returned fire as best they could, they could not hold that position on the upper floor for long. They quickly assessed the positions of the Soviets who were raking them with fire and made their way down to the doorway to get out as soon as possible. Upon seeing the men's attempt to escape, fire was once again concentrated on the doorway, seriously wounding Walli in the right leg and forcing the men to retreat towards the increasingly precarious shelter offered by the walls of the battered building. They managed to drag the wounded man inside the house, where they staunched the profusely bleeding wound. But it was only a temporary solution, and they lacked the means and the time to treat the wound properly. Walli, at his own request and so as not to jeopardise his comrades' attempt to escape, would remain behind with his weapons to defend himself to the end, once the Russians reached the house.

As the exit through the gateway was clearly far too dangerous for the safety of what remained of the *Einheit*, the four Spaniards resolved to sell their lives dearly and decided to use their remaining *panzerfausts* to disrupt the Russian positions as much as possible.

Meanwhile, on the other side of the bridge, many men who had witnessed the explosion of the tanks and the intense fire raging on the north bank had decided to attempt to cross it. Men from the *Kriegsmarine* were the first to cross, followed by others taking advantage of the situation, among whom were possibly some of the Spaniards who had not crossed initially.

Faced with this flood of disorganised troops crossing the Spree, the Russians retreated a few metres, while continuing to harass them. This allowed the arrival of fresh Soviet troops led by new armoured vehicles coming from Karlstrasse. With these reinforcements, the Soviets would, within a few hours, almost annihilate the desperate men in a frantic flight through the ruined streets of northern Berlin. On Friedrichstrasse and Schönhauser Allee, several of the German armoured vehicles that had managed to cross the Weidendammer Bridge were destroyed.

As the fugitives advanced, the compact group that had set out from the Government District began to break up. In many cases, the small groups had to move on all fours, crouching behind the piles of rubble that littered the city and making use of every ruined house that allowed them to hide from the enemy's view. The danger of being shot by the Soviets grew with every metre they advanced in search of the freedom offered by the outskirts of the German capital, as the Soviets had become aware of the German movement and had begun to reinforce the possible escape routes. Furthermore, in the places where civilians had taken shelter, uniformed troops were not welcome, due to the risk of being discovered by Soviet troops, with the danger that they would all be shot for harbouring them.

Amidst the inferno of fire that erupted in the minutes that followed, Ezquerra and *Sergeant* Pinar lost track of Gracia and Carranchas. They would never meet again, so the *Einheit Ezquerra* now consisted solely of Ezquerra himself and his faithful sergeant. Some men from various units joined them on a strictly temporary basis, so that together they might attempt to reach their common objective: Stettiner Bahnhof, so close and yet so far away.

As the street where they were located was completely under heavy automatic gunfire and with Russian grenades literally raining down on them, they decided to approach their objective through the interiors of the houses. Using the ubiquitous *panzerfausts*, they manage to blast holes in the walls connecting one building to another, large enough to pass through. By this method, widely employed during the Battle of Berlin even by the Soviets, they reached Elsastrasse without coming under enemy fire, where they emerged back into the open. And from there, in just a few metres, they managed to reach their objective. The final order received by the *Einheit* had been carried out, at the cost of losing all its men except for the leader and Pinar.

But Stettiner Bahnhof was nothing more than a carbon copy of other stations where many civilians had taken refuge, as well as soldiers who had discarded their uniforms in the face of imminent capture by the Soviets.

Once they arrived, Ezquerra, Pinar and the men accompanying them decided not to give up on their mission and that they would try to continue their escape from Berlin. To do so, they decided to continue through the dark underground tunnels. But as this area of Berlin was already Soviet-occupied territory, at least nominally, they encountered enemy forces that prevented them from advancing through the underground. This forced them to reassess the situation once more, and they decided to retrace their steps, though not without having suffered considerable casualties in the encounter.

Soviet soldiers during an attack on the streets of Berlin. The attackers must have suffered heavy casualties in the face of the tenacity of the defenders of the German capital. (Dmitry Chernov. Public Domain)

They decided to risk venturing outside and continue their advance northwards. They formed two lines of men, and, hugging the buildings closely, one line advanced along each pavement. And although they were advancing, they could not really know where they were heading. Where might the Soviets be positioned? Could they make contact with other groups of men to break through that cordon that was suffocating Berlin? Although, clearly, after the multiple battles and subsequent retreats they had faced in the last few hours, with hardly any rest, morale was low, the idea of fulfilling your duty for some, or the simple struggle for survival for many others, still kept the men united in such a difficult undertaking.

They reached the bunker at Stettiner Bahnhof, only a short distance away and where some German troops still remained, and placed themselves under their command. But they could do little under their new commanders, as by this stage the German soldiers' fighting spirit had been completely shattered. It is here that they were finally captured by the Russians, unable to make any further attempt to break through the increasingly densely manned Russian lines. At this point Ezquerra and Pinar parted ways, never to see each other again. Although it had been hours since the unit had ceased to exist as such, it is here that it was truly reduced to just him. We next hear of Pinar when he was released by the Soviets in December 1955; recounting his stories of having taken part in the defence of Berlin (as Ezquerra himself acknowledges in his work) and even of having seen a wrecked tank in which he recognised Bormann himself. His account says:

> On the night of 1/2 May, we advanced under heavy Soviet fire. In the middle of a street, a tank had been disabled by a Russian tank; someone shouted that Bormann was in it. I jumped onto the tank, opened the hatch and saw two bodies inside. I lifted the first one and carried him to the side of the street. When I looked at his face, I recognised Bormann. I did not have time to search his pockets for identification documents or other personal items. But I am certain that it was Bormann. You can be sure that Bormann died.

A small Soviet formation showing a 76mm ZiS-3 gun and an M4A2 (76)W Sherman tank. Although the photograph was taken on the streets of Vienna, the resemblance to the streets of Berlin is apparent. (Public Domain)

The sad fate of this column of German prisoners (in this case *Volkssturm*) from Berlin, passing by a T-34 of the 7th Guards Tank Corps, would be the Soviet Union. The small number of guards relative to the large number of prisoners allowed many of them to try to escape, with varying degrees of success. (Vladimir Paulovich. mil.ru)

Well-known photograph showing the Soviet flag flying over the Reichstag. (Public Domain.)

After the Russians arrived, Ezquerra was captured, along with other soldiers who were in the bunker and who offered no further resistance. They were taken outside, where they were lined up in rows of eight, to be transported under guard to prisoner-of-war assembly areas. These formed endless lines of captives who walked along the ruined streets of Berlin, exhausted from the hardships they had endured.

Ezquerra, for his part, after spending several days in captivity, managed to escape from the poorly guarded groups of prisoners. After many vicissitudes and having passed himself off as one of the thousands of forced labourers the Germans had, he reached Spain via the Pyrenees.

Wednesday 2 May

In addition to the attempt to break through the encirclement in Sector Z of Berlin heading north (Weidendammer Bridge), a second route heading west was also planned. With regard to this westward breakout, the time for the escape attempt was set for 04:00 on 2 May, with men from various units beginning to assemble in the area of the zoo's anti-aircraft tower. The units on which the burden of the breakout attempt would fall was what remained of the *18. Panzergrenadier Division* and the *Müncheberg Division*. The breakout could only be carried out via the Charlotten or Schulenburg bridges, which allowed the crossing of the Havel as they were the only ones remaining intact; the Charlotten Bridge in the Spandau area (and on the westernmost side of the Moabit District) was definitively chosen. For this counter-attack, the Germans managed to muster some armoured vehicles, notably including a pair of *Königstigers* from the *SS-Pz.Abt.503*. It does not appear that many of the Spaniards took part in this attempt, although by this stage of the fighting the unit was already scattered.

The outcome of both breaches of the Soviet encirclement was similar, as most of those who broke out were killed before completing their attempt or were captured, and only a few small groups of men and armoured vehicles managed to break through the encirclement and escape from Berlin, most of them eventually falling into Soviet hands, while only a small group of lucky ones reached the part of Germany in the hands of the Western Allies. Many of those who had managed to cross the Weidendammer Bridge but were unable to escape Berlin retraced their steps, regrouping in the area of the Schultheiss brewery, where they were eventually surrounded and subsequently taken prisoner by the Soviets.

The Battle of Berlin is over and the victorious Red Army soldiers celebrate on 2 May 1945. The celebrations and laxity among the Soviet troops allowed many captured defenders to escape. (Bundesarchiv Bild 183-E0406-0022-018)

Almost simultaneously with the attempts to break the encirclement of Berlin, an hour after midnight, a German delegation was sent to cross the Soviet lines to discuss the terms of surrender. The meeting was with the Soviet negotiator, General Chuikov, at Schulenburgring, and at which the unconditional surrender of all German troops stationed in Berlin was demanded. It is at this point that Ezquerra recounts having been one of the members of the group of German parliamentarians sent to negotiate with the Russians as a special guest. It really does not seem to make any sense that the commander of a small military unit would accompany *General* Krebs, as Ezquerra himself spoke German with difficulty and no Russian at all. On the other hand, what Ocañas mentions in his book regarding his encounter with Ezquerra (when the lieutenant was already a prisoner), as well as Ezquerra's attempt to take him to the German lines – though unsuccessfully due to the Soviets' refusal – does lend credibility to this account. Whether or not this encounter took place, what is known is that any attempt at negotiation during those days resulted in the same outcome as that described here.

Soviet soldiers on the attack in a Berlin street; facing them, German troops await in numerous more or less fortified positions, defending every metre of the German capital. (mil.ru)

Furthermore, taking advantage of the dwindling number of defenders in the building, the 79th Rifle Corps launched the final assault on the Reichstag, where resistance had already diminished dramatically. Only a few small groups of armed men, determined to resist to the end, held out in some of the rooms. Finally, the Soviet flag was raised on the roof of the building.

Image of the north-south *S-Bahn* tunnel in the Landwehr Canal behind Anhalter Bahnhof, which was blown up on 2 May 1945, causing numerous civilian casualties among those taking refuge there. (Bundesarchiv Bild 183-R97751)

The underground tunnels were destroyed by the Germans to prevent the Soviets from advancing through them. The north-south axis of the *U-Bahn* lines was deliberately flooded (the flooding affected the route from the BHF, reaching to beyond Mehringdamm on Line 6 and to Südstern on Line 7), although it also affected the east–west axis (from Potsdamer Platz to Frankfurter Allee on Line 5 and to Rosenthaler Platz on Line 8). Additionally, other stations and sections of lines were flooded at various locations across Berlin's suburban network.

It appears that troops belonging to the Waffen-SS were responsible for this action which, while on the one hand achieving its objective of halting the Soviet advance, also caused civilian casualties, as the latter were taking shelter from the bombing in the underground stations.

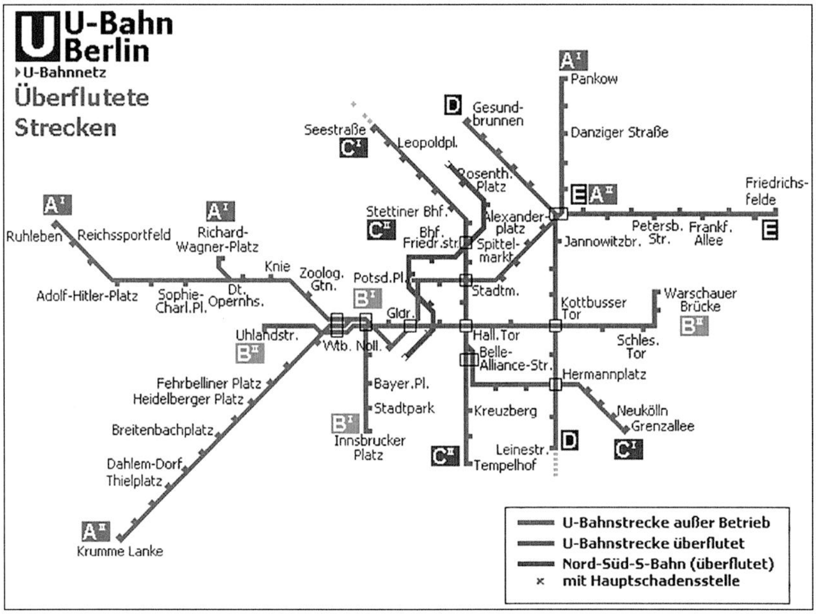

Map of the Berlin underground in 1945 showing the sections of line that were flooded during the Battle of Berlin. Grey: Underground line out of service. Blue: Flooded underground line. Green: North-south S-Bahn (flooded), with the worst-affected points marked with an X. (Marcus Schomacker. Public Domain)

TASS photojournalist Yevgeny Khaldei (centre) in Berlin, near the Brandenburg Gate. In the background, an IS-2 from the 7th Guards Tank Brigade. (Waralbum.ru. Public Domain)

Following these clashes with Soviet troops, *General* Weidling surrendered, officially ending the resistance in Berlin at around 13.00 on Wednesday 2 May. Although some scattered groups of men would continue to fight, they would eventually be overrun by the Soviets. The lucky few would manage to slip through the Russian lines and escape the city.

Marshal Zhukov ordered a ceasefire and the guns fell silent; the ruins of the capital were plunged into a 'deafening' silence.

The Battle of Berlin was over, and Stalin concluded the Red Army's daily order, in which the fall of Berlin was announced to the entire Soviet Army, with these words:

> Today, 2 May 1945 at 11.30, the capital of our homeland, Moscow, salutes the First Belorussian Front and the First Ukrainian Front with 323 artillery salvos from 24 guns to honour their great success in the capture of Berlin.[43]

As Pinilla recounts, an unknown member of the *Einheit Ezquerra* who was being treated for his wounds at the emergency hospital set up in the Reichsbank described his capture by the Russians on 2 May as follows:

> The medics ordered us to remain in our respective wards, and those who still possessed weapons were told to hand them over, along with all kinds of ammunition .... It wasn't long before the first Red Army soldiers arrived; pistol in hand and completely drunk, they demanded watches, high boots, lighters, penknives, etc. Moreover, they went round asking one by one for those who belonged to the SS. Naturally,

Friedrichstrasse in March 1945 following the Allied bombing raids in March 1945. This street was one of the escape routes taken by the Germans in their attempt to break through the Berlin encirclement on 1 and 2 May. The group consisted of the last tanks and men of the *Nordland Division*, plus men from various units, notably those of the *Wachregiment Grossdeutschland* and the *9. Fallschirmjäger Division*, all supported by a single *Königstiger* from *SS-Pz. Abt.503*. (Bundesarchiv Bild 183-J31399)

43 Order of the Day 2 May 1945, https://www.marxists.org/reference/archive/stalin/works/1945/05/02.htm

epaulettes and other insignia had already been torn off by their owners, and the Germans, in complete camaraderie, did not betray any of their compatriots. Nevertheless, they took away from my room around a dozen men, chosen at random, whom they believed might belong to that unit, even going so far as to literally riddled with bullets, from their submachine guns, a young man who was unable to follow them because he was seriously wounded...[44]

Soldiers and T-34/85 tanks of the 12th Guards Tank Corps of the 2nd Guards Tank Army in a Berlin street after the fighting had ended. (Anatoly Arkhipov. Public Domain)

During the course of the day, most of the men of the *Einheit Ezquerra* had either fallen in battle or disappeared into the ruined streets of the German capital (those attempting to slip through Soviet lines would, if possible, shed their uniforms, and if this was not possible, at least their national decorations and insignia, as foreign volunteers in the Waffen-SS were treated with greater cruelty by Soviet soldiers). Among those still holding out, alongside other soldiers from a motley collection of units that defended Berlin – including the *9. Fallschirmjäger Division*, and *18. Panzergrenadier Division* – were the last remnants of a battalion of Latvians who defended the area around the Air Ministry and who tried, unsuccessfully, to break through enemy lines, or the badly battered survivors of the *Müncheberg, Nordland*, part of the *9. Fallschirmjäger Division*, and the *18. Panzergrenadier Division*,

44 Ángel González Pinilla, *La Legión Clandestina: Españoles en la Wehrmacht Y Las Waffen-SS 1944–1945* (Madrid: Gutiksland, 2021), pp.172–173.

who launched an assault on the bridge over the Havel in West Spandau (known as the Charlottenbrücke) to escape the encirclement. Mingled among them were civilians who saw crossing that bridge – still defended by a few detachments of the Hitler Youth – as their last chance to escape the city, come what may.

This attempt to break the encirclement took place under relentless artillery fire from the Soviet 47th Army stationed on the opposite bank, resulting in utter carnage. Despite this, the desperate need of those under siege and the vast crowd of civilians and military personnel determined to cross the bridge at all costs managed to drive the Soviet soldiers stationed on the western bank of the Charlottenbrücke from their positions. Only a few managed to reach the 'safety' of the territory occupied by the Western Allies; the vast majority perished in the attempt and the few survivors were captured by the Soviets. The latter were condemned to a living death in captivity in the gulags, where, despite threats, torture, murders, starvation and countless punishments, the Spaniards, led by Captains Teodoro Palacios Cueto and Gerardo Oroquieta Arbiol, managed to keep their spirits high throughout their nine-year imprisonment.

Ezquerra's case is unique, as he managed to emerge alive from such a brutal battle and escape to Spain after evading Soviet captivity. Among the few fortunate ones who were able to return to their homeland, the only option was to try to remain anonymous, or run the risk, as happened to one man, of being court-martialled for 'abandoning his post', as a consequence of disobeying the regulations issued by the Spanish Government in this regard – although the man was eventually acquitted a couple of years later.

Image showing the state of ruin in which the city of Berlin was left following the battle of April and May 1945. (Courtesy of Juan Carlos Ocaña and the website HistoriasigloXX.org)

Thursday 3 May

Soviet soldiers - a private and a lieutenant - with a Soviet flag in Berlin against the backdrop of the Brandenburg Gate. (Yevgeny Khaldei (TASS). Public Domain)

On Thursday 3 May, the Soviets distributed among the German survivors of the Battle of Berlin an information leaflet written in German for the German population, which began:

> Berlin has been taken. – The troops of the First Belorussian Front (under the command of Marshal Zhukov), together with those of the First Ukrainian Front (under the command of Marshal Konev), have defeated the defending forces in Berlin, the capital of Germany, the centre of German imperialism and the source of German aggression. The city held out until 3 pm on 2 May, when the commanders of Berlin's defences (General of Artillery Weidling and his General Staff) were taken prisoner. By 9 pm on the same day, Soviet troops had taken more than 70,000 prisoners...[45]

Ivan Stepanovich Konev, Marshal of the Soviet Union, who, together with Zhukov, led the forces primarily responsible for the capture of Berlin in April–May 1945. (Public Domain)

Despite the defeat, some groups of soldiers continued to fight the Soviets in small pockets of resistance within the city, attempting, in most cases in vain, to flee from the Soviets or at least avoid capture. In the case of the Spaniards, as related in the following chapters, some were captured and others managed to escape, in some cases even after having initially been taken prisoner. The chaos reigning in the German capital and in the country in

45 Virgilio Ortega, *La Segunda Guerra Mundial: tomo 8: Un nuevo orden mundial* (Barcelona: Plaza & Janés, 1989), pp.75 & 280.

general gave rise to these events, despite the fact that they remained within territory dominated mainly by the Soviets.

The cost in human lives during the battle was enormous, both for the defenders and the civilian population, and for the Soviets, who, from 16 April to 8 May, suffered losses of missing, wounded and sick personnel totalling more than 280,000 men, plus some 70,000 men killed and at least 2,000 tanks and 500 aircraft lost. Although the actual casualties during this period are probably even higher.

Further evidence of the end of the fighting in Berlin: a Soviet soldier (Maria Timofeevna Shalneva) directing the movement of military personnel near the Reichstag in Berlin. The state of destruction of the streets bears witness to the ferocity of the previous fighting. (Yevgeny Khaldei. Public Domain)

4

After the Defeat

The few Spanish soldiers who were still fighting when Berlin surrendered tried to avoid capture by discarding their uniforms and donning civilian clothes. Although this may seem like an ineffective plan, the reality is that thousands of people were involved in massive movements from one part of Germany to another, in many cases trying to reach areas occupied by the Western Allies, so in some cases the plan was successful. From these territories not occupied by the Soviets, after months as refugees and generally facing great difficulties, they usually managed to reach Spain, as was the case with Ezquerra, who was in Madrid by September 1945.

With the Soviet occupation of Berlin, a number of Spanish soldiers, including Ramón Mandado, Cipriano Sastre and Ramón Fernández Palacios among others, managed to initially avoid capture. Although in some cases, as the months passed, some were eventually captured by the Soviets. Some even managed to gain access to the Spanish Embassy building (which, as we know, had been abandoned but was occupied by homeless civilians), obtaining 'legal' documentation with which they could prove they were

An IS-2 tank of the 2nd Guards Tank Army in Berlin, near the Brandenburg Gate after the street fighting had ended. (Public Domain).

forced labourers in Germany and thus avoid being taken prisoner on the grounds that they had not been combatants.

On the other hand, some survivors of the *Einheit Ezquerra* who managed to avoid captivity remained in Berlin in hiding, engaging in looting and taking advantage of the chaos in the city. As González Pinilla's work records, in early September 1945 16 Spaniards were arrested on charges of looting in the US occupation zone.[1]

THE
GROOPER
WEEKLY NEWSPAPER, OFFICE OF MILITARY GOVERNMENT FOR GERMANY (U.S.)
VOLUME 1, NUMBER 19 BERLIN 1 DECEMBER 1945

Header from *The Grooper*, the weekly newspaper published by the US Military Government Office in Germany. This is issue 19 of volume 1, dated December 1945, which reported on the existence of 'gangs of outlaws' made up of Spanish soldiers. (Public Domain)

González Pinilla's work also references an article published on 1 December 1945 in issue 19 of *The Grooper*, the newspaper produced by the US occupation forces, which stated:

> Berlin police take action against organised crime by former SS members. Berlin police forces are continuing raids this week in an attempt to dismantle an underground group, which has sharply increased the crime rate in the city. The investigation has led to the arrest of Erasmus Medina, a member of the Spanish SS Blue Division. Medina, who fought in the final days of the resistance here [Berlin], went into hiding after the city's fall. When he was arrested last week, Medina had managed to form a criminal gang from a group of former SS members, who are believed to be responsible for at least 40 robberies over the past month. Eight other members of the gang were arrested alongside Medina, and seven further criminals were apprehended in subsequent raids. Although police action has virtually wiped out this gang, official reports indicate that this group is one of many spreading crime and terror amongst the citizens of Berlin. According to the report, all of Medina's members are Spanish nationals and former members of the Blue Division, which was created by Franco to fight on the Eastern Front.... A large proportion of the robberies, assaults and many other crimes committed on the streets of Berlin during the winter nights are attributed to gangs of SS and SA men who went underground rather than face Allied military justice. Unable to obtain food, money, clothing or accommodation through regular channels, these men, well-versed in violence during the years of Nazi rule, turned to crime to earn a living.[2]

1 Ángel González Pinilla, *La Legión Clandestina* (Madrid: Gutiksland S.L., 2021).

2 *The Grooper*, 1 December 1945.

According to reports from the time, the number of Spanish detainees accused of looting rose to 51 men (not necessarily all belonging to the *Einheit Ezquerra*, although this information cannot be verified), who were tried in the Soviet zone and sentenced to eight years' imprisonment for 'vandalism'.

Berlin Police Cracking Down On Crime Rings of Ex-SS Men

Berlin's police force this week continued a series of raids in an attempt to smash underground gangs which have sharply raised the city's crime rate.

Prize catch of the police investigation was Erasmus Medina, former member of the SS Spanish Blue Division. Medina, who fought in the last days of resistance here, went underground after the fall of the city. When he was taken into custody last week Medina had succeeded in forming a large group of ex-SS men into a criminal band which was charged with at least 40 robberies in the past month.

Seized with Medina were eight other members of the band and subsequent raids netted seven more of the criminals. Although these police measures have practically knocked out the gang, officials pointed out that this group is only one of many who are spreading crime and terror through Berlin's civilian population.

According to the report, all members of the Medina gang are of Spanish nationality and are former members of the volunteer Blue Division which was raised by Franco to fight on the Eastern Front.

Still at large and leading a large well-armed bandit gang is Paul Haeusler, former S. A. Truppfuehrer. Two months before the end of the war, in March, renegade Hitler Youths formed this band and, taking advantage of the chaotic conditions in Berlin, launched a wave of armed robberies. In June, a large portion of the gang was arrested, but Haeusler soon formed a new group of Hitler Youth, SA and SS men, equipped them with rifles, pistols and automatic weapons.

The Haeusler band's headquarters, according to the police, are in the air raid shelters of the Army camp at Berlin-Doeberitz. The group operates mainly in the Russian zone in the Alexanderplatz district.

The police, who have so far been unable to corner Haeusler himself gained the information on the gang from one of his lieutenants — Horst Zoberbier. Zoberbier, a former Hitler Youth organization officer, who was seized as he attempted to attack and rob a German civilian woman.

Some weeks ago, Hans Dominowski, former driver of Nazi Labor Front Leader Dr. Ley, was seized by the police and charged with heading a gang trading in black-market motorcars. At the time of his arrest he had five former Nazi party members working with him.

A large portion of the robberies, assaults and the many other crimes being carried out in Berlin's streets during the winter nights are attributed to the gangs of SS and SA men who have gone underground rather than face Allied military justice. Unable to obtain food, money, clothing or lodging through regular channels these men — well-versed in violence during the years of Nazi power — have turned to crime for an existence.

Story from *The Grooper*, issue 19 of volume 1, dated December 1945, concerning Spanish soldiers who belonged to a 'gang of outlaws' in Berlin. (Public Domain)

5

Prisoners

The first few days of captivity in Soviet hands allowed many of the members of the long formations of prisoners, escorted by only a handful of Soviet guards, to slip away and attempt to escape. In the case of non-German combatants, they generally tried to reach their respective countries; this was the case with Botet and Ezquerra, who, not without great difficulty, managed to reach Spanish territory within a few months. For some other prisoners, these columns meant certain death, as the guards were in some cases merciless and ended up executing prisoners who, exhausted, could

The sad end for many of Berlin's defenders was their capture. The photograph shows a column of prisoners following the capture of the city passing by a Soviet armoured vehicle. The large number of prisoners and the euphoria of their guards following the victory allowed many of the prisoners to escape from these long columns bound for the Soviet Union. (Yevgeny Khaldei. Public Domain)

Berlin has fallen and the Soviets are in control of its streets. Meanwhile, small groups of German soldiers and civilians were trying to flee the city. Only a minority of them managed to escape westwards and surrender to the Western Allies. (Public Domain)

no longer keep up with the column. Those who survived had little hope of continuing life either, as they were sent into the Soviet 'labour camp' system.

The various Spanish prisoners held captive by the Soviets were distributed in small groups across different 'labour' or concentration camps, being transferred from one to another. It is estimated that there were possibly around 500 Spanish prisoners, comprising members of both the Blue Division and the 'Irreducibles'. The Spaniards were held in concentration camps at: Cherepovets, Norilsk, Odessa, Kadievka, Griazovets, Vologda, Rostov, Borovichi, Voronezh, Krasnogorsk, Sverdlovsk, Stalino, Gorky, Dzhezhazgan, Akmolinsk, Moscow and Kiev. In the final period before their release, they were gathered in Odessa.

Life for the prisoners proved very harsh due to the conditions to which they were subjected by the Soviets. In addition to the hard labour, ill-treatment, poor food and inadequate care, one must also consider the Soviet tactic of undermining the Spaniards' morale. However, in this regard, the heroic efforts of officers and non-commissioned officers to keep them united and always hopeful of returning to their homeland (despite the fact that many prisoners of other nationalities had already begun to return home) succeeded in preventing the majority of the detained Spaniards from falling under the control – not only physical but also mental – of their captors.

Alphonse Van Horembeke, a member of the *Einheit Ezquerra*, recounted in his memoirs how harsh captivity was from the very outset:

> ...by a small fire they had lit on the ground where everyone was burning their documents and insignia, I did the same, forgetting the 80cm of silver cord that trimmed the collar of my tunic. It was 'Guaje' who was tasked with holding a white cloth through the basement doorway, and from that moment on we were prisoners of the Russians. We were then taken to a nearby park, where they were interested in nothing but each person's nationality; and invariably, whatever nationality was given, everyone was sent to the same pile. 'Guaje' was walking in front of me and, when asked the ritual question, he replied proudly: '*Ich, Spanier*' (I am Spanish). He was the only one they separated from the others and sent to the other side of the street. Seeing what was happening, I said I was Belgian, and they sent me to the pile. A few minutes later I saw poor 'Guaje' fall, struck down by a burst of machine-gun fire fired at point-blank range, simply for being Spanish...[1]

Another account of the harsh conditions endured by the Spaniards in the labour camps comes from one of the last defenders of the Berlin Chancellery bunker, SS-*Oberscharführer* Rochus Misch. Misch mentions Juan Pinar (who at that time was assuming the false identity of 'Captain Roca'):

> At the beginning of my stay in Borovichi, I had close contact with the recipient of the Knight Cross, de la Rocca, of the Spanish Blue Division. The behaviour of the Spaniards in captivity impressed me greatly. They were made up of two groups of enemies. The first were the so-called 'Red Spaniards', anti-fascists who had fled eastwards at the end of the Spanish Civil War or, perhaps as children, had been taken there by their guardians. Their lot in Russia was a harsh one, confined to camps and subjected to forced labour. The Spaniards of the Blue Division, with a fascist and anti-communist background, had fought for the Germans as volunteers. However, whenever a Spaniard was taken away for interrogation, the others would accompany him and also provide information. Without exception. There were no longer any 'Blue' or 'Red' Spaniards, only Spaniards. They stood united. The Japanese did too. There was little the Russians could do about it; they could hardly shoot them all. There was nothing of the sort among the Germans. If one of us was taken away for interrogation,

1 Ángel González Pinilla, *La Legión Clandestina* (Madrid: Gutiksland S.L., 2021), p.174.

A column of prisoners captured during the fighting for Berlin in April–May 1945 marching along Berliner Strasse in Reinickendorf-West. The sad fate of the survivors among these men was several years' imprisonment in Soviet labour camps. (Bundesarchiv Bild 183-R77366)

he went alone; no fellow countryman cared about him. I saw another death sentence looming when I was accused, along with de la Rocca, of having instigated a mutiny. For weeks we were given nothing but cornmeal to eat. Cornmeal, cornmeal and more cornmeal. Although we remembered worse times of hunger we had experienced in Borovichi, we could not bear the smell, the sight or the thought of eating corn. The mere sight of the mushy ration made us want to vomit. The other prisoners were given the same. Someone had singled out de la Rocca and me as the ringleaders. Shortly before a full-scale revolt broke out, the camp administration changed its mind; the cornmeal came to an end and they served something else.[2]

---

2 Rochus Misch, *Hitler's Last Witness* (Barnsley: Frontline Books, 2014), pp.180–181 & 184.

6

Repatriation

The process of returning home was, as we can imagine, extremely complicated. The circumstances of the occupation of the former Reich by both the Soviets and the Western Allies, coupled with the destruction of much of its infrastructure, made smooth movement across the country virtually impossible; yet the prevailing chaos, with thousands of people moving from one place to another, in a way enabled many combatants to travel thousands of kilometres to finally reach Spain. Those who arrived via the Pyrenees were generally detained on arrival in Spain for illegally crossing the border and not carrying documentation.

The first stage of the journey for the surviving members of the *Einheit Ezquerra* involved fleeing from the Soviet-occupied zone to the Western Allies' sector. Their membership of the SS would work against the Spaniards in the Western sector, but would have meant certain death in the eastern sector. Shortly before the surrender, several Spaniards (among whom, according to Ezquerra, there were some 30 members of his unit) managed to leave Berlin and subsequently Germany, thanks to the assistance of the Spanish Consulate in Berlin. A handful of men managed to reach Spanish soil after numerous vicissitudes. Other groups of Spaniards (possibly those remaining in the Alpine region), after being released from their oath of allegiance to Hitler, were issued with passports to neutral Switzerland, where they were interned in the camps at Oerlikon-Zurich and Laplaine-Geneva. After obtaining the necessary authorisations, they secured, through the mediation of the Spanish Government, a train that departed from Bern and arrived at the French station of Chambéry on 17 June. While at this station, the train was attacked by forces of the former *maquis*, forcing it to return to Switzerland, where they were once again interned in the camps at Laplaine-Geneva and Bühler-Appenzell. They had to wait until 3 December before they managed to return to Spain aboard the ship *Plus Ultra*.

Some Spaniards, after being captured by the Western Allies, had to spend time in prisoner-of-war camps before being subsequently released. This was the case with some of the men who had served in the mountains of northern Italy.

Thus, from 1945 onwards, there was a trickle of returns of various Spanish volunteers from the Reich, not just of the combatants in Berlin. But many Spaniards had been taken captive by the Soviets, and the conditions would not be the same. In the gulags, they had to survive through hard years that seemed never-ending, subjected to all manner of abuse and deprivation.

The Spaniards who remained in the area controlled by the Western Allies generally fared better than those held captive by the Soviets, as, despite the difficulties, there was none of the mercilessness shown by the Soviets towards their captives. Even by mid-1946, many Spanish nationals remained in German territory controlled by the Western Allies, without the victors having allowed them to return to their country. Those wishing to return were urged to contact UNRRA (the United Nations Relief and Rehabilitation Administration, a United Nations agency that existed from 1943 to 1947, whose main function was to assist in the repatriation of people displaced by the Second World War). As a result, in October and December of that same year, three expeditions were organised from the UNRRA camp in Mittenwald, with a total of 314 people returning to Spain by sea from Genoa to Barcelona. *SS-Untersturmführer* Ricardo Botet returned to Spain on the first of these expeditions.

Following Stalin's death in March 1953, the prisoners' living conditions improved and rumours began to circulate of a possible repatriation. A year later, the prisoners were gathered at the port of Odessa, 18 decided of their own accord to remain in the USSR, as did 65 deserters who, fearing reprisals, would not return to their homeland either. On Friday 2 April 1954, the Spanish prisoners of war, who had managed to survive after being held for 10 or 12 years in the Soviet gulags under endless hardships, returned to Spain following contacts between the Soviet and Spanish Governments. This long-awaited return took place on the Greek-owned, Liberian-flagged, vessel *Semíramis*, chartered by Spain and organised by the International Red Cross, which, setting sail from the port of Odessa, disembarked 286 people at the port of Barcelona. These were made up, according to their origin, of:

A contingent of 248 male prisoners of war:

219 who had belonged to the Spanish Division of Volunteers.

7 who had belonged to the Spanish Legion of Volunteers.

21 from Waffen-SS troops.

1 from the *Azul* Squadron.

The remaining 38 people were:

4 'war children'.

internees. These were in turn made up of:

19 sailors, most of them crew members of the motor vessel *Cabo San*

Agustín, a ship that transported shipments of gold from the Bank of Spain to Odessa. There were also sailors from the Republican Fleet who, at the end of the Spanish Civil War, found themselves on Soviet territory.

12 men who had been students at the Kirovabad Aviation School and who, after the end of the Spanish Civil War, did not renounce their Spanish citizenship; they were declared dissidents and interned in camps.

3 workers captured in Germany at the end of the Second World War.[1]

It was at 5.35 a.m. that the ship docked in the port, disembarking men who were thin and emaciated after such a long captivity but thus bringing to an end their 'adventure' in their fight against the Soviets.

They were greeted by a large crowd, including family members and other close associates. On behalf of the Head of State, the Minister-Secretary General of the Movement, Raimundo Fernández Cuesta, and the Minister of the Army, *Teniente General* Muñoz Grandes (first commander of the Blue Division), came on board to welcome them, accompanied by Agustín Aznar, National Health Delegate. A thanksgiving ceremony was held in the Basilica of La Merced, attended by the Archbishop-Bishop of Barcelona, Modrego.

The return of the repatriates on the *Semíramis* was witnessed on the quayside in Barcelona by thousands of people. (Courtesy of L. E. Togores)

However, the *Semíramis* did not bring back all of the prisoners remaining in the USSR, as it is known that a number of Spaniards – the exact number is difficult to determine – were still alive as late as 1955. In fact, one of the men who fought in the *Einheit Ezquerra* during the Battle of Berlin, Juan Pinar, was only released in December 1955. Despite the poor relations between the Soviet and Spanish Governments, thanks to the mediation of the Red Cross, some 2,500 Spaniards were eventually repatriated in seven 'voyages' between September 1956 and May 1959 (in September, October, November and December 1956; January and May 1957; May 1959), most of which were carried out by the *Crimea* and were bound for the port of Castellón. However, these other returnees, due to Spain's position in the world at that time, have gone almost unnoticed over the years right up to the present day, never having had their moment of glory in the newspapers or news programmes

1 Data taken from the article published in issue 46 of *Revista Española de Historia Militar* entitled 'Semíramis, 1954: The Return of the Captives of the Blue Division'.

of the era. It is noted that amongst the Spaniards (mainly minors, political exiles and some divisionaries) on the ship that arrived on 18 December 1956 was a Spanish soldier who had been taken prisoner in Berlin.

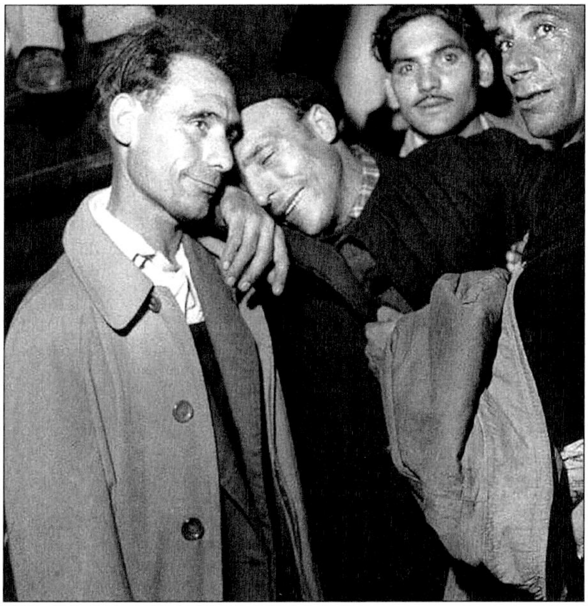

The emotion is evident on the faces of the Spanish repatriates aboard the *Semíramis*. (Courtesy of L. E. Togores)

Muñoz Grandes at the reception held for the returnees of the *Semíramis* at the Ministry of the Army. (Courtesy of L. E. Togores)

7

Reception of the Volunteers in Spain

The difficulty of reaching Spain after the war ended was, in itself, very complicated for Spaniards who had fought with the Third Reich, but for those who managed it, the problems did not end there. Remember that Spanish legislation was very clear regarding Spaniards who served under other flags.

The Royal Decree promulgated on 24 July 1889 remained in force during this period; it stipulated that any citizen of the Kingdom of Spain who served in a foreign army at war would lose their Spanish nationality, unless the citizen in question held a special permit from the Head of State. Specifically, Article 25 of Title I of Book I of the Spanish Civil Code states as follows (published by the Royal Decree of 24 July 1889):

> 1. Spaniards who are not of Spanish origin shall lose their nationality:
> a) When, for a period of three years, they exclusively use the nationality they declared they had renounced upon acquiring Spanish nationality.
> b) When they voluntarily enter military service or hold political office in a foreign state contrary to the express prohibition of the government.
>
> 2. A final judgement declaring that the person concerned has committed falsification, concealment or fraud in the acquisition of Spanish nationality shall render such acquisition null and void, although this shall not give rise to detrimental effects for third parties acting in good faith. The action for annulment must be brought by the Public Prosecutor's Office ex-officio or following a complaint, within a period of 15 years.

As we have seen, this Article 25 is largely consistent with the widespread view that the Spanish Government had rendered a significant number of Spaniards who chose to continue fighting stateless; however, the difficulty in accepting this fact as certain lies in the title of this article, which clearly states: *Los españoles que no lo sean de origen perderán la nacionalidad*

(Spaniards who are not of Spanish origin shall lose their nationality). We can therefore see that the article is not directed at Spaniards who are Spanish by birth, or in other words, the vast majority of Spaniards.

In any case, the Spanish Government, while perhaps not going so far as to admit that all those who performed military service for belligerent governments would lose their Spanish nationality, considered that support for the Axis powers was becoming less productive by the day and that it would be the more politically correct course of action to avoid, as far as possible, the presence of Spanish military units in the conflict. This situation was reflected in the Spanish Government's official statement of January 1944, in which it expressed its opposition to Spaniards remaining in the various military branches operating in Germany. (I do not have the text of that official statement, but its existence is recorded in the various texts dealing with the subject.)

This official statement was intended to put an end to the clandestine crossing of the Spanish-French border by Spaniards who had been encouraged by the German secret services in Spain and by falangist leaders to join the German armed forces.

However, Clyde Clark notes that Spanish legislation in force between 21 December 1943 and 1 January 1945 guaranteed amnesty to those recruited by other countries or deserters who remained abroad.[1] Although we must refer to the legislation in force at the time, which was that published by the Royal Decree of 24 July 1889, as previously noted; and which was possibly misapplied to achieve the government's intended purpose.

All this legislation had sought to prevent this exodus of Spaniards to the Reich, but the fact is that after the war ended, the Spanish Government gradually changed its attitude towards these men. Thus, as early as September 1945, a pardon was proposed for 'those charged with serious crimes or offences of desertion committed that year, and who presented themselves to the military authorities before 1 January 1946', with this deadline being extended until 1948 (with these men being accepted even at Spanish diplomatic missions abroad). In February 1946, a new decree was enacted which 'granted permission to regain Spanish nationality to those who had lost it by fighting without authorisation from the Spanish authorities in the armed forces of the states involved in the world war.' Thus, 'Spaniards who had lost their Spanish nationality for having served from 7 September 1939 to 7 May 1945 in the armies of the belligerent nations could apply for reinstatement at the Civil Registry within a period of six months from the publication of the decree, either in Spain or at embassies or consulates abroad.' Thus, the ruling used in Spain to prevent Spaniards from serving in the armies of other nations was now officially repealed.

What can certainly be considered true is that these men's return to Spain was far from amicable. There were several cases in which the repatriates,

1 Clyde Clark, *Evolution of the Franco Regime* (Washington DC, US State Department, 1950), pp.442 & 555–556. Digitised via Project Gutenberg.

having belonged to the Spanish Army and having abandoned their positions, had to answer to the military authorities. Although these cases were eventually 'forgotten' and the men returned to normal civilian life.

In the brief biographies of some of the key figures presented in Chapter 14 below the specific fate of some of these indomitable volunteers is related.

Part II

8

Uniforms

The uniforms worn by the men of the *Einheit Ezquerra*, as a result of the situation in Germany at that time were extremely varied. 'Quartermastering' was practically nonexistent, so within the ranks of the *Einheit*, green SS uniforms were intermingled with camouflage uniforms of various designs and even some clothing from the *Wehrmacht*. In any case, the Spaniards were issued with M44 mottled camouflage uniforms in Potsdam, consisting of a four-pocket jacket very similar to the *Feldbluse M43* and straight-leg trousers, both made of rayon fabric printed in five colours – various shades of green and brown.

A group of German soldiers taken prisoner by the British during the fighting in Arnhem (British paratroopers can be seen in the background behind the prisoners). Of interest to us in this photograph is the M44 mottled camouflage uniform they are wearing. This type of uniform was issued to the Spanish unit in Potsdam, just before their participation in the Battle of Berlin. (Public Domain)

A Spanish soldier from the Blue Division wearing camouflage on his helmet observes enemy positions through his binoculars. The unit's regulation insignia can be clearly seen, which was the same as that worn on the left arm by some of the men of the *Einheit Ezquerra*. (Collection of J. Arráez)

Some of the men still retained their blue shirts, which had already become standard issue, worn beneath the German-made uniforms used by the men who made up the Blue Division. This shirt was the uniform of the *FE de la JONS* and was used continuously despite contravening the, albeit increasingly lax, regulations towards the end of the conflict, regarding military attire. There are also accounts mentioning the use of certain elements of the Spanish Army uniform, such as the regulation belt of the Spanish Legion. As for footwear, apart from a few who retained their high boots, the most common at this stage of the conflict were short boots with gaiters.

The belts used initially were the standard SS issue, although some from the *Wehrmacht* cannot be ruled out. There are also accounts of former legionaries from the tercio who continued to wear their belts with the arquebus and crossbow badge, as well as their leather wristbands.

The headgear used consisted of the Model 35/40 and Model 42 helmets, with or without a visor, or the peaked cap introduced in 1943 for greater comfort.

However, the fact is that, as there are no known photographs of the Spanish during the Battle of Berlin, all we know comes from the accounts of the survivors and other eyewitnesses. Although, in general, like other foreign formations that fought with and were integrated into the German armed forces, they would have been uniformed much like the rest of the German soldiers, and more specifically like those belonging to the Waffen-SS who fought in Berlin, such as the men of the *33. Waffen-SS Grenadier-Division (Französische Nr. 1) Charlemagne*.

The distinctive features worn by the Spanish were the badge on the left sleeve (as was standard in the Waffen-SS) bearing the national colours with the word *España* at the top. It is possible that not all men wore it, given the diverse origins of the troops in the *Einheit Ezquerra* (though the majority of those who had served in the Division or the Blue Legion did so), and in many cases it was simply pinned to the uniform rather than sewn on. In other cases, the badge was placed on the right sleeve, contravening the established regulations. Within this badge, there were various designs, which might feature an embroidered yoke with arrows, an Iron Cross or swastikas.

Unofficial variant of the badge used by the men of the Blue Division, Blue Legion and *Einheit Ezquerra*, featuring the yoke and arrows over the colours of the Spanish flag. (Public Domain)

The badge used by soldiers in Spanish units serving Germany. In the *Einheit Ezquerra*, as was standard in all SS units, it was worn on the left sleeve with the national colours and the word *España* at the top. It is possible that not all men wore it, given the diverse origins of the troops in the unit. (Public Domain)

Above the shield was to be the standard eagle of the Waffen-SS, into which the Spanish unit was integrated.

Other insignia that might be seen on the uniforms included armbands on the right arm indicating the destruction of an armoured vehicle in combat; as well as Spanish or German decorations (the latter in the case of former members of the Blue Division or the Blue Legion) that each individual might possess, or emblems of the *Falange* or the SEU.

Another factor to bear in mind regarding the varied appearance the Spanish soldiers might have had at that time is that volunteers from the legion often wore tercio belts, leather wristbands and a string of decorations scattered across their tunic. Although, of course, it is not possible to generalise on this point.

9

Decorations

It is not really known which decorations the men of the unit might have worn on their uniforms, but bear in mind that many of them had already taken part in numerous battles, either in units under Spanish or German command during the Second World War or in Spain, during their time in the Spanish Army, from when they might also have received decorations that they were entitled to wear.

Apart from the Spanish decorations, it is worth noting the number of medals awarded to the men of the Blue Division, some of whom served in the *Einheit Ezquerra*:

one Knight Cross with Oak Leaves.

one Knight Cross.

two German Crosses in Gold.

2,497 Iron Crosses (of which 138 were First Class).

2,216 Crosses of Military Merit with Swords (of which 16 were First Class).

Medal (ribbon missing) for participation in the Russian campaign awarded to members of the Blue Division by the German state. Its name was the *Erinnerungsmedaille für die Spanischen Freiwilligen im Kampf gegen den Bolschewismus* (Commemorative Medal for Spanish Volunteers in the Fight against Bolshevism). (Public Domain)

Medal (ribbon missing) for volunteers of the Blue Division, awarded by the Spanish Government to Spanish volunteers who had fought against Bolshevism. (Public Domain)

Furthermore, it appears that most of the men who took part in the defence of Berlin were awarded the Iron Cross Second Class for their participation in that battle. Ezquerra mentioned in his first book that he was awarded the Iron Cross First Class following a mission in the Normandy area. He recounted it as follows:

> I had to leave them because I had been urgently summoned to Paris to attend to other duties. When I arrived at the *Hôtel Lutetia*, I met Stammer, who was expecting me. Without wasting any time, he gave me the good news, saying: 'You have been awarded the Iron Cross First Class.' He pinned it to my chest and embraced me with remarkable vigour, then added, 'Take a hundred thousand francs; if you need more, let me know.'[1]

As for the Knight Cross, Ezquerra claimed to have received it from the Führer himself, although there is no record of this nor any witnesses (the only Spaniards to have received it, apart from Ezquerra, were the two commanders of the Blue Division). The fact that he received it from Adolf Hitler seems very strange, and the lack of any evidence appears to disprove it, but did he receive the Knight Cross of the Iron Cross? To me, it had always been just another of Ezquerra's fantasies, but Vincent Hunt sent me this excerpt from a statement by *SS-Obersturmführer* Atis Neilands, a Latvian who fought alongside the Spaniards and acted as a translator

1 Miguel Ezquerra Sánchez, *Luché Hasta El Fin: Memorias de un voluntario español en la guerra 1939–1945, Berlin a vida o muerte* (Granada: García Hispán, 1999), p.37.

during the surrender negotiations. To look at his comments on the matter after returning from those negotiations, which took place on 1 May:

> Having returned to the Reich Chancellery, I reported to *General* Mohnke on what had happened. Having heard my report, he ordered me to take charge of the defence of the Air Ministry building. My *kampfgruppe* would include units of the French and Spanish SS and a company of naval infantry. I knew that the commanders of the French and Spanish units were both *SS-Hauptsturmführer*, so they outranked me, and furthermore, both had been awarded Knight Cross of the Iron Cross. Seeing my surprise, Mohnke replied that I had more combat experience. Returning to the security headquarters, I thought about my new order of battle. I had never seen the naval infantry before, and, as it turned out, I never saw them afterwards either.[2]

Adolf Hitler's final public appearance. Ezquerra recounted that he had several encounters with Hitler during the Battle of Berlin, during which he received decorations from him. There is no evidence of these, although the whole matter of the decorations received by Ezquerra is a subject of some debate. (Public Domain)

Clearly, there was only one commander of the Spanish unit, and that was Ezquerra. He began the Battle of Berlin as an *SS-Hauptsturmführer*, although he later states that he was promoted first to *SS-Sturmbannführer* and subsequently to *SS-Obersturmbannführer* (possibly another of his fantasies), and the other captain (or *SS-Hauptsturmführer*) must have been Henri Fenet, who had received that decoration on 29 April. You will understand that my doubts regarding that decoration being in Ezquerra's possession are somewhat lessened. This report comes from a Latvian soldier who had no interest whatsoever in glorifying anyone, let alone a Spanish combatant. Obviously, there is no official documentation to confirm this, but having heard this account from Vincent Hunt, I sincerely believe that Ezquerra wore that medal during the final days of the Reich. Whether it

2 Information from Vincent Hunt.

was officially awarded or whether he obtained one and wore it, we may never know, but he did indeed wear that medal during the Battle of Berlin.

This does not imply that Ezquerra did not embellish his tales with further decorations. According to Ezquerra – and therefore this must obviously be viewed with great caution – between April 1944 and May 1945 he received the following German decorations:

> Oak Leaves to the Knight Cross of the Iron Cross.
>
> Knight Cross of the Iron Cross.
>
> Iron Cross First Class.
>
> German Cross in Gold.
>
> Knight Cross of the War Merit Cross with Swords.
>
> War Merit Cross with Swords, First Class.

Knight Cross of the Iron Cross. This is the decoration that Ezquerra claimed in his memoirs to have received from Adolf Hitler, the veracity of which claim has always been highly questioned. However, the testimony of the Latvian *SS-Obersturmführer* Neilands in this regard once again raises the question of whether Ezquerra actually wore this decoration. (By Bruce Marvin. Public Domain)

To briefly outline below the reasons for which each of these medals was awarded:

> The Second Class Iron Cross was generally awarded for meritorious service in combat, requiring at least one act of bravery in the face of the enemy or actions beyond the call of duty. The ribbon was normally fastened to the buttonhole of the second button on the tunic.
>
> The First Class Iron Cross was awarded after three or four acts of bravery (unlike the Second Class, which required only one). It thus carried greater prestige for the recipient.
>
> To be awarded the Knight Cross, one had to already hold the First Class Iron Cross, as well as demonstrate bravery and excellence in a sustained series of outstanding actions in combat beyond the normal demands of service.
>
> The 2nd Class War Merit Cross with Swords recognised those military personnel whose acts of valour went beyond the call of duty, although they did not meet the criteria for the Iron Cross. These acts could involve acts of valour not under enemy fire or the planning or direction of combat operations. When the Cross without Swords was awarded, it was generally for acts of merit in general.
>
> The Spanish Decoration for Divisionaries and the German Decoration for Divisionaries. Awarded respectively by the Spanish and German Governments to members of the Spanish Divisionary Corps who took part in the fight against Bolshevism in Russia.
>
> The Eastern Front Medal, which was awarded to those who met the following criteria on the Eastern Front: 14 days of combat participation or 60 days of service in a combat zone (even without having taken part

in combat), or having sustained injuries or frostbite severe enough to qualify for the Combat Wound Badge.

The Combat Wound Badge was awarded in three grades: black, silver and gold. The grade awarded depended on the number of wounds sustained in action or on the severity of the injuries. The black badge was awarded for 1 or 2 wounds sustained, the silver for 3 or 4 wounds, and the gold for 5 or more wounds.

A badge for having taken part in an assault, awarded for participating in 3 attacks on different days. In the case of more than three attacks, it bore a gold number at the bottom, indicating the number of attacks.

Tank destruction badges existed in two grades. In silver for having individually destroyed an enemy tank using a portable weapon, and in gold, awarded for having destroyed 5 enemy tanks using a portable weapon. This decoration was not awarded to troops from anti-tank units.

10

Main Weaponry of the *Einheit Ezquerra*

In the confusion and turmoil of the final days of the Reich, the weapons issued to the troops varied more according to available stocks than actual needs. It is therefore difficult, if not impossible, to say with certainty which weapons the Spanish contingent used in this battle. It is known, however, that they were fairly well supplied with weaponry, given the circumstances, upon arriving in Berlin, among which the StG44 or MP44 assault rifles stand out. These weapons proved highly useful in the Berlin street fighting due to their high rate of fire and greater reliability at short and medium ranges. It was an ideal weapon for attempting to hold back the vast mass of Soviet soldiers flooding into Berlin, with a limited number of defenders, albeit well-equipped ones.

Although this image was taken during the Battle of the Bulge, it is included because of the MP44 carried by the soldier in the foreground. A weapon with a high rate of fire, which proved lethal in urban terrain. (Bundesarchiv Bild 183-1985-0104-501)

The other outstanding weapon used by the Spanish was the *panzerfaust*, which earned a deadly reputation amongst the ranks of Soviet armoured units, who suffered incessantly from them in the streets of Berlin. It was most effective at short to medium range, and its design allowed for its use by soldiers hidden amongst the rubble and ruins that littered the streets.

Perhaps the most notable feature of the weaponry carried by the Spanish was its abundance; it was not unusual for many men to carry one or two pistols and to be equipped primarily with automatic weapons as well as the aforementioned *panzerfaust*.

Given below is an overview of the technical characteristics of some of the weapons used by the men of the *Einheit Ezquerra*.

StG44

Also known as the MP43 or MP44, the StG44 can be considered the first assault rifle. Its development was driven by the need to increase the firepower of infantry. The weapon was gas-operated, with the gas acting on a piston that operated a cylinder on the barrel. This rifle has had a significant influence on infantry weapons developed after the war.

A view of both sides of the MP44 or StG44 assault rifle used by Spanish soldiers during their assault and defence operations in the streets of Berlin. Its high firepower partly compensated for the small number of men in the *Einheit Ezquerra*. (Collection of The Armémuseum, Stockholm. Public Domain)

Principal features:

Length	940mm
Weight	5.12kg
Barrel	420mm
Calibre	7.92mm Kurz
Rifling	4 grooves/right-hand
Operation	Gas operation
Feeding	30-round curved magazine
Sight	Sliding; up to 800 m
Muzzle Velocity	647 m/s
Rate Of Fire	500 rounds/min
Fire Mode	Single shot and burst

MP40

The MP40 (and its variants, the MP38, MP38/40, MP40/2 and MP41) was already a proven weapon by this stage of the war, making it highly sought-after by both the German and Soviet troops. By the end of the war, approximately 1,047,000 units had been manufactured. All of which made the MP40 one of the most famous weapons of the Second World War. It offered great accuracy, even at ranges of 50–100m. Its main advantages were its ease of maintenance, durability and lightness.

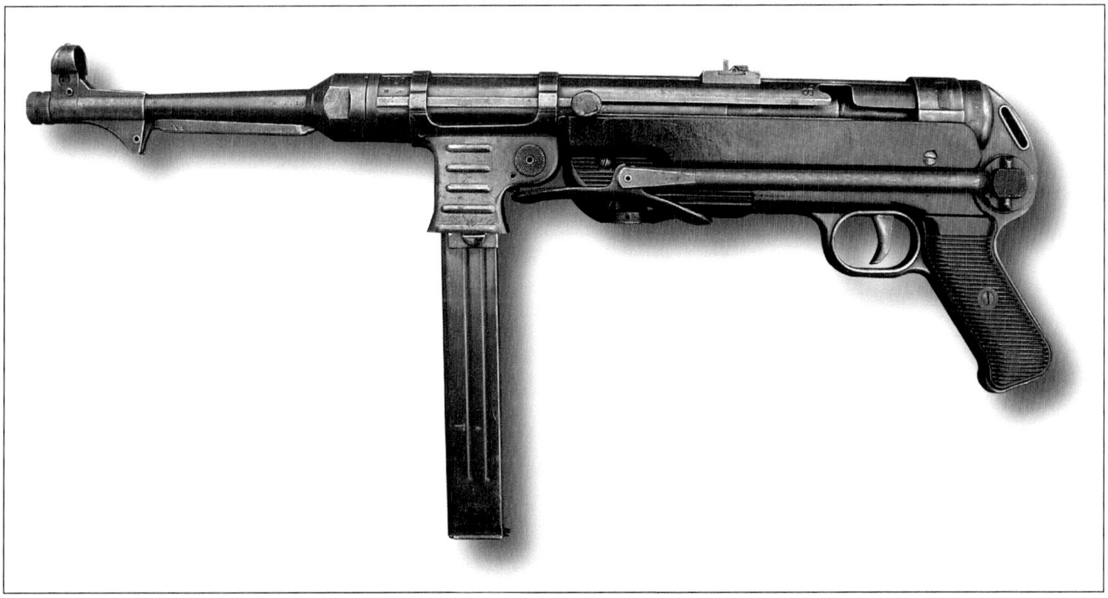

The *Maschinenpistole 40* or MP40 was another of the automatic weapons issued to Spanish soldiers for the Battle of Berlin. It was an ideal weapon for close-quarters combat. (By Quickload. Public Domain)

Principal features:

Calibre	9mm Parabellum
Selector	Automatic
Feeding	32-round straight magazine
Weight (Empty)	4.03kg
Loaded Weight	4.7kg
Length	833mm
Rifling	6 grooves/right-handed
Sight	Folding; 100–200 m
Rate Of Fire	450 to 550 rounds/min
Muzzle Velocity	381 m/s
Effective Range	200m

Walther P38

This pistol was manufactured to replace the famous P08 Luger, resulting in a robust weapon characterised by significantly better handling and maintenance than its predecessor. It soon became a very popular weapon, finding its way into various branches of the *Wehrmacht* and the SS.

Principal features:

Calibre	9mm Parabellum
Overall Length	214mm
Barrel Length	125mm
Weight, with empty magazine	950 g
Weight, with full magazine	1050 g
Feeding	8-round magazine

Kar 98k

This was the standard issue rifle in the German Army throughout the war. It was developed in response to the need for a more manoeuvrable rifle than the Mauser *Gewehr 98*, which had been used in Germany for many years. The final model was a shortened version of the *Gewehr 98*. These were reliable and easy-to-handle rifles, although throughout the war (and even more so in its final stages) their limited firepower became apparent when compared to the new automatic and semi-automatic weapons that were emerging. Despite this, production continued until the final year of the war (the last examples were manufactured less than a month before the end of the conflict), totalling more than 11.5 million examples across its various variants.

Principal features:

Calibre	7.92mm
Overall Length	1,110mm
Barrel Length	600mm
Weight, with empty magazine	3.8kg
Weight, with full magazine	3.94kg
Feed	5-round cartridges

Gewehr 43

The 7.92mm *Gewehr 43* semi-automatic rifle was used by some of the men of the *Einheit Ezquerra*. It was a simple, reliable and lightweight weapon. Very suitable for urban combat in Berlin. (Collection of the Armémuseum, Stockholm. Public Domain)

After obtaining examples of the Soviet Tokarev SVT 40 semi-automatic rifle, the German authorities decided that their army needed a weapon with similar characteristics because, in the face of the Russians' overwhelming numerical superiority in their counter-offensives, it was necessary to provide the defending troops with a greater volume of fire than their current weapons were capable of delivering.

It was the only semi-automatic rifle produced in significant numbers during the Second World War in Germany. Its main characteristics were its robustness, accuracy and high reliability. The fact that it did not reach front-line troops in greater numbers was due less to its potential limitations than to its coexistence with what would come to be known as assault rifles, which were less powerful but more practical to use, and offered greater firepower.

Principal features:

Calibre	7.92
Type	Semi-automatic gas-operated
Operation	Semi-automatic
Total Length	1,117mm
Barrel Length	545mm
Weight (unloaded)	4.3kg
Feeding	Magazine with a capacity of 10 rounds
Rifling	4 right-hand grooves

MG42

Despite the excellence of its predecessor, the MG34, the machine gun was designed for ease of handling and maintenance, even in the most extreme conditions such as mud, snow, dust and water. Furthermore, it had a rate of fire of around 1,200 rounds per minute, higher than that of the MG34, making it a weapon of devastating effect.

Principal features:

Calibre	7.92
Type	Automatic machine gun
Length	1.2 m
Weight	11.56kg
Rate Of Fire	1,200 rounds/min
Muzzle Velocity	762 m/s
Range	800m on bipod; 3,000m on tripod with telescopic sight
Action	Recoil

Panzerfaust

Panzerfausts in their original box at the Sotamuseo, Helsinki. The defenders of Berlin used this weapon both against enemy armoured vehicles and to blast holes in the walls of buildings to create safe 'corridors' that would shield them from enemy fire. (Public Domain by BALCER)

The *panzerfaust* was the first anti-tank weapon, easy to manufacture and proven effective. It was in fact a recoilless rifle consisting of a steel tube with a firing mechanism, inside which the round and a cartridge of black powder were placed. The round was a hollow-charge type and had a wooden tail with four steel fins.

To use it, the rear sight was raised and the firing mechanism cocked; the trigger was pulled and the powder charge propelled the round. It was a disposable weapon, as it was cheaper to make a new *panzerfaust* than to reload the empty tubes.

It could have devastating effects in expert hands. To make it easier to use, all *panzerfausts* had a label stuck to their 'head' with illustrations and instructions on how to use it. It was greatly feared by Soviet armoured forces in general, and even more so in urban combat terrain, which provided the ideal setting for its use in skirmishes and ambushes. However, the Soviets also made good use of captured versions during the Battle of Berlin. Its exact characteristics varied according to the model.

Principal features:

Model	Date of manufacture	Barrel diameter	Range	Propellant	Penetration	Weight
Pzf 30 Klein	August 1943	10cm	30m	70g	140mm	3.2kg
Pzf 30 Grosse	August 1943	15cm	30m	100g	200mm	5.2kg
Pzf 60	August 1943	15cm	60m	130g	200mm	6.8kg
Pzf 100	November 1944	15cm	200m	200g	200mm	6.8kg
Pzf 150	March 1945	10cm	150m	200g	+300mm	7kg

11

Soviet Troops

The Soviet forces that took part in the assault on Berlin belonged to Marshal Zhukov's First Belorussian Front and Marshal Konev's First Ukrainian Front. The forces of the former encircled the capital from the north, east and west, while the latter did so from the south, east and west.

The troops the Spanish would face belonged mainly to Konev's Front and Zhukov's Front.

In the fighting that took place on 27 April in the Saarlandstrasse area, the Spanish encountered troops from Colonel-General Chuikov's 8th

Anhalter Station and Anhalterplatz in the years leading up to the war. The station's walls witnessed numerous battles during the Russian siege of the German capital. (Waldemar F-Hermann. Public Domain)

Guards Army; at Moritzplatz, they faced men from the 9th Rifle Corps of Colonel-General Berzarin's 5th Shock Army.

When the Spanish moved to defend the area around Anhalter Station on 28 April, they once again clashed with their 'old acquaintances' of the 8th Guards Army.

On 29 April, the Spanish soldiers would face Soviet advance units from the 26th Guards Rifle Corps (part of the 5th Shock Army) in the Reichsbank area. As the men of the unit retreated through the Anhalter area, they clashed with men from the 8th Guards Army and the 92nd Guards Tank Regiment.

Subsequently, the general rout, the prevailing chaos and the collapse of the defences would lead to the fragmentation of the unit's components; although they would likely continue to face these same Soviet units advancing through the streets of central Berlin.

In the final chapter of the unit's history, the remnants of the unit, while attempting to reach Stettiner Station, came into contact with Soviet forces of Colonel-General Kuznetsov's 3rd Shock Army.

The ethnic composition of the Soviet troops was quite diverse, as they hailed from the many republics that made up the USSR, and with the main exception of the elite Guards regiments, they could vary greatly in appearance, language and dress. Among them were Russians, Belarusians, Ukrainians, Karelians, Azerbaijanis, Armenians, Georgians, Tatars, Uzbeks, Kazakhs, Bashkirs, Mongols, Cossacks, Siberians, et cetera.

Their uniforms, much as those of the German Army, were also quite varied. Thus, alongside the predominant dark brown uniform, there were also khaki ones. As for headwear, we find everything from metal helmets to leather helmets with ear flaps, fur hats and khaki caps, all in the most varied states of repair after the many months these troops had spent at the front.

12

Urban Combat Tactics in Berlin

Throughout history, urban terrain has witnessed how small, poorly-trained forces can halt or even drive back larger regular armies. Something similar occurred in Berlin, but the heterogeneous defensive forces – which included veterans of the *Volkssturm*, children from the Hitler Youth, women, in addition to the remnants of the various regular troops of the *Wehrmacht* and the Waffen-SS – despite inflicting countless casualties on the Soviets, were unable to hold back forces that were so overwhelmingly superior in terms of both weaponry and numbers. Furthermore, it must

A Berlin street following the fighting in April–May 1945. The vast amount of rubble that enabled the defenders to 'ambush' both armoured vehicles and Soviet infantry on numerous occasions is obvious. (Public Domain)

be borne in mind that a highly motivated defender can prove a very tough nut to crack because of their knowledge of the terrain and their unyielding determination to protect their territory against an invading soldier.

In the case of the Soviets, they faced the double handicap of being unfamiliar with the terrain, as well as being aware that the end of the war was approaching, which heightened their fear of being killed or wounded with so little time left before returning home victorious. All these factors influenced the fighting that took place between late April and early May 1945 in the capital of the Reich, although they were not, in practical terms, decisive in terms of the outcome, due to the aforementioned Soviet superiority in all respects.

Three men of the *Volkssturm* armed with *panzerfausts*. This anti-tank weapon was one of the main obstacles encountered by Soviet armoured troops as they attempted to capture Berlin. (Bundesarchiv Bild 183-J31320)

The Germans' tactics in urban combat were therefore based on the knowledge gained during so many years of war and on the physical characteristics of the city, with its numerous bridges and waterways. Most of the city's central districts consisted of blocks of buildings, some with inner courtyards, set along more or less straight streets interspersed with canals, parks and railway lines. Elevation would not represent a significant advantage in these battles (apart, of course, from the formidable anti-aircraft defence towers located in the city), as the city is completely flat with very few hills, and these of little consequence. The men of the *Einheit Ezquerra* employed the same offensive and defensive tactics as their comrades in the German Army, perhaps with the advantage of their powerful weaponry.

The tactics followed by the Soviets did not recommend sending tank units into a city held by the enemy, as their movements are severely restricted by the layout of the urban environment, while such terrain is perfect for the creation of barricades and anti-tank obstacles that further 'channel' the direction of the armoured vehicles' advance. Another important factor is that any building can become a heavily defended stronghold, which will inevitably result in a high number of casualties.

In the case of the Battle of Berlin, various defensive and offensive tactics were developed, drawing on the lessons learnt after each engagement. Above all, the Soviets were unprepared for the constant ambushes and counter-attacks by the defenders, which in the early stages of the Battle of Berlin had already inflicted a very high number of casualties (both human and material). These high casualties were a direct consequence of the tactics employed by the defenders, who exploited the Soviets' narrow lines of advance through streets lined with ruined buildings that were perfect for ambushes.

A heavy 203mm B-4 howitzer advances towards Berlin to take up positions and destroy the defenders' buildings and fortified positions. (Public Domain via Mos.ru)

Let us hear here, in Ezquerra's own words from his memoirs, an account of one of their actions in which they ambushed Soviet troops, inflicting a large number of casualties, both human and in terms of armoured vehicles:

> At a certain point, from behind a barrier of wrecked tanks, the Soviet soldiers, howling and screaming like rabid animals, charged towards us. We let them advance to the middle of the square and level with us, and at the same time we all fired, the 'iron fists'. It was an astonishing clash. Few survived that first wave. That blow was decisive because the fighting gradually subsided, with only a barrage of fire remaining on the Russian side to cover their retreat. The square, littered with corpses and twisted metal, was now ours. That marvellous feat did not come for free; it was paid for with the lives of many comrades and by increasing the number of wounded, who were, on both sides, carried to safer places.... At that moment, an orderly approached us, crossing an open street. He was marching so recklessly and so exposed to the bullets that it was a miracle he arrived alive... My men, exhausted, were already in the Europa building, and I did not know to what

> extent I could count on their depleted strength. Moreover, there was a shortage of ammunition, and above all we lacked 'iron fists'. But as the situation was critical and a Russian breakthrough in that sector could lead to a dire situation for all of us, we went back on the offensive.... Upon reaching the site under attack, Lieutenant Múgica, who was in charge of defending a group of houses, his face blackened and his uniform torn, shouted to us, raising his arm: 'Hurry, comrades!' The situation was almost desperate. We ran faster and Múgica exclaimed when he saw us arrive: 'Without your help, we would all die'.... The Russians, their tanks silent, showed signs of drunkenness and advanced in compact masses without the slightest caution. It was a pleasure to blow them to smithereens and remind them that walking in Berlin is not the same as treading the steppes. I ordered them to take up positions and aim carefully at that mass. When the time seemed right, I ordered the firing.... As they tried to regroup, a second volley struck them again, completely scattering the attacking mass. There was no one to hold them back and they retreated in disorder, leaving hundreds of dead behind. Our automatic weapons finished the job.... The tanks, which were unable to manoeuvre, were destroyed and piled up, joining the many hundreds of corpses covering the pavement of the square.[1]

Initially, the Soviets used their powerful armoured force to advance through Berlin's wide avenues and streets. The infantry provided support for the tanks and anti-tank vehicles, but German tactics claimed a multitude of armoured vehicles, which were destroyed mainly by the ubiquitous *panzerfausts* (referred to as *puños de hierro* by Ezquerra, a literal translation of the German name) and, to a lesser extent, by the *panzerschrecks*. The defenders used these two weapons from positions where their field of fire was wider and it was difficult for the armoured vehicles' guns to target them (because of the minimum elevation angles of the guns), such as from basement vents or from piles of rubble. These positions also allowed the defenders to go unnoticed by the advancing tanks and thus get closer to their targets, as proximity was necessary to hit them with accuracy. In narrow streets (or due to rubble blocking access), once the first, or first two, tanks at the vanguard had been destroyed – as they were travelling in single file – the way was blocked for those following behind, who would attempt to turn back, provided the defenders did not take some of them as casualties. Following this temporary retreat, the next Soviet move was to tow away the wreckage of the armoured vehicles blocking the way to allow the next attack.

1 Miguel Ezquerra Sánchez, *Luché Hasta El Fin: Memorias de un voluntario español en la guerra 1939–1945, Berlin a vida o muerte* (Granada: García Hispán, 1999), p.78.

Soviet artillerymen preparing a new salvo of rockets from their Katyusha. The extensive damage caused by these rockets overwhelmed the German defences, destroying their defensive positions. (Mark Redkin. Public Domain)

The importance of the *panzerfaust* during the Battle of Berlin is reflected in one of the short articles in *Der Panzerbär* concerning this weapon, which was easy for any citizen to use and capable of inflicting great damage on the Soviet advance:

> Afraid of tanks? No, there's no need to be. Afraid of tanks? Well, we aren't; it's an excellent weapon, by the way, and it's only dangerous for Ivan. They're lying in ambush everywhere, with *panzerfausts* at the ready. The enemy himself has created an ideal battlefield for them: death and destruction now lie in wait for him in the ruins of Berlin. The soldiers, especially those from the Eastern Front, await the attack with steely calm; the men of the *Volkssturm*, among them many veterans of the First World War, wait in cold blood from their cover, while the lads burn with fighting zeal. But they all know a single slogan: 'The enemy shall not pass!' They know that their beloved Führer is among them, in their Reich capital. This fuels their determination to resist to the utmost…. Yes, such are the defenders of Berlin! Their lives do not belong to them. They belong to Germany and to the freedom of their homeland.[2]

Clearly, the advance of the Soviet tanks was not yet so restricted in the outlying areas of the capital, due to the large number of parks, gardens, and

2 *Der Panzerbär*, 27 April 1945.

The ruined streets of Berlin became the perfect setting for the creation of numerous positions for small groups of defenders who launched fierce attacks against both armoured vehicles and enemy infantry. (Bundesarchiv Bild 183-J31347. Public Domain)

the like; this allowed them to bypass potential points of German resistance and attack from the flanks. However, as they penetrated deeper into the city, the higher density of buildings and the narrowness of the streets significantly reduced the armoured vehicles' manoeuvrability. The only areas allowing a greater degree of freedom were the wide avenues, which do exist in Berlin, although these were littered with anti-tank obstacles and featured various defensive strongpoints.

Following the heavy losses that they were suffering, the Soviet General Staff decided to change their tactics in Berlin, organising assault detachments that combined a battalion of tanks or self-propelled guns, a rifle battalion, an artillery battalion, a platoon or company of engineers, and a flamethrower platoon. On occasions, 203mm howitzers with massive destructive power could be deployed, although their use in very close-quarters combat was limited as there was no time for their shells to explode. To this force, the Soviets added the support of other artillery pieces (mainly 85mm, 122mm or 152mm – the most common calibres) and anti-aircraft artillery tasked with destroying positions where enemy resistance was more difficult for infantry and armoured units to neutralise, that is, enemy deployed on rooftops and upper floors. With the destruction of the buildings, the defenders were in many cases buried under the rubble, and clouds of dust so thick that everyone was blinded and suffocated, unable to speak or move. Those who managed to survive appeared like spectres covered in earth and dust (the dust hung in the air, originating from the explosions and collapsed buildings, giving it the consistency of a kind of mist), but despite the initial disorientation, they resumed their positions, now amidst the rubble, and it all began again as a new Soviet attack advanced. In all this, one must remember the importance of the snipers on both sides who, always 'on the prowl', claimed numerous lives, many of them having managed to survive the collapses and fires of the buildings where they had been positioned defending a sector.

It was common practice for the Soviet infantry to advance close to the sides of the streets, sometimes sheltered by the smoke of the fighting and in other cases by smoke screens created specifically to try to get as close as possible to the defensive positions without being detected. Unfortunately for them, the defending troops often managed to spot them, turning the fighting into a veritable bloodbath for the Soviets. But when an assault unit was repelled, a new Soviet attack on the same sector would follow shortly afterwards, with the clear intention of wearing down the defending troops both physically and mentally. On other occasions, the Soviets managed to reach the defenders' positions and then, if the defenders did not retreat, violent close-quarters combat would ensue, which often turned into life or death hand-to-hand fighting.

Each building was the responsibility of a combat group of around 10 men or so, depending on requirements. In addition to their machine guns and rifles, they made good use of the *panzerfaust* or *panzerschreck*, despite the fact that their use in confined spaces was dangerous because of the release of gases when the round was fired.

Buildings in which men could not be deployed for defence were usually turned into traps for the Soviets, and explosive devices were placed within them, in particular grenades, mines or demolition charges. Explosives were usually incorporated into obstacles on access routes or in the corridors of these buildings, serving both to defend the building and as an alarm to indicate the presence of the enemy within. The aim of these booby traps was not so much to inflict casualties on the enemy as to slow them down and instil fear in Soviet infantry soldiers, affecting their morale and fighting spirit.

Tanks in the central areas primarily played a supporting role to infantry and artillery forces. It was the infantry themselves who had to first eliminate any resistance in the adjacent buildings, thereby allowing the armoured vehicles to advance in more safety. This was effectively a combined attack by infantry and tanks, which latter could advance once their flanks were protected. Thus, the idea was that, when faced with a pocket of resistance, it was the engineers and infantry who were tasked with attacking it, with artillery support and troops armed with flamethrowers; this was intended to overwhelm the defending troops, who would be unable to confront the armoured vehicles as they passed through that sector. SS troops did not usually build barricades near street corners if the streets were straight, as they could be attacked by artillery fire from elevated positions on other buildings, putting them at a very dangerous disadvantage. Instead, they positioned snipers and men with machine guns on rooftops and upper floors of buildings, which, as well as protecting them, in most cases made it impossible for the guns of the Soviet tanks to achieve a sufficient elevation to fire at them. Similarly, men armed with *panzerfausts* or *panzerschrecks* positioned in low-lying areas, such as rubble at the base of buildings or basement windows, could 'seal off' the entire defensive system designed to ambush Soviet armoured vehicles and soldiers.

Understandably, these tactics were emulated by the other defending troops in Berlin – the *Wehrmacht*, the *Volkssturm* and the Hitler Youth; although evidently not with the same effectiveness as battle-hardened troops of the SS could demonstrate, though no less bravely. One of the problems the defenders faced was poor coordination between the *Wehrmacht* troops, the *Waffen-SS* and the *Volkssturm*, due to internal tensions between the high command of each.

It was impossible for the Soviets to apply the same tactic at every single stronghold they encountered; therefore, there had to be certain variations depending on the specific circumstances of each case. Thus, at times the initiative was led by tanks that could advance along two or three streets, allowing for a greater degree of mobility among the attacking troops, although the armoured vehicles were also left unprotected by the scant infantry that might accompany them. Once the agreed distance had been covered, the front line was stabilised by the attacking troops taking up strategic positions. If necessary, they would storm any area that posed an obstacle to their advance.

The Soviets emphasised the importance of not spreading the attacking troops too thinly, to prevent them from being attacked while locally outnumbered; as well as attacking along a relatively narrow front with each assault group.

As mentioned above, ambushes against Soviet armoured vehicles and troops were common, even usual, and to counter these attacks – which were costing them so many vehicles and men – the Soviets began to station men armed with submachine guns on top of the tanks, with the task of unleashing a hail of bullets on literally every door and window from which the defenders might operate (on the downside, these crew members significantly restricted the turret's ability to rotate quickly when necessary). Another solution was to exploit their clear superiority in attack aircraft and artillery, so that aerial bombing and howitzer shells would literally 'crush' any defences that might arise in any building on any Berlin street.

With these tactics, Soviet infantry began moving from house to house rather than advancing in a straight line along the streets. Their movements would be dictated by the terrain, namely, ruined buildings with endless rubble blocking the pockmarked streets. They also learnt, just like the defenders, that it was often unnecessary to go out onto the street to move from one building to another. Since it was obviously very dangerous to advance through the streets, the abundance of *panzerfausts* (among both the Germans and the Soviets upon capturing depots containing them) allowed for the creation of 'corridors' parallel to the streets by opening gaps in the walls of buildings, which were much safer than the streets themselves. While these troops advanced 'at ground level', other men took up positions on the upper floors of the buildings so that the attics could also be used as links between one building and another.

Despite the theoretical merits of these tactics, the reality is that the Soviets had to face hundreds of ambushes, which caused them a high number of casualties in both armoured vehicles and men.

Badge of the *11. SS-Freiwilligen-Panzergrenadier-Division Nordland*, to which the Spanish unit was attached during the Battle of Berlin. (Artwork by Willtron. Public Domain)

As for the Spanish troops who took part in the defence of Berlin, their role was what has come to be known as a 'fire-fighting unit'. That is, heavily armed units sent to one sector or another of the front line that was in danger of being breached by enemy troops. These same missions were carried out by troops from the *Nordland*, the *Sturmbataillon Charlemagne* and the Latvian Battalion.

At this stage of the conflict, and because of the deplorable state of Berlin's streets, movements from one side to the other had to be made on foot through streets littered with craters and rubble and under enemy fire, or via the underground tunnels.

In the former case, the advance had to be made, as far as possible, by trying to stay close to the walls of the buildings – or what remained of them – to minimise the time spent in the open under fire. For, even when moving through streets within the German defensive perimeter, the heavy Russian artillery fire was capable of causing heavy casualties. The men, as Ezquerra recounted in his book, moved in single or double file, presenting as small a front as possible to enemy fire. And it was due to this incessant pounding of the artillery that, on certain occasions, it was necessary to abandon the advance on the surface – faster and more direct – in favour of the Berlin underground tunnel system.

The area where the Spaniards fought had an extensive underground network, as well as various stations serving as entry points to it. Moving through these tunnels was sometimes difficult because of the various obstacles posed by the darkness, as well as the crowds of people taking shelter in the stations.

Given this situation, it was necessary to use torches and for the men to move through the tunnels in single file, as close to one another as possible. Although this advance was not as direct as moving through the streets in broad daylight, it was clearly safer.

Once they reached the area where they had been ordered to deploy, the main priority was to ascertain the positions of neighbouring friendly units, as well as of the advance of enemy troops.

The Soviet enemy's advance guard consisted of infantry and armoured forces, so the defensive priority was to take out the infantry in order to leave the tanks unprotected; a moment that would be exploited by the men tasked with destroying the tanks.

To this end, the defenders made use of craters and rubble that could offer cover, as well as walls, windows, rooftops and any nook or cranny in the buildings where they could hide while firing their weapons. The Spanish, armed with assault rifles, rifles, machine guns, et cetera, could generate a powerful volume of fire concentrated in small areas through which the Soviets were advancing. This barrage of fire served, on the one hand, to cut down a multitude of infantrymen, while forcing many others to seek cover or retreat. And it was precisely at that moment that the men armed with *panzerfausts*, who until then had been taking cover behind whatever protection they could find, emerged, advancing as close as possible to their prey so as not to miss their shots at the armoured monsters. Clearly, to ensure these shots were successful, they had to be aimed at the tanks' weakest armoured areas: the top, rear and sides. The men of the *Einheit Ezquerra* made good use of these primitive but effective anti-tank weapons, this being one of their main missions: to halt the Soviet tanks at all costs.

This entire process was carried out under the cover of fire provided by their comrades, which continued while the soldier who had attacked the Soviet tank returned to his original position.

In his memoirs, Ezquerra recounts various incidents such as the one in the Anhalterplatz area, which may have taken place on the morning of 29 April, although it cannot be fully confirmed. He says that he gathered some 30 men from the Spanish unit, forming what he himself called 'mobile groups' ready to be deployed to any part of the front:

> I formed a group of 30, selecting the best men: Múgica, Pinar, Ferrer, Gracia, amongst others. Having laid out the plan, we took up position next to a tall building overlooking Anhalter Square with the intention of crossing it at the opportune moment. To get to the other side, we had the advantage of being out of range of automatic weapons. Walli was with us but did not accompany us on this daring attack as he had another mission to carry out.... The street continued to be pounded by hellish rifle fire, and some of the buildings hit by artillery were burning or beginning to burn.... The scene outside offered no better prospects, for at every moment, in a diabolical succession, new columns of tanks arrived at Anhalter Square, firing in all directions. We already had some dead and quite a few wounded, which made our precarious situation even worse. Behind us, the fire raged with increasing intensity by the minute; in front of us, apart from the exit, a torrential rain of shrapnel.... Beside me were Gracia, Ferrer and Pinar, waiting for the best moment to fire.... *Luftwaffe* soldiers approached to relieve us. Walli came with them and congratulated me with a hug.[3]

During these clashes, Ezquerra reports that he and his men destroyed several tanks with the ubiquitous *panzerfausts*. Although it is impossible to know the number of armoured vehicles destroyed by the Spanish, it does seem plausible that it was a significant number, given the size of the Spanish unit and their continuous use of the *panzerfausts*.

When the Soviet armoured vehicles were held back by the Spanish tactic while advancing in a staggered single file, they would switch, in their next

3 Miguel Ezquerra Sánchez, *Luché Hasta El Fin: Memorias de un voluntario español en la guerra 1939–1945, Berlin a vida o muerte* (Granada: García Hispán, 1999), pp.107–108.

attack, to a single file of 7 or 8 tanks in a line, albeit almost touching one another, in an attempt to provide greater defensive capability.

These fragile defensive groups, while capable of halting the Soviet onslaught, had to be flexible and ready at the right moment to withdraw in an orderly fashion to regroup a few metres further back and again stand their ground against the enemy. After all, tactical retreat is another – and quite significant – aspect of an army's manoeuvres during combat.

The use of the *panzerfaust* and *panzerschreck* meant that some Soviet armoured vehicles had to prepare for a dangerous enemy, who would appear hidden from the most unlikely positions. Consequently, tank crews began to develop protective screens (perforated metal sheets resembling the springs on which mattresses rest) and attached them to the turret and hull. These protective measures proved highly effective against portable anti-tank weapons, although they were not implemented across all Soviet armoured units in Berlin, with each unit devising its own solution to this problem. As Medina notes, 'Every corps, division, regiment and battalion fought its own battle in the streets of Berlin, often without any meaningful information beyond the radius of one or two blocks for which it was responsible.'[4]

On certain occasions when, despite their efforts, the Soviets breached the defensive lines, some of the men could find themselves behind enemy lines, with the consequent higher risk of being captured or killed. Faced with such a situation, the possible solution lay mainly in one of two approaches: either attempting a forced breakthrough – more feasible when the number of men involved was high; or waiting for the right moment, preferably under cover of darkness, to sneak across enemy lines – a more practical method for men alone or in small groups.

After the fighting, once the enemy advance had been halted and the front lines re-established, the men were relieved from their positions by other army units, to await deployment to another vulnerable section of the front. On the Soviet side, a failed attack was followed by another, and so on, in an attempt to wear down and drive back the defending troops.

This continuous fighting, combined with a lack of proper rest, caused the soldiers to lose all sense of time. Their world was one of endless alerts, bombardments, explosions, fires and ruins. For them, the question of the future no longer arose. They saw no future other than destroying tanks, firing on Soviet troops and holding out – holding out until the end.

---

4 Francisco Medina, *Berlín 1945* (Santiago de Compostela: Sátrapa Ediciones, 2009), p.56.

13

Berlin Battlefield

The once-majestic capital of the German Reich had for many months been methodically bombed by the British (night-time missions) and the Americans (daytime missions), with over 70,000 tons of bombs dropped, leaving a large proportion of the buildings destroyed or damaged. But the Soviet presence just a few kilometres from the city seemed like a final blow.

Scherl Publishing House building, on the corner of Jerusalemer Strasse and Zimmerstrasse, destroyed by an air raid. This image of darkness and fires in the city would become a common sight during the Battle of Berlin, largely due to the Soviets' use of flamethrowers. (Bundesarchiv Bild 183-J30142)

The siege of Berlin had begun and the outlying districts were under attack. Bombing raids on the city continued unabated and Soviet artillery fire was already reaching the city centre. There were countless casualties among both civilians and military personnel, who were buried (when possible) in large mass graves. With the arrival of the Soviets and their massive artillery barrages, combined with continuous infantry and armoured attacks, the initial darkness of the Berlin night gave way to the vast inferno into which the city had been transformed. Entire neighbourhoods were ablaze, as were many of the destroyed tanks, serving as torches. A sinister light hung over the entire city, now bathed in a reddish glow against which the flames rose. The air was unbreathable; thick smoke and red brick dust that got into one's mouth and throat pervaded everything. Dust and clouds of smoke covered the sky, causing the ruins and skeletons of the buildings, silhouetted against the incandescent sky, to take on unreal and hallucinatory forms. Burnt-out cars at the roadside, trams torn from their tracks (and in many cases used as barricades), burst water pipes and debris of all kinds from the homes of Berliners. Enemy aircraft dropped flares over the battle zones and the combatants also used illumination and tracer rounds. To all this must be added the continuous roar of artillery shells, air raids, rocket launchers and all manner of gunfire that ceased only on rare occasions.

The Soviet Il-2 Sturmovik ground-attack aircraft became a real threat to the troops defending the capital of the Reich. (Mark Redkin, Public Domain)

Der Panzerbär informed Berliners that the city had become the front line of the battle:

> Ever since the days when our Berlin bear donned his armour and began to face the Bolshevik enemy with a *panzerfaust* and shovels [referring to the literal translation of the newspaper's name, the Armoured Bear carrying a shovel and a *panzerfaust* on each shoulder], the capital of the Reich has become a front-line city. The last vestiges of a time when the front was far away that we Berliners had clung to, even through all the

> years of bombing, have now gone out the window in the final phase of this struggle, where the front line runs through the centre of our city.[1]

In Berlin, there was great confusion regarding news of the progress of the fighting, and although the morale of the defending troops was generally low – except perhaps for some SS units and the boys of the Hitler Youth – there was a widespread determination that the city must be defended. Despite the political and military harangues directed at the troops and the population, the war was lost, and only the initial hope of German troops arriving to save Berlin, and later the more utopian hope that the Western Allies would reach Berlin and be able to confront the Soviet troops, kept that flame alive in many Berliners.

Although most Berliners were prepared to fight to the death, there were also a great many civilians who longed for the fighting to end, even if the Soviets were to emerge victorious, as seemed inevitable. Both civilians and soldiers carried out their duties day and night like automatons, sleeping, eating and drinking whenever they could. The defenders were utterly exhausted from lack of sleep, from hunger and from thirst, yet despite this they held their positions with determination and maintained a high level of aggression in the face of enemy attacks. It was not only the *Volkssturm* or the Hitler Youth who were fighting, women dressed as men were also fighting in the houses and on the barricades erected in the streets, wielding all manner of weapons.

Civilians conscripted into the *Volkssturm* work to reinforce an anti-tank barrier at the Hermannstrasse *S-Bahn* Station in Neukölln in March 1945. These defensive positions inflicted heavy casualties on both Soviet infantry and armoured units at the hands of the defenders. (Bundesarchiv Bild 183-J31319)

1 *Der Panzerbär*, 25 April 1945.

In its issue of 25 April 1945, *Der Panzerbär* conveyed to Berliners the significance of the historic moment they were experiencing and extolled the resistance against the Soviets:

> The impregnable defence of the Reich capital and the determination of German soldiers and civilians to repel the Bolshevik attack against the Reich within the walls of the Reich capital are highlighted with ever greater clarity in all American and British newspapers and news agencies, as well as in reports from Moscow. The strength and indomitability of Berlin's defenders is acknowledged, among other things, in an almost identical slogan carried by all enemy newspapers, which reads: 'The resistance in Berlin offered by the *Wehrmacht*, the SS, the *Volkssturm*, the police and the Hitler Youth is unprecedented in the history of European nations!'

Although the higher authorities intended for life to continue in Berlin, the destruction to which the city was being subjected now that it was under direct fire from Soviet artillery had turned the streets into vast labyrinths where facades or even entire buildings had collapsed, leaving rubble everywhere, the remains of vehicles, animals, destroyed tanks and the dead from both sides. Shells rained down on the entire city, like a veritable hurricane of steel that caused walls to shake under the explosions until, in many cases, they collapsed. The rubble was often used by the defenders to create barricades and positions to face the enemy. But it was also necessary for the defenders' mobility that the streets remain passable despite such extensive destruction, so the civilian population was urged to assist with these clearance tasks, as reflected in this article from *Der Panzerbär*:

> Keep the streets clear! The people of Berlin are asked to seize every opportunity to do their bit by clearing the streets buried by artillery fire and bombing. Above all, it is important that fallen overhead cables are removed and cleared from the road. As soon as there is a lull in the fighting, this clearance work can be carried out.
>
> Men and women of Berlin, lend a hand! Let us help keep the roads clear so that military movement within the city is assured, as well as the much-needed vehicle traffic to maintain supplies.[2]

Contrary to what one might suppose, Berlin as a whole did not display the panic and nervousness one might expect given the terrible situation it faced. In fact, according to witnesses, the general population 'showed absolute indifference and insensitivity to whatever might happen… people hurried to places of danger without a trace of drama, with the naturalness

2 *Der Panzerbär*, 26 April 1945.

of those who have foreseen and accepted death.'[3]

In fact, life in Berlin, despite the incessant artillery fire directed at it, was becoming tragically routine, as this article from *Der Panzerbär* attests:

A Soviet soldier raises the red flag over the captured Reichstag, 2 May 1945; the flag later became known as the Victory Flag. (From waralbum.ru, photographer unknown)

> 'Life has become very basic,' the Berliner used to muse as he emerged from his cellar after an Anglo-American air raid and realised that, once again, so much had changed in the meantime. Well, these days, life has become even more basic, and it must be said: Berliners – whether men, women or children – have adapted to the new situation with the same speed they have shown on other occasions. While the air-raid shelter had previously, fortunately, been used only for guests, it now serves in many places as permanent accommodation, which means that 'the steps of the staircase have worn thin'. Entire flats have even been set up in basements, and it is noted that even candlelit situation meetings are possible. Outside, on the street, the situation has become extremely uncomfortable. The low-flying planes that Ivan sends whizzing through the area can cause some to kiss Mother Earth for the first time or, as the Landser puts it, 'stick their snouts in the ground'. Surprisingly quickly, life has adapted to these pesky moths. If there is imminent danger, people wave to motorists and make holes in the air with their index fingers. Then everyone runs for cover.[4]

3 Antony Beevor, *Berlín: La caída, 1945* (Barcelona: Editorial Crítica S.L., 2002), p.97.
4 *Der Panzerbär*, 26 April 1945.

Another tragic example of the 'normality' of life among the civilian population is recorded in this *Der Panzerbär* article:

> In north Berlin, a hundred metres from the front line, an innkeeper offered his services. In his former café, he, his wife and the waiters served the defenders deployed in that area.... Amidst artillery and machine-gun fire, in front of a house, passers-by have to cross the street in giant strides. 100 metres away, tanks are being knocked out and two dead men lie in a corridor. A kind person asks, 'Would you like pudding or beetroot for dessert?', and shortly afterwards, 'Can I bring you your coffee now?' When the two men jokingly 'ask' where the cake is, they quickly receive the reply, 'It's still in the oven. Right now we're making portions for 60 men from the *Volkssturm*, who are about to come for dinner.' Here we can only say that: the front-line city, Berlin, surpasses itself in perseverance, camaraderie and composure.[5]

The trams had stopped running and the underground was being used to transport troops and supplies to the front lines, leaving Berlin transformed into an apocalyptic landscape where only the Germans' extreme organisation allowed it to continue resisting the powerful Soviet onslaught. Many neighbourhoods lacked water and electricity, while others were still being supplied thanks to underground factories. Where the electricity had been cut off, which was the case in most parts of the capital, both civilians and military personnel had reverted to a cave-dwelling existence, living in the basements of homes or government buildings under extremely precarious conditions. At the end of April, it was still cold and there was persistent rain, heating was important for the population, but with no coal available, furniture from homes was used as fuel.

The relentless strain to which the defenders were subjected day after day, hour after hour, the virtual absence of any hope combined with the hellish atmosphere created by the fires, bombings and the Soviets' continual ground attacks, as well as the intense smell of gunpowder and death (many of the victims of the fighting and bombings were left in the streets without being collected), brought soldiers and civilians to the brink of collapse. A veteran of the *Nordland* Division recalled this hell into which Berlin had been transformed: 'The whirlwinds of stone, the metal debris and fragments of bloodied human bodies made the air unbreathable, filling it with the dense dust of rubble and the fumes of gunpowder.'[6]

In this chaotic environment, which left no time for the defending troops to rest, the use of Pervitin continued, just as it had been used for years in the German Army. Pervitin was a type of methamphetamine widely

---

5 *Der Panzerbär*, 25 April 1945.

6 Thomas Fischer, *Berlin 1933–45 avec Wilhelm Mohnke* (Paris: Éditions Heimdal, 2013), p.55.

distributed among German soldiers to boost their stamina, reduce fatigue and eliminate fear in combat; it kept the Germans awake for several days, making them more aggressive and violent, and causing them to attack with greater ferocity than usual.

Another important factor for the defenders was no longer surviving the fighting, but merely surviving. We refer here to the great difficulties that both military and civilians faced in obtaining food and water for drinking – not for shaving or washing.

The interruption of the drinking water supply could force the use of water from rivers, lakes or ponds, with the consequent danger that such water sometimes contained pathogens such as typhoid fever or dysentery, and could become the cause of diseases and epidemics. Consequently, water from rivers, lakes or ponds had to, under all circumstances, be boiled to eliminate any pathogens before drinking.

In the case of troops in combat, it was often impossible for them to gain access to any source of water, so thirst took its toll; on many occasions, their saviours were local residents who, risking their lives, provided them with some water and, on occasion, food. Food supplies for the military were scarce, so they ate whatever they could find, whenever they could find it. It was a common sight to see civilians queuing at public fountains or at the state-run public kitchens in the street, at the mercy of fire from Soviet troops; only to then remain deep within a shelter like an animal in its burrow until it was necessary to venture out again for food or water. Many people had nothing but the clothes on their backs and slept wherever sleep overtook them, in the most hidden corners. A multitude of infectious diseases broke out due to the problems of the water supply, and the fighting continued day and night. The underground hospitals were overflowing and received more wounded every day, who were cared for in subhuman conditions.

14

Biographies of Some of the Main Participants

Below, we will briefly relate the biographies of some of the protagonists of our story. These biographies include some events not mentioned in previous chapters, and thus provide a useful complement to the above.

Miguel Ezquerra Sánchez

This biography of Ezquerra is based on verifiable facts and others taken from his biography and the interview conducted by Javier Nart for *Interviú* magazine.[1] As the source of the latter is Miguel Ezquerra himself, they must be considered at least partially true, though certain doubts remain regarding their plausibility in some respects.

Born in Canfranc (Huesca) on 10 January 1913, he was a former member of the Falange who worked as a teacher (he studied teacher training in Pamplona and spent some time teaching in Lodosa). On 2 January 1935, he joined the army in Jaca and was assigned to the 4th Company of the 2nd Battalion of the *Regimiento de Infantería América No.14.* When the Civil War broke out with the mutiny of the troops in Africa on 18 July 1936, he met with his falangist friends in a café, where they caught up on events in the country. The following day he registered at a recruitment centre and was assigned to the 7th Falange Battalion, with which he served throughout the Civil War. He took part in fighting on the fronts in Madrid, Aragon and Extremadura. During the war, he rose to the rank of *alférez provisional.* When the war ended, he was posted to Málaga with the company he commanded, where he was discharged at his own request, and he returned to his profession as a state school teacher. He began a new life when he married Consuelo, with whom he had two daughters, Consuelo and Pilar.

1 *Interviú* no. 339, Madrid, November 1982.

Later, through the Ministry of Foreign Affairs, in 1940, he was posted as a Spanish teacher to the French city of Bayonne. After the end of the German invasion of Russia, Ezquerra returned to Spain with the intention of enlisting in the Blue Division. However, he was unable to do so at first, as there was an enormous number of volunteers who far exceeded the available places in the division. It was in late 1942, following the necessary rotations among the division's personnel, that he was finally able to seize his opportunity.

Initially, he enlisted as a private, though he was eventually able to depart with his former rank of *alférez*, in Millán's battalion, leaving his wife and children behind in Seville. Now a member of the division, and serving as an *alférez* in an anti-tank unit in the Leningrad area in early September 1943, he was awarded the Second Class War Merit Medal. His very brief stint as a divisional officer came to an end after he was wounded in his right foot and groin in late September 1943 from the explosion of an enemy mortar bomb while serving with the 2nd Divisional Anti-Tank Company (Anti-Tank Group 250) on the Kolpino Front. After receiving appropriate treatment in the unit's first-aid post, he was subsequently evacuated to the Spanish Hospital in Riga, where he remained for about 15 days, and was then transferred to the hospital in Königsberg, where he stayed for a month until he was repatriated to Spain on 21 December, at which point he was discharged from the Blue Division.

After being repatriated, he joined the legion. However, he did not yet consider his involvement in the Second World War to be over, as he felt a deep feeling after his time on Russian soil defending his ideology against communism; consequently, he made preparations for his clandestine departure from Spain towards the Reich. Throughout 1943 and part of 1944, he spent his time with his wife and two daughters, devoting himself fully to family life, and during this time they moved to Seville. On 2 April 1944, he took the difficult decision to return to the war, which meant leaving his wife and two daughters in Seville. It was via Irún that, on 2 April, he secretly crossed the Pyrenean border into France. As a result, both Ezquerra and his companions achieved their long-sought goal, although he had to fire several shots into the air to prevent the civil guards on border duty from capturing them. It was these shots that alerted the German soldiers guarding the border on the French side, who immediately located them and pointed their weapons at them. The Spaniards, now on French soil, threw down their weapons and raised their arms towards the German soldiers, who took them prisoner and to a nearby Gestapo barracks. Once in German-controlled territory, after being investigated and their military past confirmed, Ezquerra and his comrades were sent to Saint-Jean-de-Luz (it was in this town that Ezquerra was first contacted by the SS), to Biarritz and subsequently to the Queen's Barracks in Versailles, where they would spend three weeks undergoing training.

From this point onwards, it is Ezquerra's memoirs that recount his experiences and 'exploits', bearing in mind that, as there is no way to corroborate some of the facts that he gives they must be treated with scepticism. What is certain is that Ezquerra is well-versed in the subjects he discusses in his memoirs, so he may well have embellished real events with details of his own making. Having made this clear, let us follow the account of his actions during and after the Second World War.

Unlike other Spaniards who were unable to confirm their previous rank in the division or the legion, Ezquerra managed to persuade the Germans to allow him to wear the stripes of an *alférez* (he mentions in the interview in *Interviú* that he was documented as *Capitán* Kronos).

After Versailles, he moved to Stablack-Süd, where he joined the Spaniards who were training there. It was at Stablack that he met Ricardo Botet Moro and Rufino Luis García Valdajos (more usually known as Luis García Valdajos), whom he would later fight alongside in the defence of the city of Berlin.

Luis García Valdajos in *SS-Obersturmführer* uniform. (Courtesy of Erik Norling)

Ezquerra, now working for the *Sicherheitsdienst* (SD, Security Service), was given the task of reporting to Sonderstab F in the south of France, where, from Cauterets, he would be responsible for 'channelling' the Spaniards crossing the border into Stablack with the aim of creating a unit of strictly Spanish volunteers. Shortly afterwards, possibly in late May 1944, he was transferred to Paris to undertake an Abwehr officers' training course (the same one that García Valdajos had completed shortly before).

It was not long after the Normandy landings that Ezquerra was tasked with organising a company of Spanish soldiers to carry out sabotage operations behind enemy lines. The unit, formed in the second half of June, was short on men and was drawn from various sources (Hall in Tirol, from the 102nd, or other units where there were Spanish soldiers[2]). These soldiers had a knowledge of English and wore civilian clothes, with the aim of going as unnoticed as possible. According to Ezquerra in *Interviú*, he commanded a unit of some 80 to 90 Spaniards, to whom were added a few Frenchmen from Doriot's party and some Russians (Ezquerra's opinion of the latter was far from positive, as he regarded them as cowards). They were attached to an SS unit (the identity of which is unknown) and from 27 June

2 When in 1944 many Spaniards were being assembled in the Reich to join the German Army, they were gathered at Solbad Hall, Tyrol. In June 1944 there were two units composed of Spaniards in Solbad Hall and that was when they received their official designation of *101. Spanische-Freiwilligen Kompanie* and *102. Spanische-Freiwilligen Kompanie*. In general, the entire unit was that usually called *Freiwillige Einheit Solbad Hall*.

carried out raids in 'occupied' territory. They laid mines, changed the directions of road signs, and blocked roads, all to slow down the Allied advance. But sooner or later it was inevitable, and they were discovered and subjected to intense artillery and even aerial fire. The hunt for the Spaniards began, but after more than 20 hours of being hounded, they finally managed to make contact with German troops. When they headed for the rear, they were once again recruited to join a Waffen-SS battalion (there is also no information to confirm which one) that was resisting the Allied attack. Again, they carried out 'guerrilla' missions, blowing up a fuel depot and neutralising potential positions that could serve as strongholds for the Allies if captured.

A week later, they were attached to the Brandenburg Division and received a new contingent of Spaniards who were possibly stationed in Versailles. Numbering more than 150 men, they continued their tasks on the Normandy Front. Casualties were heavy, and the unit was eventually out of action, and withdrawn to Paris. From there, on 25 August 1944, as Allied troops were entering Paris, Ezquerra and a few other Spaniards attempted to leave the city in a car, but not before coming under fire from the French resistance near the Opera and the Place de la Concorde; after their tyres were punctured, they were forced to abandon the vehicle. They finally left the city, having even seen the Allied troops (including tanks manned by exiled Spanish Republicans) making their presence felt on the streets of Paris.

After leaving Paris, Ezquerra went first to Vienna and then to a *Luftwaffe* barracks in the Czechoslovakian town of Wutweiss.[3] He was subsequently called to Berlin to lead a secret mission to South America, which never took place, so he was placed in command of a unit of Spanish commandos that took part in the start of the Ardennes offensive in December 1944 within the *Brandenburgos* (German Army Special Operations Division), which had by then been incorporated into Otto Skorzeny's *SS Jagdverbände*.

The Ardennes offensive began on 16 December 1944. The men commanded by Ezquerra located US infantry troops and artillery in the Ardennes forest. Ezquerra divided the Spaniards into two groups and launched the assault. The first group blew up the American ammunition depot, causing confusion, while the second group attacked the tents. As the Americans emerged from their places, the Spaniards shot them, continuing until all of the Americans had been eliminated or surrendered. The surprise attack by the Einheit Ezquerra cost them at least three dead and two wounded, but the Americans suffered 300 casualties, most of them as prisoners, and the loss of an ammunition depot for an entire division. It had been a great victory for the small group of Spaniards, though it would be of little use, as the Ardennes offensive eventually ground to a halt and then saw a retreat back to the same lines from which the offensive had begun.

3 Wutweiss is the name that Ezquerra recorded in his memoirs – it is probably Budweis.

During these operations, Ezquerra suffered frostbite to one foot, which became infected, so he was transferred to Wiesbaden in Germany, where he underwent an operation. Once recovered, he was sent to what would be his new posting in Berlin.

Between February and March 1945, thanks to the efforts of *General* Faupel, who was in charge of the Ibero-American Institute, he was tasked with forming a unit of Spaniards for the Waffen-SS, comprising any Spaniards he could persuade to join. Faupel may well have provided financial assistance to Ezquerra to facilitate his recruitment efforts. Among those recruited were surviving veterans of the *Wallonien* as well as students and some workers from the *Organisation Todt*; it is even possible that some of those recruited had outstanding legal issues with the German authorities. In *Interviú*, Ezquerra states that he had an authorisation signed by Heinrich Himmler, the head of the SS! With his recruits, he formed a unit, which, to facilitate its integration into the organisation of Berlin's defence, was named after its leader.

Just as Ezquerra was 'recruiting' men to bolster his unit's ranks, there was another Spaniard in Berlin engaged in a similar activity, albeit with a very different purpose. This was Gonzalo Rodríguez del Castillo, a Spanish journalist and the last Spanish diplomatic representative in Berlin. In reality, the Spanish Diplomatic Corps should have been under the command of Diego Bohigas, who was the acting Ambassador of the Spanish diplomatic mission, but he had informed Rodríguez del Castillo at a meeting that on 30 March 1945 the diplomatic corps would depart for Bregenz, on Lake Constance (close to neutral Switzerland). It was in Switzerland, due to the war situation, that the new Spanish ambassador to Germany was to be based. This decision had been taken given the critical situation the city was in and the even worse prospects on the horizon. Bohigas offered del Castillo the chance to join this 'convoy', which comprised most of the Spanish delegation in Berlin, but he declined, effectively remaining, as mentioned, the last Spanish diplomatic representative in Berlin. During his time as head of the Spanish diplomatic mission in Berlin, del Castillo was engaged in numerous negotiations with the *Organisation Todt* and the German Labour Front (*DAF*) to secure safe-conduct passes, train tickets and food vouchers for many Spanish citizens who belonged to these organisations. According to Vadillo, he managed to get 200 Spanish workers onto trains to secure their repatriation between 12 and 16 April 1945 alone.[4] Evidently, this work clashed head-on with that of Ezquerra, whose intention was to recruit those protected by Rodríguez del Castillo. Again according to Vadillo, in a face-to-face encounter between Ezquerra and the diplomat, they were on the verge of coming to blows due to their disagreement.

General Wilhelm von Faupel maintained an important relationship with Spain, holding, among other posts, that of Director of the Ibero-American Institute, from which he had close ties with the Spanish who continued to fight for the Reich from 1944 onwards. (Public Domain)

4 Fernando Vadillo, *Gran Crónica de la División Azul en los Irreductibles* (Granada: García Hispán, 2008).

With the unit that would bear his surname composed of two companies of men well equipped with light weapons, he took part in the swansong of the Reich capital, rising to the rank of *SS-Obersturmbannführer* in the Waffen-SS (again, according to his own account).

In his interview, Ezquerra again states that his unit (which was apparently still being formed) took part in the fighting that took place in Stettin, where for several days they defended a German bridgehead on the Oder; there, 'the battle against the Russian tanks was terrible and served to toughen up my soldiers'.

Following these skirmishes, they were sent to Berlin and incorporated into the *Nordland* Division. Once in Berlin, after various engagements against Soviet armoured forces, they were converted into a reserve unit, stationed in the cellars of the Air Ministry. He received several awards for his bravery in combat, including being awarded the Knight Cross of the Iron Cross and German citizenship, granted personally by Adolf Hitler, according to Ezquerra's own account; consequently, this must always be regarded as dubious.

Regarding his conduct during the fighting in Berlin, we have widely varying accounts ranging from a heroic attitude worthy of decorations (the version given by Ezquerra himself and by some other members of the unit) to a completely wretched attitude and one of being isolated from the fighting, as reflected by the journalist Ramón Lobo, a relative of Julio Antonio Lobo Varela (a member of the *Einheit Ezquerra*), about whom he writes:

> In the final days of the Third Reich in Berlin, he fought in the *Einheit Ezquerra*, of which only a handful of soldiers remained. He had experience with anti-tank weapons, and that was his mission: to try to stop the Russian tanks. Although Ezquerra claimed credit for destroying several armoured vehicles, my uncle said that was a lie, that Ezquerra never went out onto the streets, that he was a bastard who spent his final days holed up in the cellars of the *Excelsior Hotel* on Königgrätzer Strasse, surrounded by prostitutes and alcohol, before disappearing and abandoning his men.[5]

He was captured, but managed to escape from his captors and return after many adventures, like a labourer crossing half of Europe. Ezquerra was forced to surrender to the Russians in the bunker at Stettiner Bahnhof (not before discarding his medals and national insignia) and, after they stole his watch and knocked out some of his teeth, he joined a column of prisoners being marched eastwards, where he encountered several Spanish comrades. Once on Polish territory, they were interned in an abandoned concentration camp. There, Ezquerra and his comrades – two Spaniards (named Jesús

5 Ramón Lobo, *Todos náufragos* (Madrid: Ediciones B, 2015).

Codina and 'the Legionary') and two Frenchmen from the Charlemagne – stole a rucksack of provisions from a German officer prisoner and also got hold of a rifle. As night fell, Ezquerra approached the lone Russian sentry on duty to speak to him; at that moment, one of the Frenchmen stabbed the sentry. Subsequently, the five escaped from the camp and found themselves free on Polish soil.

Free in Poland, Ezquerra and his companions came across a group of thousands of prisoners liberated by the Russians. Among them, they met a Jewish man who had been in a German concentration camp; he joined the group and even managed to get them food, although Ezquerra never knew where it came from. Upon reaching Germany, Ezquerra and his companions ditched the Jewish man and fled without saying a word to him, as they suspected he might betray them if they were discovered. On another road, they came across French soldiers who had been prisoners of the Germans; the two Frenchmen accompanying Ezquerra lied, claiming that they too had been prisoners and that their Spanish companions had been forced labourers. The French, without even suspecting that they were Waffen-SS, fed them and took them in their lorry so they wouldn't have to walk. Near Berlin, the group of escapees parted ways for good; the two Frenchmen managed to get a pass to return to France, the two Spaniards decided to carry on their own, and Miguel Ezquerra, now alone, returned to Berlin.

In Berlin Ezquerra was hidden by a family of friends and obtained documents from the Ibero-American Institute that allowed him to pass as an Argentine citizen. At the end of May, Ezquerra and other companions were transported to Magdeburg in Russian lorries to be supposedly repatriated to Argentina. At the border between the Soviet and British zones, British soldiers refused to let those of Argentine nationality cross; however, some former British prisoners who had befriended Ezquerra intervened on his behalf and he was finally allowed to pass. In Magdeburg, some American journalists asked the Spaniards if they knew a certain Miguel Ezquerra, to which they replied that they did not know him, suspecting a possible trap to capture him. After various adventures, Ezquerra managed to reach a sector controlled by the British, and from there he was sent to Brussels, where he parted ways with his companions. But he soon made contact with new people, who happened to be Spanish Republicans dissatisfied with communism (all of this is still following the work of Miguel Ezquerra).

Ezquerra, attempting to regularise his far from regular situation, made his way to the Argentine Embassy to explain his uncomfortable and dangerous situation, before subsequently going to the Spanish Embassy. At that time, not all embassy staff were willing to take risks to help a fugitive, which is why neither embassy was of much assistance, although he eventually managed at least to secure a new identity as a Spanish Republican released from a concentration camp. This version, taken from his book, differs from that given to Interviú, where Ezquerra obtained the documents by 'fabricating' them himself using stamps and official paper at the Ibero-

American Institute. In any case, Ezquerra's new identity would be that of Fernando Reyes Calvo, an Argentine national.

During his escape, Ezquerra realised that Argentine nationality was perhaps not the best choice he could have made, as Perón's government was regarded as fascist by the Soviets. Despite this, he was placed with a group of former American and British prisoners of war who were to be sent to Northern Germany within the American occupation zone. With his new companions, everything went well until a couple of British men became suspicious of Ezquerra, but he was not reported (Ezquerra notes that they, like him, harboured a certain hatred for the Soviets due to the numerous atrocities they had committed against the German civilian population), and he arrived with his secret undiscovered in the Belgian city of Liège. From there, he travelled to Brussels, where, during his stay, he happened to meet some Spanish communists who entered the restaurant where Ezquerra was sitting. Realising he had been discovered and to avoid further trouble, he had to leave the Belgian capital and head for his familiar Paris, this time posing as a refugee.

In Paris, some Spanish friends, some of them former Republicans, provided him with a pass allowing him to travel freely throughout France (according to his interview in Interviú, it was a Spaniard named Ricardo Bruguera who gave him his own documents; a fact that is actually quite strange and is dubious, unless Ricardo Bruguera's identity was also false). Despite this, he was far from safe on French soil, as anyone arousing suspicion was systematically arrested and interrogated (Ezquerra himself states in his account that he was at the top of the most-wanted list, a fact that should at least be questioned). With the help of various villagers, he made his way towards the Spanish border, hiding in roadside ditches, woods and areas with little traffic. He reached Dax, where he worked in a sawmill until one day he decided to steal a bicycle, which he used to reach the outskirts of Hendaye, where he abandoned the bicycle and crossed over the Pyrenees on foot. Returning to his interview, Ezquerra says that to finally cross the border he had to hold a pistol to the heads of two gendarmes, whom he forced to guide him to the border after disarming them (a story suspiciously similar to his departure from Spain, a fact that is indeed more credible). Upon finally reaching the border, the civil guard rushed out to pick him up and he finally entered Spain.

Due to the regulations in force regarding Spaniards who had served in the German Army following the withdrawal of the Blue Legion by the Spanish Government, Miguel Ezquerra had lost his Spanish citizenship, so he chose to head for Portugal, where he published a book about his experiences in the conflict.

It appears that in the 1950s he worked in North Africa (Algeria and Morocco) for the Spanish secret services under the command of *General* Beigbeder; in the 1960s, he returned to his profession as a teacher. Once in Spain, and again according to Ezquerra's own account, he worked for the Spanish secret service and then enlisted in the French *Légion étrangère's* intelligence services by joining the *Bureau de Sécurité Territoriale*;

eventually working as a double agent for the Spanish in Algiers (as Ezquerra put it, 'the Spanish consul in Oran was a comrade-in-arms from the Blue Division', so collaborating with him proved easy). He was subsequently drawn into the Indochina War between the Mekong and Red River deltas, where he spent almost a year in what he described as 'nightmarish' combat conditions. He later managed to return to Algeria, where, now a *sergent*, he left the *Légion étrangère* after a year's service. He was contacted again by the *Bureau de Sécurité Territoriale* to continue working with them, but Ezquerra refused. He moved to Casablanca, where he was arrested by the *Bureau de Sécurité Territoriale* at the entrance to the Spanish Consulate. There, Ezquerra spent 90 days detained in a prison he describes as filthy, with five square metres for a dozen other prisoners alongside him. Finally, after three months in captivity, he was transported in a van to the Spanish zone of the Protectorate – his destination: Ceuta prison. From there he was transferred to the mainland, though only to remain in prison, this time in Carabanchel. He was held for a crime unknown to us but shortly afterwards was released (Ezquerra mentions, again in his interview, that the reason for his imprisonment was related to 'matters concerning the secret services which it is best not to go into in detail').

His next steps took him from Madrid, where he stayed only briefly, to the Caribbean, where he trained the 'Caribbean Anti-Communist Legion' for the Dominican Republic's dictator, Leónidas Trujillo, after being hired in Spain to form a so-called Caribbean Anti-Communist Legion – an idea that initially appealed to Ezquerra. But the reality did not convince him and as soon as he could, following incidents of an unknown nature, he left the Dominican Republic and headed for neighbouring Haiti. From there he travelled to Venezuela and finally ended his journey through the Caribbean countries in Brazil, where, thanks to his contacts with German exiles (very likely former SS members settled in the South American country) based in the town of Santa Catalina at the confluence of the borders of Paraguay and Brazil, he remained for a while. Santa Catalina was a large logging settlement that was physically isolated from the rest of the world by the dense jungle surrounding it; in fact, only those who were vouched for by some of the residents or who could reliably confirm their actions during the Second World War were allowed to enter. According to Ezquerra and the mythology that emerged at the end of the war, many of the German leaders who fled following Germany's defeat were said to have settled there in the post-war period (among them, he mentions in *Interviú*, Martin Bormann, whom he also claims to have seen fleeing Berlin, and Dr Mengele). Ezquerra did not stay there long, as thanks to his contacts with the Spanish ambassador in Asunción (Paraguay), Giménez Caballero, he was granted a logging concession in the Upper Paraná, in Colonia Strössner. He remained there for a couple of years, although it was not profitable, mainly due to the constant struggle with the jungle and the worst bureaucracy he had ever had to face. After leaving, he lived for some years in Argentina and then in Chile before returning permanently to Spain.

Back in his homeland, he joined the CEDADE (Spanish Circle of Friends of Europe), taking part in a congress in Madrid in 1973, where he wore his World War II decorations.

He died on 29 October 1984 and was buried in the Almudena Cemetery in Madrid, alongside his comrades in the Blue Division Pantheon.

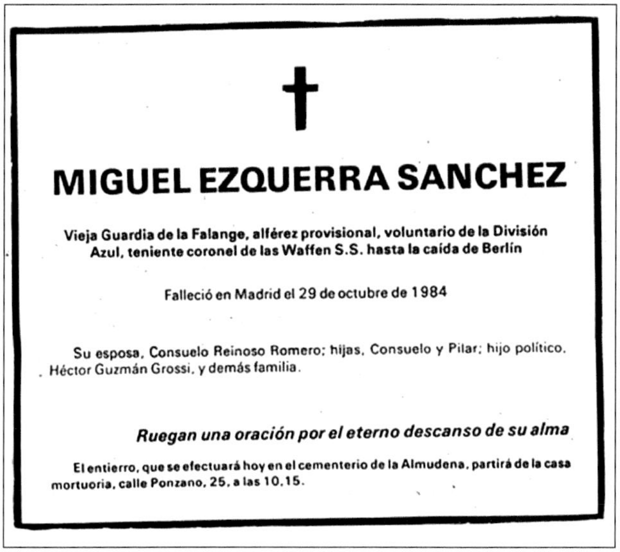

†

MIGUEL EZQUERRA SANCHEZ

Vieja Guardia de la Falange, alférez provisional, voluntario de la División Azul, teniente coronel de las Waffen S.S. hasta la caída de Berlín

Falleció en Madrid el 29 de octubre de 1984

Su esposa, Consuelo Reinoso Romero; hijas, Consuelo y Pilar; hijo político, Héctor Guzmán Grossi, y demás familia.

Ruegan una oración por el eterno descanso de su alma

El entierro, que se efectuará hoy en el cementerio de la Almudena, partirá de la casa mortuoria, calle Ponzano, 25, a las 10.15.

Obituary of Miguel Ezquerra Sánchez. (Public Domain)

Ezquerra was a man with a remarkable, very intense life and, although, as noted, his biography contains various facts that cannot be verified and are often inconsistent, he does deserve a certain degree of trust and his word should usually be taken at face value, given that he was indeed serving Germany in the final years of the Reich, as we have seen throughout these pages.

Ricardo Botet Moro

Ricardo Botet Moro was born in Barcelona in 1921, the son of a Spanish father and a mother of German descent. From an early age he felt drawn to military life, joining the ranks of the National Army in the Spanish Civil War at the age of 16. Little is known of him after that until his enlistment in the 'Blue' Division, part of the force which took part in operations between 1941 and 1942. He served in the II/269th Infantry Regiment as an interpreter as he spoke French and German fluently. He was promoted to *sargento* for his conduct in the fighting on the Volkhov River, and was awarded the Iron Cross Second Class on 22 April 1942 and the Assault Badge. He would later be one of the Spaniards to remain after the repatriation of the Division, as a part of the 'Blue Legion', in which he served on the General Staff of the 1st Battalion.

When the legion was repatriated, Sargento Ricardo Botet Moro, together with Rufino Luis García Valdajos and other comrades (a total of 53 men), decided to jump from the train bound for Spain on 5 April near Hanau, and were eventually assembled with other Spaniards at the 'Queen's Barracks' in Versailles.

It is possible that around 15 April 1944, as was the case with García Valdajos, he went to Stablack-Süd. Although there is no record of this he may have followed in García Valdajos' footsteps by joining the SD, as shortly afterwards there are reports of both men operating on French territory in a special operation that led to the capture of an American officer acting within the ranks of the maquis.

In late October 1944, thanks to his fluency in French as well as German, he acted as an exceptional interpreter for García Valdajos at the meeting they held with Léon Degrelle at the Adlon Hotel in Berlin, with the aim of recruiting new men for his recently formed 28. SS Wallonien Division.

Botet was to serve as one of the section leaders in the Spanish Company attached to the Wallonien Division, holding the rank of *SS-Oberscharführer*, under the command of García Valdajos; this unit was later redesignated as the 3rd Company of the 1st Battalion of the *70. SS-Grenadier-Regiment* of the Wallonien. He took part in the fighting at Stargard and Stettin (February and March 1945), subsequently attaining the rank of *SS-Untersturmführer*.

He was awarded the ribbon of the Iron Cross 2nd Class, earned on the Volkhov Front, during his time with the Blue Division (1941–1942), and the Iron Cross 1st Class, awarded on the Pomeranian Front in 1945, while commanding one of the platoons of the 3rd Company of the 1st Battalion of the *70. SS Regiment* of the *28. SS-Freiwilligen-Panzergrenadier-Division Wallonien*.

After being withdrawn from the *Wallonien* Division, he was stationed in Potsdam, where he joined the unit commanded by Miguel Ezquerra.

With Ezquerra's unit, he took part in the defensive fighting in the city during late April and early May 1945. Apparently, in the final days of the Battle of Berlin, he received orders to make contact with German units outside the siege of the German capital, though he failed to complete his mission successfully. At the end of the war, he managed to escape capture by the Soviets, wandering thereafter, posing as a forced labourer, through German territory, until he was finally captured by British troops in the Allied control zone. He spent a year as a prisoner of the British and in 1946 returned to Spain, arriving on 24 October, on the first UNRRA expedition, a country he had not set foot in since he left in 1941. During this period, he only travelled to Berlin to see his German family (his grandmother and uncles). He continued his life in Spain with no contact whatsoever with other veterans of the Eastern Front. He died in Málaga on 18 July 2008.

Juan Pinar Torregrosa

Juan Pinar Torregrosa was born in Ceutí, Murcia, in January 1922. In July 1942, at the age of 20, he enlisted in the Spanish Volunteer Division for Russia and was assigned to the 2nd Company of Anti-Tank Group 250, where he was wounded in May 1943. After completing his service in the Blue Division, he joined the Blue Legion as an *obergefreiter*, posted to the General Staff of the 3rd Battalion. Following the disbandment of the legion, he enlisted in the German Army and, after a spell at Hall in Tirol, ended up in the *Einheit Ezquerra*, where he served as an *SS-Unterscharführer*, before being captured by the Soviets in the German capital. During his captivity, he used various false identities, notably that of 'Captain Roca', and confronted his captors on numerous occasions, which meant he was unable to return to his compatriots in April 1954; he had to wait until December of that year when, through the mediation of the Spanish Consul, he returned to Spain by air on the 20th.

Wilhelm Faupel

Wilhelm Faupel, a German military officer and director of the Ibero-American Institute, was born in 1870 in Berlin and died in 1945.

A career soldier, he took part in the German expedition against the Boxer Rebellion in 1901. Subsequently, from 1904 to 1907, he was posted to the German Protectorate of South-West Africa, before going on to serve as an instructor to the Argentine forces. In 1911, he joined the teaching staff at the Argentine War College in Buenos Aires. At the outbreak of the First World War, he returned to his country, where he was posted to the General Staff on the Western Front, eventually rising to the rank of *oberstleutnant*. After the war, he went on to serve in the *freikorp*s that proliferated in Germany, before returning once more to Argentina, where from 1921 to 1926 he acted as military adviser to the army and in 1926 held a senior post in the Brazilian Army. From 1927 to 1930, he served the Peruvian state as the inspector general of its army.

He returned to his homeland in 1931, where, thanks to his involvement with the NSDAP, Adolf Hitler summoned *General* Wilhelm Faupel to the Chancellery in Berlin in 1934, appointing him director of the Ibero-American Institute in Berlin. This first period of the institute's leadership in relations with Spanish-speaking America spanned from 1934 to 1936.

In November 1936, Hitler appointed Faupel as the first ambassador to Franco's headquarters in Salamanca, serving as the Reich's chargé d'affaires in Spain. Despite having received precise instructions from the Third Reich's Foreign Minister, von Neurath, not to interfere in Spanish political affairs, he found himself, with the support of his wife Edith Faupel, embroiled in political intrigues backing dissident factions within the Falangist Party, particularly the Hedillist faction. Faupel observed with great displeasure how, in his view, the authentic revolutionary fascism he saw in the Spanish

Falangists was progressively turning into a conservative, Catholic, clericalist orientation. During this period, Faupel maintained close relations with some falangists, attempting to instil in them the authentic National Socialist spirit; he subsequently took some of them to Berlin as translators and journalists.

All these activities led Francisco Franco, with whom he had initially maintained good relations, to regard him as *persona non grata* as the Reich's representative; Franco forced his replacement in the summer of 1937, and he was succeeded by the more conservative Eberhard von Stohrer.

On his return to Germany, Faupel was reinstated in the management of the Ibero-American Institute, replacing Albrecht Reinecke, where he would serve a second term from 1938 to 1945. It was during this second period that his close relationship with men such as Martín de Arrizubieta evidently developed, and during which he supported the formation of the unit under the command of Ezquerra.

Since its creation in Berlin in January 1930, the Ibero-American Institute had been a centre for scientific research and cultural exchange between Germany and the countries of Latin America. In commemoration of the 'beginning of relations between the New and the Old World', the opening ceremony was held on 12 October, the day of Columbus's discovery of America, also known as *Día de la Raza*.

Prior to Faupel's arrival, the institute's cultural life was rather modest due to the meagre state funding it received. Under Faupel's leadership, the institute would no longer merely fulfil its cultural mission, but broadened its scope of interests by aligning them with the Reich's domestic and foreign policy, placing itself at the service of the regime. From being an institution founded on Hispanic studies, it became a major organ of National Socialist propaganda and dissemination into Spanish-speaking countries. From there, Faupel organised the publication of three journals on Ibero-American topics, two of them in Spanish (these were the interdisciplinary journal *Ibero-Amerikanisches Archiv* from 1930 and, from 1939, *Ensayos y Estudios*, a journal of culture and philosophy in Spanish and Portuguese). From 1944, a new publication entitled *Enlace* was published; this was a weekly aimed at Spanish workers in Germany. In its early days, this latter publication was 'controlled' by the *FET-JONS* apparatus in Germany. Martín de Arrizubieta was in charge of the weekly *Enlace*, and it was from there that proclamations were issued in favour of a new order led by Germany, leaving Franco's Spain in a poor light, which prompted various protests from the Spanish Diplomatic Corps.

From his privileged position at the Ibero-American Institute, Faupel established good relations with the SS as well as with the SD. From as early as 1942, he devoted himself to helping, to the full extent his position allowed, Ibero-American and Spanish students, as well as members of the Spanish Volunteer Division and the more than 10,000 Spanish workers recruited since 1941 who were working within the Reich; for whom he secured more than 800 grants and scholarships.

A final task undertaken by the institute was to serve as a point of reference and meeting place for Spaniards who, after February 1944, wished either to maintain ties with other Spaniards or to contact the Waffen-SS in order to join its ranks. At the same time, they helped to boost, as far as was possible, the morale of these men who were fighting and dying so far from their homes.

Enlace had a section entitled 'Soldiers of an Ideal' which reported on and for the Spanish volunteers fighting for Germany. Here, many combatants saw their letters published, mainly from the front, or the replies they received. As for the staff acting as journalists for this publication, Sourd tells us that they wore German uniforms, both SS and *Heer*, depending on each individual's circumstances, bearing in mind that many of them were veterans of the Spanish Volunteer Division. Regarding the names of these men, apart from the incomparable Martín Arrizubieta, Sourd mentions others: Juan Ximénez, Ramón Farré, José Salazar, Eduardo Pérez, Eugenio Pinero and R. Monzón – the latter being Central American, unlike the rest, who were Spanish by birth.

The situation towards the end of the conflict in Europe evidently limited the institute's cultural activities, as its staff had been greatly reduced. This was not the case in political and military matters, as Faupel's assistance to Miguel Ezquerra appears to have been decisive in the formation of the Spanish unit which, under the SS rune, would defend the streets of Berlin against the Soviet onslaught. The Faupels committed suicide once the Russians reached the capital of the Reich, fearing they would be taken alive.

Rufino Luis García Valdajos

Rufino Luis García Valdajos was born on 4 May 1918 in Tordesillas, Valladolid, into a middle-class Catholic family. At the age of five, he moved with his family to Madrid. In 1936, he began studying law at the City University; he was on holiday in Valladolid when the National Uprising began on 18 July of that year. As this area was quickly taken by Nationalist troops, he, as a falangist, promptly enlisted as a civilian volunteer in the civil guard. At the end of August, he enlisted in the Falange Militia, going on to serve in the Bandera de Castilla. With his unit, he fought on the Madrid Front in the Las Rozas sector. On 11 January 1937, he was selected to take part in a training course for *alférez*, which was to be held in the city of Granada. He subsequently began serving in his new rank with the Batallón de Cazadores de Montaña Serrallo, part of the 11th Division; with this unit, he took part in the battles they fought on the Extremadura Front and later on the Madrid Front until the end of the Civil War. His service during the conflict was recognised with various medals.

By July 1939, he had been promoted to the rank of *teniente de complemento* and was assigned to the 1st Regiment, which was stationed in the capital, where he served for the next three years.

From the outset of the German invasion of the USSR, a volunteer movement began to organise in Spain to head to the Russian front to fight against the Soviets. This movement took shape in the formation of the Blue Division in June 1941, and García Valdajos applied to be included in its ranks, though without success. He tried again to join the division in the summer of 1942, with the same result; he finally succeeded in September 1942, though he was unable to retain his rank from the Spanish Army and had to accept entry as a private. On 12 September 1942, he arrived in the city of Logroño, where his replacement battalion was stationed, and where he managed to be quickly promoted to cabo. On 22 November 1942, his train crossed the French border carrying the 18th Marching Battalion, into which he was to be integrated. His destination was the Leningrad Front, where, upon arrival, he was assigned to the 11th Company of the 2nd Battalion of the 269th Regiment on the Leningrad Front. During a year of fighting, he took part in various engagements against the Soviets, most notably the Battle of Krasny Bor; gaining combat experience that would prove invaluable to him in the future. In the Blue Division, he served in the cartographic section of Coronel Rubio's command post.

In November 1943, the Blue Division was withdrawn from the front and repatriated to Spain, leaving behind the new Blue Legion. Upon the dissolution of the Division, Valdajos volunteered for the legion and was assigned as a non-commissioned officer in the legion until its dissolution. When the legion was repatriated, Valdajos and other comrades, including Sargento Ricardo Botet Moro, decided to remain in Germany. A report dated in Madrid on 3 June 1944 lists 52 legionaries, classified as deserters, as of early May of that year.

After jumping off the train bound for Spain near Hanau on 5 April, Valdajos made his way to the nearest Wehrmacht post, where he was sent to the Queen's Barracks in Versailles, which was where Spaniards crossing the border to join the German forces were concentrated.

From there, on 15 April 1944, García Valdajos and 40 other comrades were sent to Stablack-Süd, arriving on the 20th of the same month. Once there, Valdajos was recognised for the first time as an oberleutnant, the rank he had held in the Spanish Army.

At Stablack-Süd, Valdajos was contacted by the SD, who offered him the chance to enlist in a special unit fighting against Spanish exiles who were acting as terrorists in France. On 7 June 1944, he travelled to Paris to undertake a two-week course for SD officers on combating the maquis. He learnt encryption and decryption techniques, as well as how to operate two-way radios. He was subsequently taught how to manufacture explosives and how to operate various types of vehicles and use various combat weapons, as well as how to read maps, et cetera; as a result, he received a high mark upon completing the course.

Once properly trained, he carried out anti-maquis operations from 23 June to 16 September and worked behind the lines on the Normandy Front. It is possible that the men under his command were, at least in part, drawn from those carrying out anti-maquis operations in the south of France as part of the Brandenburg Division. After operating in the north, García Valdajos would shift his 'theatre of operations' to central and southern France.

There, he and his unit would monitor and take action against the increasingly numerous maquis groups populating the French countryside. Here, together with Ricardo Botet, he took part in a special mission to capture an American officer operating within the ranks of the maquis.

He was subsequently called to Berlin, where he was congratulated on his magnificent fulfilment of the many missions entrusted to him and invited to attend an officer training course.

On 4 October 1944, García Valdajos was in Berlin awaiting a new mission and was possibly attached to the Ibero-American Institute headed by General Wilhelm Faupel, the former German Reich Ambassador to Spain. From there, he coordinated the activities of Spaniards living and working in Germany.

While in Berlin, Ricardo Botet convinced García Valdajos of the importance of contacting Léon Degrelle, the Rexist leader, who was in the Reich capital at the time trying to recruit new men for his recently formed 28. SS *Wallonien Division*. They finally met in late October 1944 at the Hotel Adlon in Berlin, with Botet acting as interpreter since he spoke German and French. Some accounts suggest that Alphonse Van Horembeke, a Belgian citizen who had obtained Spanish nationality after fighting in the Spanish Civil War, may also have been present at this meeting. Ultimately, the wishes of both the Walloons – to secure new men for their unit – and the Spaniards – eager to join combat formations – were fulfilled. After reaching an agreement with García Valdajos, Léon Degrelle appointed him commander of the Spanish soldiers to be incorporated into the *Wallonien Division.*

Once the agreement had been 'signed', the Spaniards, led by García Valdajos, were sent to Breslau around 1 November 1944, where the Belgian Division's Depot Unit was based. The men who initially arrived at the unit did so mainly via two routes: some came from the Spanische Ausbildungsbataillon (Spanish Training Battalion) based in Solbad in Hall in Tirol, and others, from Spanish workers already in Germany. Just one week later, they were transferred westward to Alfeld (Leine), in Lower Saxony. Valdajos began organising his company, appointing Ricardo Botet and other former officers of the Blue Division, such as Lorenzo Ocañas and Rafael Lafuente, as section leaders; they were granted the highest non-commissioned officer rank, SS-Oberscharführer. The unit consisted of at least 100 men, though according to other accounts this number may have reached as many as 240. Shortly afterwards, around mid-November, they were transferred to the Hemmendorf/Altendorf training camp, while García Valdajos was summoned to Berlin to carry out administrative duties.

Following the Ardennes offensive, on 25 December the Spanish Company, like the rest of the *Wallonien Division*, was placed on ready alert in anticipation of a possible advance into Belgium. García Valdajos, having returned to the Spanish Company, accompanied Léon Degrelle, along with members of his unit, on a reconnaissance mission of the area of operations in case the situation called for the deployment of the Wallonien into Belgium.

On 7 January, the offensive ground to a halt and the reconnaissance group returned to their barracks, with García Valdajos returning to Berlin to assess the current state of affairs.

It was in late January 1945, following the rapid advance of Soviet troops through the north of the Reich, that a combat group was formed comprising the two regiments of the Wallonien, numbered 69 and 70, as well as the 28. SS-*Artillerie-Abteilung*. This combat group was immediately sent to Pomerania, to attempt to halt the Soviet offensive.

The Spanish Company was incorporated into the 3rd Company of the 1st Battalion of the 70. SS-Grenadierregiment commanded by SS-Untersturmführer Rudi Bal, a Belgian officer who had been born in Argentina and spoke Spanish. This was due to the absence of García Valdajos, who was in Berlin at the time, where he was to marry a German citizen named Ursula Jutta-Maria Turcke, and had to complete all the bureaucratic requirements demanded of any SS officer to carry out the marriage (his application having been registered on 2 February). The 70. SS-Grenadierregiment was under the command of SS-Obersturmführer Robert Denie.

The fighting that followed was very intense, causing heavy casualties on both sides, one of whom was Rudi Bal on 6 March. He was possibly replaced in command of the Company by SS-Untersturmführer Albert Steiver, also of Walloon origin, who later recorded in his memoirs that he commanded the 'Spanish Company' in the fighting around Stargard.

It was not until February, during the fighting in the Arnswalde sector, that Valdajos re-joined his unit following his stay in Berlin. Few Spaniards managed to emerge alive or unharmed from these clashes; only around 60 men were withdrawn from the front for subsequent reorganisation, among whom was García Valdajos.

On 16 March, Valdajos reported to the headquarters of the 'Alfeld (Leine)'Wallonien Division and ordered them to assemble in Potsdam pending further orders. It was thus in mid-March 1945 that the separation of the Spaniards from the *Wallonien Division* came to pass, with orders received to station themselves in Potsdam.

As previously mentioned, between 100 and 150 Spaniards eventually gathered in Potsdam; García Valdajos would not command them, as command was handed over to Miguel Ezquerra Sánchez, with García Valdajos remaining as the Spaniards' liaison officer with the SS headquarters. However, by the end of April, we find García Valdajos once again with the troops commanded by Ezquerra for the defence of Berlin.

He survived the fighting and, following the Soviet capture of the city (his German military records state that he took part in the battles to defend Spandau and in the Tempelhof-Potsdamer Platz area during the Battle of Berlin), managed to remain in hiding until 9 May 1945, when he sought refuge at the Spanish Embassy. There he was unable to obtain help, as it was controlled by Spanish communists. He left the embassy on 13 May 1945 and remained in hiding in the ruined streets of Berlin until 8 June, when he managed to cross a Soviet checkpoint to leave the capital. García Valdajos disguised himself as a forced labourer and, dressed in civilian clothes, made his way to Stendal, in the Soviet zone of influence. By November 1945, he managed to make contact with the British Forces Headquarters in Berlin, who attended to him and listened to his story. He managed to arrange with them his admission to a refugee camp for displaced persons. He travelled through similar camps in various countries, including Germany, The Netherlands, Belgium and finally France.

On 14 December 1945, having reached the Spanish-French border at Irún, he managed to cross the bridge separating the two countries. At the Irún border post, he was detained for three days until his identity could be verified. Once back in his homeland, just five days later he reported to his former barracks. Due to his 'desertion', he was court-martialled in 1946 for abandoning his post; however, he was not imprisoned, was acquitted by a judgement dated 27 January 1947, and was finally granted full freedom on 1 March 1947.

After this period, little else is known of the life of the man who experienced first-hand the organisation of various Spanish units into battalions within the forces of the Reich, following the return of the Blue Legion. He died in Madrid on 27 October 1988.

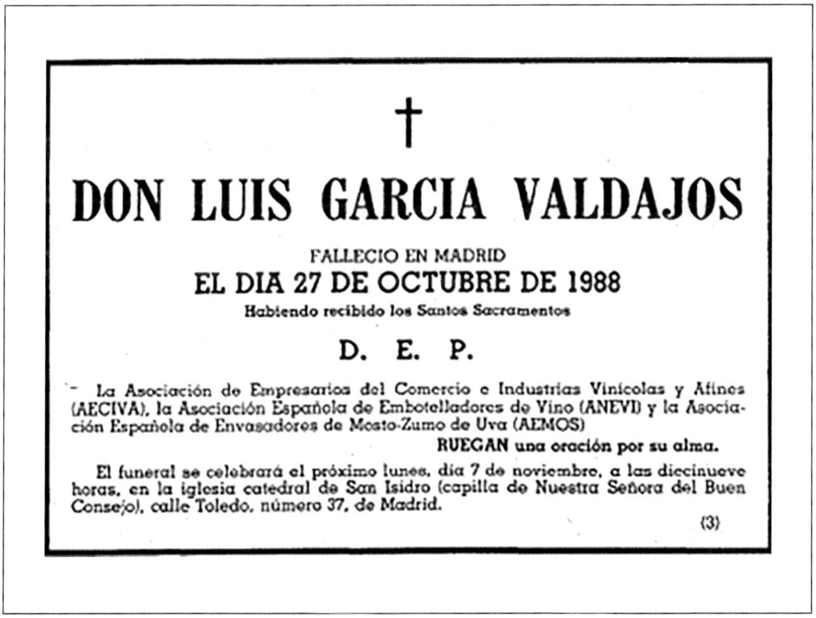

†

DON LUIS GARCIA VALDAJOS

FALLECIO EN MADRID

EL DIA 27 DE OCTUBRE DE 1988

Habiendo recibido los Santos Sacramentos

D. E. P.

La Asociación de Empresarios del Comercio e Industrias Vinícolas y Afines (AECIVA), la Asociación Española de Embotelladores de Vino (ANEVI) y la Asociación Española de Envasadores de Mosto-Zumo de Uva (AEMOS)

RUEGAN una oración por su alma.

El funeral se celebrará el próximo lunes, día 7 de noviembre, a las diecinueve horas, en la iglesia catedral de San Isidro (capilla de Nuestra Señora del Buen Consejo), calle Toledo, número 37, de Madrid.

(3)

Obituary of Luis García Valdajos. (Public Domain)

Erik Norling wrote a very interesting piece on Garcia Valdajos, which served as the basis for this profile.

Lorenzo Ocañas Serrano

Lorenzo Ocañas Serrano was born in April 1915 in Montoro, Córdoba. During the Spanish Civil War, he enlisted in a Falange unit, ending the conflict with the rank of *alférez*. He subsequently decided to enlist in the Spanish Volunteer Division for the militias of Castellón, joining in July 1941. In December 1941, he was wounded at Posad, on the Russian front. During his period of service in the Soviet Union, Lorenzo Ocañas Serrano was hardened by the fierce fighting there between German and Soviet forces. Upon his return to Spain, his anti-communist convictions led him down the path that others had already blazed: returning to Germany to continue his hitherto 'unfinished' struggle against communism. In July 1944, he met in a café in Madrid with four other officers who had also served in the Blue Division, and they decided to return to Germany.

They arranged to meet on 1 August 1944 in Barcelona, to cross the border on the 4th or 5th of that month. Ultimately, the latter date was chosen, and at 7 o'clock in the morning, accompanied by *Alférez* La Puente, they crossed the border at Port Bou.

After passing through Cerbéres and Banyuls, they reached Perpignan. They were then directed towards Innsbruck, to reach the Spanish camp at Hall in Tirol, where, together with more comrades-in-arms, they honed their skills in handling the various weapons supplied to them at that time by the German state.

In November 1944, they were assigned to the *Wallonien*, arriving in Cologne where a company of Spanish soldiers had been formed; Ocañas was appointed section commander. He took part in the fierce fighting in which the *Wallonien* was engaged near Stettin, until, in February 1945, he was posted to Potsdam, where he joined the unit commanded by Miguel Ezquerra. On 28 April 1945, while taking part in fighting – according to his

Muñoz Grandes giving a welcome speech to the repatriates from the *Semíramis*. (Courtesy of L. E. Togores)

own account, in command of a section and holding the rank of SS-*Untersturmführer* – against the Russians near Berlin's *Hotel Excelsior*, he was captured by the Soviets. He remained a prisoner from that moment on, passing through various gulags until he finally returned to Spain on 2 April 1954 aboard the *Semíramis*.

The reception at the Ministry of the Army for the returnees on the *Semíramis* in 1954. (Courtesy of L. E. Togores)

On his return to Spain, Ocañas was subjected to proceedings. The interrogation was conducted by *Coronel* Joaquín Huidobro.

When the prisoners from Córdoba in the Blue Division arrived in Córdoba, they were received with honours, which was not the case for Ocañas.

He applied to rejoin the armed forces, but his application was rejected due to his 'record' during the final period of the World War. He found work at the Bank of Spain's Córdoba branch, and there he lived in the Lepanto neighbourhood, his life further unremarked and unnoticed.

Ocañas married, becoming a widower and again in his second marriage. He had no children. He died on 16 December 1981 at the Hospital de los Morales in Córdoba from a chronic lung condition, contracted during his time in Russia.

His remains rest in San Rafael Cemetery, where another comrade from his final days defending the Reich, Martín de Arrizubieta, is also buried.

Alphonse Van Horembeke

Alphonse Van Horembeke was a Walloon who had served in the 4th Battalion of the Tercio and later in the 67th Company of the 17th Battalion, taking part in the fighting in the Bielsa pocket during the Spanish Civil War. In 1940 he worked for the Deutsche Reichsbahn (German Reich Railway), returning to his country in August 1941 to enlist in the *Wallonien* Legion, where he remained until he was demobilised following the Caucasus campaign. He subsequently served with the SD in Liège and Ghent, and in 1944 he was secretary of the *Frente de Juventudes* in Vizcaya. There he was entrusted with the mission of enlisting a group of members of the Falangist Youth who wanted to join the German armed forces. Van Horembeke therefore attempted to contact some friends to ensure that these volunteers were integrated into the ranks of the *27. SS-Freiwilligen-*

Grenadier-Division Langemarck (Flemish *Langemarck* SS Division). The reason for choosing this unit was that it had been stationed alongside the Blue Division in the Leningrad area from 1941 to 1943. Accompanying Van Horembeke was Juan Beltrán de Guevara; they arrived first in Versailles, where the latter left to join a group of German and Romanian soldiers en route to the Eastern Front. Despite the problem this departure caused for the mission, Van Horembeke pressed on with it. He moved towards Lichterfelde West, Berlin, where he knew the *Langemarck* reinforcement battalion was stationed. And there an event occurred that would mark and alter the fate of his mission, as Van Horembeke spoke neither Flemish nor German, which led to a lack of interest among the Flemish in the idea presented to them by the *Wallonien*. Consequently, he was referred from the *Langemarck* to the barracks of the *Wallonien*, where he would evidently be understood and possibly attended to.

Back in July 1944, at the Heidelager Camp in Poland, Van Horembeke bumped into an old friend by the name of Paul Kehren, whom he had served with in the tercio. After informing him of his mission, the two of them finally set off to make contact with Léon Degrelle. The latter, always in need of men to bolster his unit, gave his approval to the task of recruiting Spaniards into the *Wallonien*. Kehren and Van Horembeke set off to begin their 'recruitment drive' at the Stockerau Barracks, where they had heard that Spanish soldiers were being collected. Upon arriving there, they met Juan Beltrán de Guevara, the other emissary who had left Spain alongside Van Horembeke. They set to work, managing to convince some of the Spaniards who were there, possibly around 36, of the step forward it would represent for them to belong to a prestigious unit such as the *Wallonien*. He continued on his way, once again accompanied by Beltrán, to recruit more men from various industries in different towns across the Reich where Spaniards might be found. Around this time, Van Horembeke came into contact with SS-*Obersturmführer* Luis García Valdajos, due to his knowledge of the situation of Spaniards in the German armed forces. In September or early October 1944, a meeting took place at the *Hotel Adlon* in Berlin with Léon Degrelle, which was also attended by Ricardo Botet.

After completing his recruitment duties, Van Horembeke joined active military service in the fierce fighting of the *Wallonien* in Pomerania. When the Spaniards marched to Potsdam to join a new unit under the command of Miguel Ezquerra, Van

Léon Joseph Marie Ignace Degrelle was a Belgian politician and military officer who became commander-in-chief of the *28. SS-Freiwilligen-Panzergrenadier-Division Wallonien*. A considerable number of Spanish soldiers served in this unit, perhaps numbering around 240–350 men by January 1945. (Public Domain)

Horembeke said of Ezquerra: 'Before Ezquerra took charge of the group, we had been sent a captain called Luis whom we did not accept, because he knew nothing more than to show off his uniform, being more of a dandy than a captain. Ezquerra, on the other hand, was a man of courage, who feared nothing.'[6] Ezquerra would fight alongside them in the defence of Berlin against Soviet troops, until Van Horembeke was finally captured. Having witnessed what had happened to a Spanish comrade who, upon being captured, was executed simply for being from Spain, he declared himself to be Belgian. He was sent to various prisoner-of-war camps until he arrived at one in Kovno. There, he was fortunate enough to be handed over to an Allied Commission that repatriated him to Belgium. There, his 'record' immediately led to a 20-year prison sentence. In the early 1950s, he was finally released and returned to his second homeland, Spain, where he obtained citizenship. For any further information on the *Wallonien* and its members – among whom were a large group of Spaniards – we would refer to Erik Norling's excellent study on the subject.

Kampfgruppe

Finally, we would like to record the meaning of the term *kampfgruppe*. This is a German term which translates into English as 'combat group'. It refers to the temporary grouping of various units of varying sizes within the German armed forces. These groups were placed under a single command for the duration of the mission or order for which they were created. They became increasingly common as the Second World War progressed, and were typically named after the military commander in charge.

6 Ángel González Pinilla, *La Legión Clandestina* (Madrid: Gutiksland S.L., 2021), p.174.

Part III

15

The Contribution of the *Einheit Ezquerra* to The Battle of Berlin

Clearly, the intervention of the unit commanded by Ezquerra was not decisive in the battle for the defence of Berlin, but it did prove to be of some importance in a manner similar to the intervention of the Latvian or French units, which were the two units most similar in their participation in the fighting. Let us briefly recall the similarities between these three non-German units that took part in these battles.

The only publicly-known photograph of Miguel Ezquerra, taken in 1982 during an interview for *Interviú* magazine. (Image kindly provided by *Interviú* magazine through its editor-in-chief, Aitor Marín, for reproduction in this book. © *Interviú*)

But let us start at the beginning; the defence of Berlin in the face of the imminent arrival of Soviet troops was not as organised as might have been expected, with the defence of the city resting primarily on the 56th Panzer Corps, comprising the battered remnants of the 9th *Fallschirmjäger* Division, the *Müncheberg* Panzer Division, the *11. SS-Freiwilligen-Panzergrenadier Division Nordland*, the *20. Panzergrenadier Division* and the *18. Panzergrenadier Division*, supported by a motley collection of smaller units from the *Wehrmacht*, Waffen-SS, Hitler Youth and the *Volkssturm*. Specifically, the *11. SS Grenadier-Division Nordland* was originally recruited with Norwegian and Danish troops, with a small contingent of Swedes. As the war progressed, the number of Scandinavian soldiers in the *Nordland* had dwindled, and the division was supplemented with German soldiers or those of German origin. It was to this unit that the French, Latvian and Spanish units would be operationally attached.

Although the various units defending Berlin displayed acts of undeniable valour against the Soviet troops, the troops that arguably offered the greatest resistance, managing to halt the enemy's advance and inflicting heavy casualties, were the men of the *Nordland*, with the French standing out above all others. This great fighting spirit was driven by various factors, although the two most important were undoubtedly their anti-communism and the uncertainty of their future should they fall into Soviet hands, particularly given the Soviets' hatred of soldiers wearing the double SS rune at their throat.

Vincent Hunt refers to this view when he quotes Gerald Reitlinger in *SS: Alibi of a Nation, 1922–1945*: 'Part of the fanaticism among those who remained in or joined the Waffen-SS was undoubtedly based on the fate of foreign volunteers should they fall into enemy hands: repatriation and, in the case of those from Allied nations, firing squads or harsh prison sentences.'[1]

Obergruppenführer Gottlob Berger as head of recruitment for the Waffen-SS was the officer who gave the order for the Spanish troops under Ezquerra's command to move to Berlin in April 1945. (Bundesarchiv Bild 183-S73321)

It is important to note that of the foreign troops who went to fight for the city of Berlin, only the Spaniards did so of their own free will. Following their deployment in Potsdam, as they were a unit in the process of being formed and had not participated as such in previous combat, they were outside the Order of Battle of the German Armed Forces. Yet they did not hesitate to accept the opportunity to fight for the capital of the Reich when their commander (Ezquerra), following his conversation with *Obergruppenführer* Gottlob Berger, conveyed to them the need for their presence in Berlin. It should be remembered that they were offered the chance not to go to Berlin just before their transfer from Potsdam to Berlin. Even the Spanish Company, which had separated from the *Einheit Ezquerra* to head for the Alpine stronghold, tried to return to their comrades in the devastated streets of Berlin to take part in the fighting when that order was cancelled. Nor should we forget that, for example, in the case of the Latvians, they tried to avoid moving to Berlin.

In the case of the Frenchmen of the *Sturmbataillon Charlemagne*, they were ordered to enter the city before Soviet troops closed off the last access routes to the German capital. Despite this, the French unit

1 Vincent Hunt, *Sent to Die in Berlin* (Warwick: Helion & Co., 2026). Details from the author; at the time of writing the book is forthcoming.

behaved with great courage and bravery, displaying high morale despite the difficult circumstances.

The Latvians tried to get around the orders they had received to fight in Berlin; two-thirds of the unit managed to do so, but one battalion (the 15th Rifle Battalion) ended up on the streets of the Reich capital, where, it must be said, they fought like 'wild boars'.

The *11. SS Freiwilligen-Panzergrenadier Division Nordland* itself, with some of its men of Danish, Norwegian or Swedish origin, eventually received orders to enter Berlin during its retreat from the Oder Front.

Soldiers from other nations who ended up fighting in Berlin (involuntarily) included the few Hungarians stationed at various training barracks in the city, or the young Ukrainians serving in the Hitler Youth and the *Luftwaffe* (the latter already deployed in training schools and the anti-aircraft towers).

This French unit was no more than a combat group belonging to the *33. Waffen-SS Grenadier-Division (Französische Nr. 1) Charlemagne*, known as the *Sturmbataillon Charlemagne*, which consisted of four companies and a *Kampfschule*, totalling around 400–500 men. These men, under the command of Waffen-SS *General* Gustav Krukenberg, were called upon to defend Berlin and managed to reach the city just before it was completely surrounded by Soviet troops. The unit would eventually come under the command of *SS-Hauptsturmführer* Henri Fenet after Krukenberg took command of the *Nordland* Division, the unit to which the French combat group was attached. As might be expected, they were the last troops to reach Berlin by land after setting out for the city on the morning of 24 April. After many trials and tribulations along the 100 kilometres separating them from the Reich capital, they managed to arrive the same day at around 22.00 (specifically, they reached the *Reichssportfeld*) after covering the final 20 kilometres on foot, having been forced to leave their lorries behind.

The small French unit, already battle-hardened after the fierce fighting in Pomerania, was sent to Berlin with the intention of their acting as a shock troop. The unit's anti-communist motivation enabled its men to maintain high morale despite heading into a city that was virtually under siege, where the defensive organisation left much to be desired. Well equipped with modern weaponry (MP44, MG42 or *panzerfaust*; some of the soldiers even wore new uniforms, similar to those of the *Einheit Ezquerra*), they were deployed as an attack force in the areas of Neukölln, Hermannplatz, Wilhelmstrasse, Friedrichstrasse, Anhalter Bahnhof, Belle-Alliance-Platz and the Reich Aviation Ministry, as well as elsewhere. These locations were generally one or two streets further east of the main deployments of the Spanish unit during the final moments of resistance in the Reich capital until dawn on 2 May 1945, when they surrendered. It was largely due to the French that the Soviets failed to take Berlin on 1 May, a highly symbolic date for them, particularly because of their fierce resistance in Sector Z near the Reich Chancellery.

Postcard of Belle-Alliance-Platz (now Mehringplatz) in 1900. It was from this square that one of the greatest efforts by Soviet troops was launched in their attack on the southern part of Berlin's Sector Z. (Public Domain)

The French unit distinguished itself through its valiant performance in the defence of Berlin, managing to halt and even drive back the Soviets in its sector (as happened in the Neukölln District), and destroying a large number of armoured vehicles during those few days of fighting. Several members of the *Sturmbataillon* were decorated for their outstanding actions. By the end of the fighting, the strength of the *Sturmbataillon* had been reduced to just over 30 men (the rest were either dead, had been captured or had managed to break through the Soviet lines and escape).

After the war, Krukenberg summed up the contribution of the French volunteers in the Battle of Berlin: 'Without the French, the Russians would have taken Berlin eight days earlier.... A compliment, no doubt, but they are credited with having destroyed some 50 Red Army tanks.'[2]

As for the Latvian unit, which would fight side by side with the Spaniards, we must go back to early April, following the defeats and retreat from Pomerania that left the remnants of the *15. Waffen-SS Grenadier-Division* (*Lettische Nr. 1*) fortifying a defensive position between Neustrelitz and Neubrandenburg, some 80 kilometres north of Berlin. On the orders of Gotthard Heinrici, commander of Army Group *Weichsel* (Vistula), the Latvians handed over all their automatic weapons, leaving them with only a few rifles for guard duty, in order to arm the German reserve units heading to the front. On 19 April, the division was ordered to form a *kampfgruppe* of three battalions for the defence of Berlin. Specifically, these battalions were: the 15th Rifle Battalion and one battalion each from the 32nd and 33rd Regiments.

2 Robert Forbes, *For Europe Revisited: The French Volunteers of the Waffen-SS, 1943–45* (Warwick: Helion & Co., 2022), p.570.

The *kampfgruppe* commanded by *Oberst* Janums encountered a major problem as there was only transport for two battalions, over which he retained command. The third battalion, the 15th Rifle Battalion (officially designated the Rifle Battalion of the *15. Waffen-Grenadier-Division der SS*) was left behind and departed later separately.

By this stage of the war, the Latvians had no intention of continuing to fight, and Janums, taking advantage of the confusion in orders and the general disorder around the Reich capital, managed to lead his two battalions around Berlin in a clockwise direction, engaging in several clashes with Soviet troops along the way until finally surrendering to the Americans in the early hours of 27 April near Lindau, close to the River Elbe.

Shoulder badge of the *15. Waffen-SS Grenadier-Division (Lettische Nr. 1)*. Spaniards and Latvians fought together in numerous engagements against Soviet troops in Berlin. (By GlibThomas. Public Domain)

The 15th Rifle Battalion managed to obtain lorries for their transport in the early hours of 20 April, but instead of joining their comrades who had left the day before, they were transported to Erkner, situated some 20km east of Berlin, where they took up positions before moving on to the centre of Berlin the following day, coming under the command of the *Nordland* Division.

The 15th Rifle Battalion, under the command of *SS-Hauptsturmführer* Walli since 25 March 1945, comprised, following its reorganisation after the fighting in Pomerania, three rifle companies totalling some 315 men, plus a mortar section (with one mortar lacking ammunition), although on the 19th part of this unit, estimated at around 180 men, departed with the lorries commanded by *Oberst* Janums. Thus on 20 April only around 135 men would set off, to whom a handful more would be added on 21 April, when the battalion's supply unit (4th Heavy Weapons Company) joined them. This was the 2nd Company, comprising 105 men under the command of German *Leutnant* Schmidt, with *Leutnants* Stauers and Titmanis and *Stabsfeldwebel* Laiviņš serving as platoon leaders (the latter would take command after Stauers was wounded in the fighting at Belle-Alliance-Platz

The Hallesches Tor in 1901. This image illustrates the importance of Berlin's canals in its defence. (By Waldemar Titzenthaler. Public Domain)

on 27 April 1945), part of the 3rd Company (originally comprising 80 men) under the command of Latvian *Oberleutnant* Rutkis; the platoons were commanded by *Stabsfeldwebel* Kamps and *SS-Obersturmführer* Neilands; and those of the 4th Company under the command of German *Leutnant* Kilp, with *SS-Obersturmführer* Liepnieks and *Kadett* Krūmiņš, who barely managed to form a platoon. From Tiergarten Station they were sent to the centre of Berlin, near the Reich Chancellery.

Although the Latvian troops did not intend to take part in the defensive fighting for Berlin but rather intended to flee westwards with the rest of their division to surrender to the Western Allies, the combat performance of the men of the 15th Rifle Battalion was excellent and appreciated by their German allies. The reason for this desperate bravery in the fighting against the Soviets was that capture by Soviet troops meant almost certain death or at best captivity in the most appalling conditions imaginable, because of the historical animosity between the two nations.

The Latvian troops did not receive more modern weaponry (as had the French and Spanish), although we know that they did receive enough *panzerfausts* with which they destroyed a good number of Soviet tanks (although this fact has never been given much prominence, as was also the case with the men of the *Einheit Ezquerra*).

Deployed in the central and south-eastern sectors of the German capital, they had the opportunity to share trenches with the men of the *Einheit Ezquerra*, with whom they fought side by side. Specifically, the Latvian unit was assigned to defend the *Hauptsicherheitsamt* [Security Office] and later the *Luftfahrtministerium* [Air Ministry], both buildings located near Hitler's bunker.

On 26 and 27 April, the 2nd and 3rd Latvian Companies fought fiercely at Belle-Alliance Platz (now Mehringplatz), near the Landwehr Canal. As with the Spanish unit, the Latvian formation took heavy casualties during the days of fierce fighting in Berlin, leaving the survivors (who numbered no more than 80 by 1 May) scattered and integrated into other units. The

An old photograph of a bridge over the Landwehr Canal, which played such an important role in the German defence of Berlin. (Public Domain)

main locations of the Latvians' fighting were the Reich Chancellery and the Air Ministry.

As mentioned above, there is some controversy regarding the German delegation sent on 1 May 1945 to negotiate the surrender of Berlin with Soviet General Vasili Chuikov, in which *General* Hans Krebs (Chief of the Army General Staff) was reportedly accompanied by *Oberstleutnant* von Dufving, some soldiers as escort, and the Latvian *SS-Obersturmführer* Atis Neilands, who would return after the meeting to take command of his unit. The presence of the latter was justified by his command of the Russian language, which was necessary for the meeting. Unfortunately for the defenders, both the battle for Berlin and the war were already all but lost, which is why the Soviets refused to negotiate and simply demanded unconditional surrender.

The few Latvian survivors of the Battle of Berlin were captured by Soviet Red Army troops in the German capital and spent many years in captivity in the USSR. However, this was not the case for Neilands and several of his men, who managed to escape from a prisoner-of-war camp in a Berlin suburb where they had been gathered to be sent eastwards, eventually reaching, with great difficulty, the area controlled by the Western Allies in West Germany.

Many of the men who fought alongside German troops in the final year of the war in Europe had sound military training and combat experience. This image shows soldiers from the Spanish Volunteer Division being trained in the use of heavy machine guns. (Public Domain)

The Spanish unit, even if we consider that it numbered as many as 80–90 men, is completely lost among the estimated 90,000 defenders in Berlin. Clearly, its role in the fighting was merely anecdotal and of no military significance whatsoever. We should, however, try to compare it with the French and Latvian units, which had certain similarities in their roles during the Battle of Berlin. As we can appreciate, compared to the 400–500 French soldiers who made up the *Sturmbataillon Charlemagne*, drawn from a unit that had fought in Pomerania, the *33. Waffen-SS Grenadier-Division*

Charlemagne (*Französische Nr. 1*), or the 300 Latvians of the *15. Waffen-SS Grenadier-Division* (*Lettische Nr. 1*), the mere 90 men of the *Einheit Ezquerra* pale into insignificance. Although all three units fought with great courage and bravery, the actions of the French went down in the history books for their valiant deeds, which managed to delay the inevitable although only for a short while, perhaps a few days. In the case of the Spaniards and Latvians, the combat operations they carried out were similar to those of their French comrades, but their smaller numbers, from which must be added the ever-increasing casualties, meant that they went largely unnoticed by historians. This is entirely understandable, as their actions bought only a few hours in the defence of Berlin. Both the Spaniards and the Latvians took part in various joint operations, largely due to the small number of men in both units, combined with the significant attrition they suffered in the fierce fighting in Berlin.

However, the strong anti-communist sentiment of the men in the Spanish unit and the individual bravery demonstrated in combat by many of them did not prevent the unit from almost disintegrating within a few days due to attrition in combat – whether through the dead and wounded, those taken prisoner, or, in some cases, soldiers who decided to abandon the fight and 'disguise' themselves in civilian clothes to pass themselves off as Reich workers.

The memoirs of Miguel Ezquerra, the commander of the unit bearing his name, are shrouded in a great deal of uncertainty. Clearly, he was indeed in Berlin in command of this Spanish unit; he was aware (long before such information appeared in various history books) of many events that took place during the fighting for Berlin; and therefore many of the events he recounts must be considered authentic (including the presence of Latvian troops and the names of soldiers from this unit). Other sources also place Spanish soldiers in the Battle of Berlin and in the fighting described by Ezquerra in his memoirs (such as the missions at the *Hotel Excelsior*, Moritzplatz, et cetera), which should dispel any doubts anyone might have had regarding Spanish involvement in that battle.

On the other hand, is the extensive fabrication that Ezquerra weaves throughout his memoirs, in which he places himself in implausible situations that no one witnessed. Being received by Adolf Hitler, his controversial award of the Knight Cross of the Iron Cross, his participation in surrender talks between the Germans and the Soviets; or his promotions from *leutnant* to *oberstleutnant* in the period between 1944 and the Battle of Berlin, make it very difficult to believe everything he says. As mentioned above Latvian *SS-Obersturmführer* Neilands said that when he took command of the remnants of Latvian, Spanish and French troops: 'I knew that the commanders of the French and Spanish units were both captains, so they were of a higher rank than me and, furthermore, both had been awarded Knight Cross of the Iron Cross. Seeing my surprise, Mohnke replied that I had more combat experience.'[3] In light of this testimony, we should not assume that what Ezquerra recounts in his second book is inaccurate regarding his receipt of the Knight Cross of the Iron Cross, as it would be highly unusual for someone to wear that decoration without having received it, especially in the vicinity of the German High Command during the Battle of Berlin.[4]

Similarly, his spotless military record both during and after the Second World War suggests that this is too much for one man (according to Ezquerra, he was awarded the Iron Cross 1st Class for his actions between June and August 1944 against the French Resistance in the Landes, the Gold Cross following the blowing up of a bridge on the Normandy Front, and the War Merit Cross with swords, 1st Class, during the Battle of Berlin, although it is not known when or why he received the Iron Cross, 2nd Class). It must be borne in mind that, after all, this is merely a memoir, in which the author recounts his adventures, exaggerating (possibly more intentionally than unintentionally) his exploits and the importance of his unit and himself in the Battle of Berlin. In the Portuguese version of his experiences during the Second World War, Ezquerra even admits to having received the Oak Leaves for his Knight Cross of the Iron Cross during fighting in Berlin, only for this decoration to disappear in the later version of his memoirs. Although, as we can see, Ezquerra's imagination was very fertile, his memoirs did serve to 'uncover' the long-forgotten and silenced presence of Spaniards in the fighting for the capital of the Reich; the core of his account is likely to be true. Although it is true that his name, like those of Ricardo Botet Moro and Lorenzo Ocañas Serrano, does appear in the scant information available on Spaniards in the streets of Berlin in April–May 1945.

As a final point regarding the greater or lesser veracity of Miguel Ezquerra's accounts, let us recall that the expert Carlos Caballero Jurado notes that Ezquerra attempted to obtain a military pension from the German Embassy in Madrid in 1965. All he could claim in that attempt was in relation to his service in the Blue Division, with no mention of his many other adventures, including his Berlin escapade. Despite the fanciful elements of his memoirs, we have been able to verify, through the various sources consulted, that a significant portion of these memoirs adhere to reality. The Spanish presence at Moritzplatz, the Europahaus building, near Anhalter and Potsdam Stations, or at the Reichsbank building can undoubtedly be said to have witnessed bloody clashes between the men led by Ezquerra and Soviet troops.

It is important to note one final detail regarding the Spanish fighters on the German side during the Second World War, namely the fact that

3 Vincent Hunt, *Sent to Die in Berlin* (Warwick: Helion & Co., 2026). Details from the author; at the time of writing the book is forthcoming.

4 Miguel Ezquerra Sánchez, *Luché Hasta El Fin: Memorias de un voluntario español en la guerra 1939–1945, Berlin a vida o muerte* (Granada: García Hispán, 1999).

no Spaniard from the Blue Division, the Blue Legion or the 'Irreducibles' was tried as a war criminal (despite frantic attempts such as that by the international Federation of Organisations in Support of the Spanish Republic, which, upon learning that a group of Spanish soldiers were detained by the Soviets in Berlin after the war had ended, requested the Nuremberg Tribunal to try them as war criminals). This fact is highly significant, regardless of their affiliation with the *Wehrmacht* or the Waffen-SS.

A1. Sdkfz 251/7 *Ausf. D, 11. SS-Freiwilligen-Panzergrenadier Division Nordland*.
Berlin, May 1945.

A2. *Flakpanzer IV Wirbelwind*. Unit unknown. Berlin, April 1945.

(Illustrations by David Bocquelet © Helion & Company 2026)

See Colour Plate Commentaries for further information

B1. Pzkw V Panther. Possibly from *Müncheberg Panzer Division*. Berlin, April 1945.

B2. Pzkw VI *Ausf B, Königstiger*. *1. Kompanie, SS-Pz.Abt.503* (503rd SS Heavy Tank Battalion). Berlin, April 1945.

(Illustrations by David Bocquelet © Helion & Company 2026)

See Colour Plate Commentaries for further information

C1. Pzkw VI *Ausf B, Königstiger*. *1. Kompanie*, *SS-Pz.Abt.503* (503rd SS Heavy Tank Battalion) Berlin, April 1945.

C2. Pzkw VI *Ausf H* Tiger I. *3. Panzer-Abteilung* from *Müncheberg Panzer Division*. Berlin, May 1945.

(Illustrations by David Bocquelet © Helion & Company 2026)

See Colour Plate Commentaries for further information

D1. Su-76M Model 1944. 11th Armoured Corps (Red Army). Berlin, April 1945.

D2. IS-2 Model 1943. 88th Independent Guards Heavy Tank Regiment. Berlin, April 1945.

(Illustrations by David Bocquelet © Helion & Company 2026)

See Colour Plate Commentaries for further information

E 1. **T-34/85 Model 1944 (with additional protection against the *panzerfaust*). Berlin, May 1945.**

E2. **T-34/85 Model 1944. Unknown unit (Red Army). Berlin, April 1945.**

(Illustrations by David Bocquelet © Helion & Company 2026)

See Colour Plate Commentaries for further information

F1. **82mm BM-8-36 'Katyusha' mounted on a 'recycled' T-40/T-60 hull. Unknown Red Army unit. Berlin, April 1945.**

F2. **82mm BM-8-36 'Katyusha' mounted on a ZIS-6 truck. Unknown Red Army unit. Berlin, April 1945.**

(Illustrations by David Bocquelet © Helion & Company 2026)

See Colour Plate Commentaries for further information

Colour Plate Commentaries

Plate A. Sdkfz 251/7 *Ausf. D, 11. SS-Freiwilligen-Panzergrenadier Division Nordland.* Berlin, May 1945.

This armoured half-track (like the various models of the Sdkfz 251) was of great importance to the German Reich during the war. They were also used in the Battle of Berlin, although the massive presence of Soviet armoured vehicles and artillery made them easy prey. The armoured vehicle pictured here is a *Pionierpanzerwagen*, an engineer half-track, fitted with mounts on the sides for carrying assault equipment.

Plate B. *Flakpanzer IV Wirbelwind.* Unit unknown. Berlin, April 1945.

These anti-aircraft armoured vehicles were widely used in ground combat, enabling the defenders to concentrate heavy firepower against enemy infantry. This particular vehicle was spotted in the Charlottenberg area.

Plate C. Pzkw V Panther. Possibly from *Müncheberg Panzer Division.* Berlin, April 1945.

The armoured vehicles of this battle-hardened division provided an important armoured reinforcement for the defenders of Berlin. Despite this, their numbers were too small to pose a threat to the Soviet forces.

Plate D. Pzkw VI *Ausf B, Königstiger. 1. Kompanie, SS-Pz.Abt.503* (503rd SS Heavy Tank Battalion). Berlin, April 1945.

This powerful tank, commanded by *SS-Unterscharführer* Geor Diers, together with the one commanded by *SS-Oberscharführer* Karl Heinz Turk, defended the Potsdamer *Bahnhof* and Stadtmitte *U-Bahnhof* sectors until the very last moment.

Plate E. Su-76M Model 1944. 11th Armoured Corps (Red Army). Berlin, April 1945.

This Soviet light self-propelled gun, equipped with a 76.2mm M1942 (ZiS-3) field gun, was used to provide armoured support to the Soviet infantry. It is worth noting that Spanish troops were on occasion deployed against this unit.

Plate F. IS-2 Model 1943. 88th Independent Guards Heavy Tank Regiment. Berlin, April 1945.

These veritable armoured behemoths were the most formidable opponents for anti-tank units armed with *panzerfausts* or *panzerschrecks*. On 28 April, the Spanish troops came into contact with the armoured vehicles of this unit as they advanced towards Hausvogteiplatz following their breakthrough at Spittelmarkt.

Plate G. T-34/85 Model 1944 (with additional protection against the *panzerfaust*). Berlin, May 1945.

Urban combat and the large number of portable anti-tank weapons such as the *panzerfaust* and *panzerschreck* led the Soviets to fit additional armour to the most vulnerable parts of their tanks to minimise the effects of such weapons.

Plate H. T-34/85 Model 1944. Unknown unit (Red Army). Berlin, April 1945.

The T-34 tanks were the principal enemy armoured vehicle that the Spanish forces had to face. These tanks suffered heavy losses in urban combat because of their limited manoeuvrability in the narrow, rubble-strewn streets of Berlin, which left them vulnerable to the *panzerfaust*, particularly when they lacked direct support from their own infantry.

Plate I. Pzkw VI *Ausf B, Königstiger. 1. Kompanie, SS-Pz.Abt.503* (503rd SS Heavy Tank Battalion) Berlin, April 1945.

The tanks from this unit that reached Berlin were deployed in the southern part of Sector Z (*Zitadelle*) in support of the troops of the *11. SS-Freiwilligen-Panzergrenadier Division Nordland*. This tank was commanded by *SS-Oberscharführer* Karl Heinz Turk.

Plate J. Pzkw VI *Ausf H* Tiger I. 3. *Panzer-Abteilung* from *Müncheberg Panzer Division*. Berlin, May 1945.

This was the last Tiger of the *Müncheberg Panzer Division*, which, after fighting in the Königsplatz area or near the Brandenburg Gate, was abandoned just a few hundred metres away, in the Tiergarten.

Plate K. 82mm BM-8-36 'Katyusha' mounted on a 'recycled' T-40/T-60 hull. Unknown Red Army unit. Berlin, April 1945.

The 82mm rockets caused widespread destruction in areas where Berlin's defenders were still trying to hold back the Soviets. This was a common tactic used to force the defenders out of their positions, although it was not always successful. This vehicle carried 24 rockets.

Plate L. 82mm BM-8-36 'Katyusha' mounted on a ZIS-6 truck. Unknown Red Army unit. Berlin, April 1945.

This truck was capable of carrying 48 82mm rockets with great destructive power. The defenders of Berlin had to get used to the deadly barrage of rockets fired at their positions.

Bibliography

Published Books

Anguiano, Felipe III, The Panzer Bear and the fall of Berlin 1945: *An English translation of all 8 Panzerbär newspapers from April 22 to April 29, 1945* (Location unknown: Privately published, 2023)

Antill, P., *Berlin 1945: End of the Thousand-Year Reich* (Oxford: Osprey, 2005)

Archer, Lee, Kraska, Robert, Lippert, Mario, *Panzers in Berlin* (Old Heathfield: Panzerwrecks, 2019)

Bahn, Karl, *Berlin 1945: The Final Reckoning* (Minneapolis MN: MBI Publishing Company, 2001)

Beevor, Antony, *Berlín: La caída, 1945* (Barcelona: Editorial Crítica S.L., 2002)

Borowski, Tomasz, *Last Blood on Pomerania* (Warwick: Helion & Co., 2016)

Boyle, D., *La II Guerra Mundial en Imágenes* (Madrid: Edimat Libros S.A., 2000)

Degrelle, Léon, *Campaign in Russia* (Newport Beach, CA: Institute for Historical Review, 1985), pp.282–283.

Duffy, Christopher, *Red Storm on the Reich: The Soviet March on Germany 1945* (Abingdon: Routledge, 1991)

Ezquerra Sánchez, Miguel, *Luché Hasta El Fin: Memorias de un voluntario español en la guerra 1939–1945, Berlin a vida o muerte* (Granada: García Hispán, 1999)

Fischer, Thomas, *Berlin 1933–45 avec Wilhelm Mohnke* (Paris: Éditions Heimdal, 2013)

Forbes, Robert, *For Europe Revisited: The French Volunteers of the Waffen-SS, 1943–45* (Warwick: Helion & Co., 2022)

Gil Martínez, Eduardo Manuel, Españoles En Las y La Wehrmacht, 1944–1945: La Unidad Ezquerra En La Batalla de Berlín (Madrid: Almena, 2011)

Glantz, David M., Djembe, Gonzalo G., Belza, Cecilia (Helmut Heiber ed. & trans.), *Hitler y sus generales* (Barcelona: Editorial Crítica S.L., 2005)

Goebbels, Joseph, *Diario de 1945* (Madrid: La esfera de los libros, 2007)

González Pinilla, Ángel, *La Legión Clandestina: Españoles en la Wehrmacht y las Waffen-SS 1944–1945* (Madrid: Gutiksland S.L., 2021)
Hamilton, Aaron Stephan, *Bloody Streets: The Soviet Assault on Berlin* (Warwick: Helion & Co., 2020)
Hargreaves, Richard, *Hitler's Final Fortress: Breslau 1945* (Mechanicsburg, PA: Stackpole Books, 2011)
Harrison, Richard W., *The Berlin Operation, 1945* (Warwick: Helion & Co., 2016)
Hinze, Rolf, *To the Bitter End* (Oxford: Casemate, 2013)
Holzträger, Hans, *In a Raging Inferno: Combat Units of the Hitler Youth 1944–45* (Warwick: Helion & Co., 2000)
Hunt, Vincent, *Sent to Die in Berlin* (Warwick: Helion & Co., 2026) (forthcoming at the time of writing)
Jacobsen, H. A. & Dollinger, H., *La Segunda Guerra Mundial en fotografías y documentos*, vol. 8 (Barcelona: Plaza & Janés Editores S.A., 1989)
Kurowski, Franz, *Hitler's Last Bastion. The Final Battles for the Reich, 1944–1945* (Atglen PA: Schiffer Military History, 1998)
Le Tissier, Tony, *With Our Backs to Berlin* (Stroud: Sutton Publishing, 2007)
Lobo, Ramón, *Todos náufragos* (Madrid: Ediciones B, 2015)
Lopez, Jean, *Berlin: Les offensives géantes de l'Armée Rouge: Vistule, Oder, Elbe (12 janvier – 9 mai 1945)* (Paris: Éditions Economica, 2009)
Marina, Alfonso, *Panzers en Berlin* (Madrid: Almena, 2020)
Medina, Francisco, *Berlín 1945* (Santiago de Compostela: Sátrapa Ediciones, 2009)
Misch, Rochus, *Hitler's Last Witness* (Barnsley: Frontline Books, 2014)
Mitcham, Samuel W. Jr, *German Order of Battle*, 3 Volumes (Mechanicsburg, PA: Stackpole Books, 2007)
Molina, L., Sagarra, P., González, O., *Cruces de Borgoña en Rusia: La Legion Valona (1941–1945)*, part III (Valladolid: Galland Books, 2024)
Muñoz, Antonio J., *Forgotten Legions: Obscure Combat Formations of the Waffen SS* (Boulder Co/London: Paladin Press/Axis Europa, 1991)
Norling, Erik, *Raza De Vikingos. La División SS Norland (1943–1945) Waffen SS Norland* (Granada: García Hispán, 2007)
Norling, Erik, *Guerreros de Borgoña* (Granada: García Hispán Editor, 2008)
Oliver, Dennis, *To the Last Bullet* (London: The Oliver Publishing Group, 2010)
Puente, Moisés, *Yo, Muerto en Rusia*: *Memorias del Alférez Ocañas de la División Azul* (Arantzazu: Ediciones Franciscanas Arantzazu, 2003)
Ryan, Cornelius, *La última batalla: La caída de Berlín y la derrota del nazismo* (Barcelona: Salvat, 2003)
Simons, G., *The Second World War: Victory in Europe, I* (New York, NY: Time Life Folio, 1995)
Skorzeny, Otto, *Luchamos y Perdimos* (Mollina: Acervo, 2003)
Sourd, Jean Pierre, *True Believers: Spanish Volunteers in the Heer and Waffen-SS, 1944–1945* (Rome: Europa, 2014)
Sourd, Jean Pierre, *Croisés d'un idéal: Volontaires espagnols de la Waffen SS, Heer et Kriegsmarine (1944–1945)* (Paris: Dualpha, 2021)

Urbanke, Axel, *Final Battle for the Reich Territory 1944–1945* (Bad Zwischenahn: Luftfahrtverlag Start, 2009)
Vadillo, Fernando, *Gran Crónica de la División Azul en los Irreductibles* (Granada: García Hispán, 2008)
Zaloga, Steven J., *Downfall 1945* (Oxford: Osprey Publishing, 2016)
Ziemke, Earl F., *La Batalla de Berlín: Fin del Tercer Reich* (Madrid: Editorial San Martín, 1982)
Zvartsev, A. M., *History of the Soviet 3rd Tank Army (3-ya Gvardeiskaya Tankovaya)* (Moscow: Voenizdat, 1982)

Journals and Magazines

Becker, Loïc, 'Les SS étrangères à Berlin' in *Batailles & Blindés* no. 125 (April–May 2025), pp.62–65
Bowen, Wayne, 'The Ghost Battalion: Spaniards in the Waffen-SS, 1944–1945' in *The Historian*, 63 (2000), pp.373–385
Caballero Jurado, Carlos, 'Los últimos de la División Azul: el Batallón Fantasma' in *Revista Defensa*, no. 114, 1987
Ferreira, Sylvain, 'Un taxi pour Berlin' in *Ligne de Front* 81, 2019
Ferrer-Dalmau, A., 'Españoles en las Waffen SS' in *Eurouniformes*, no. 14, diciembre-enero 2002-2003, pp.57–58
Noblanc, Erwan, 'The Last Stand. Foreign SS Volunteers in the Hell of Berlin,' in *Frontline*, No. 83, January–February 2020, pp.56–65
Various, 'Berlin 1945 (I)' in *Desperta Ferro Contemporánea* 38 (2020)
Various, 'Berlin 1945 (II)' in *Desperta Ferro Contemporánea* 39 (2020)
Zgoda, Tomasz, 'The Oder Bridgeheads' in *After the Battle* 184 (Barnsley: After the Battle, 2019)

Electronic Resources

Axis History Forum. Nevenkin, Kamen and others. https://forum.axishistory.com/
https://www.history.navy.mil/research/library/online-reading-room/title-list-alphabetically/g/german-defense-berlin.html
https://www.feldgrau.net/
https://waralbum.ru
https://www.zweiterweltkrieg.org
https://historyimages.blogspot.com.es/2011/09/1945-soviet-army-last-stages-ww2.html?m=1
http://www.allworldwars.com/The-German-Defense-of-Berlin-1945-by-Wilhelm-Willemer.html
https://weaponsandwarfare.com/2018/09/08/from-warsaw-to-the-oder-planning-for-the-inevitable-i/
https://weaponsandwarfare.com/2020/03/09/the-schwedt-bridgehead/
https://en.wikipedia.org

https://zbiam.pl/artykuly/cedynia-1945/?fbclid=IwAR10uM43Yleq2-oeMIaoa-w5J200Cjy-F8zfgxpqMJVRnTVx3doaM6XJP-0
https://albumwar2.com/
https://www.berlinexperiences.com/featured-berlin-experiences/visit-the-seelow-heights-memorial/
http://fdra.blogspot.com/2020/08/sgm-skorzeny-en-la-cabeza-de-puente-de.html
www.forosegundaguerra.com
https://www.gehm.es/segunda-guerra-mundial/trommelfeuer-infierno-artillero-en-los-altos-de-seelow/
https://www.worldwarphotos.info/gallery/ussr/tanks-2/t-34-85/t-34-85-germany45/

About the author

Eduardo Manuel Gil Martínez has been passionate about Spanish History for many years, mainly the Second World War and the Reconquista (the Middle Ages in Spain). Over many years he has written history articles in Spanish and Italian magazines and more than 40 books about the Second World War in several languages (Spanish, English, Italian and French) for a number of leading publishers: Helion, Almena, Key & Publishing, Pen & Sword, Kagero, Schiffer, Heimdal, et cetera. With Helion he has published six previous works: *Assault on East Prussia, 1944-1945*, *The Blue Squadrons. The Spanish in the Luftwaffe. 1941–1944*, *Fallschirmjäger in the Defence of the Oder, 1945*, the two volumes of *The Spanish Civil War in the Air* and *The Fall of Moorish Seville, 1023–1091*.

About the artists

Marco Capparoni is an artist and illustrator for wargames, fiction & nonfiction publishers, and private commissions. Specialising in history and military history, Marco's works also include natural history, portraiture, and book illustrations.

David Bocquelet has worked as a graphic designer since 2007. He has worked with many different publishers in the creations of illustrations depicting tanks and many other armoured fighting vehicles as well as ships and naval aircraft.